Why Can't Somebody Just Die Around Here?

Why Can't Somebody Just Die Around Here?

A story of war, deprivation, courage, perseverance, and triumph

GERHARD MAROSCHER

Second Edition

Book Design & Production: Columbus Publishing Lab
www.ColumbusPublishingLab.com

First edition published 2015. Second edition 2019

ISBN: 978-0-9816079-9-3

Printed in the United States of America
1 3 5 7 9 10 8 6 4 2

Dedicated to my children, Geoff and Christine,
my grandson, Kyle, and my nephews, Eric and Kirk.

Contents

Author's Notes

Why Can't Somebody Just Die Around Here? is the story of my family: Mom, Dad, my older brother Günter, and me. We are shown in the picture on the cover, taken in American-occupied West Germany circa 1950. I'm the boy on the left. This story begins just before WWII and includes the war itself, the difficult time after the war, coming to America, and achieving our dreams in the freedom offered by this country. The first chapter describes our simple but good life in rural Romania. WWII dramatically changed our lives. We faced danger, the loss of our homeland, and deprivation, yet we survived against all odds.

This book is a combination of my personal memories and my brother's, Mom's, and Dad's reminiscences. Mom's memories were preserved in the form of handwritten notes I took when interviewing her over a period of decades. The last few interviews were recorded on audiotape. Whenever Mom's translated words are used verbatim, her comments are set apart from the rest of the text with a block quote. My older brother vividly remembers life in the old country and the horrific events during the war. His first-person accounts are also block quoted within the text. My memory starts shortly after the war, during a time when we faced starvation and deprivation.

The book concludes with our lives in the United States, immigrating as refugees and adapting to a new country and a different culture, and succeeding here as Americans. The impact the war and deprivation had on each of us is presented, as is the expression of our love and loyalty to America.

I have included pictures, documents, and excerpts of letters in the text and appendix. The letters are from a time after the war, when Mom and Dad had been separated with no assurance of an eventual reunion. The letters speak of hope, desperation, love, and hardship.

This is an honest book. Although the book relies heavily on our collective memory, it is historically accurate and corroborated by documentation and research. People are not perfect; at least I have yet to meet such a person. Events are portrayed accurately, and people in the book are portrayed as I perceived them, warts and all.

Background

My parents grew up in the Transylvanian region of Romania. Their Transylvanian Saxon ancestors had migrated to Romania in the twelfth century from what today is central Germany. The last thing they expected was to be driven from their beloved homeland by WWII in the twentieth century. The Saxons' native language was a twelfth-century dialect of German. Many Saxons also spoke Romanian, Hungarian, Yiddish, and High German (which was the language of educated Saxons). For a more detailed summary of Transylvanian history, see the appendix, 41.

Mom was born in Bistritz, Romania, a city of about sixteen thousand inhabitants, where her father was a barber. She was one of ten children. Dad was born in the village of Deutsch-Budak, Romania, and grew up an only child. His father, a teacher and minister, died when Dad was only two years old. His mother never remarried. Not long after she lost her husband, she moved to Bistritz, where she owned a small farm at the outskirts of the city.

Dad attended a Lutheran seminary, earning dual teaching and divinity degrees at the age of nineteen. He began his teaching in 1936. Mom finished eight years of education and then completed a nursing course, receiving a nursing certificate. For more detail on the history of my immediate family, see the appendix, 42.

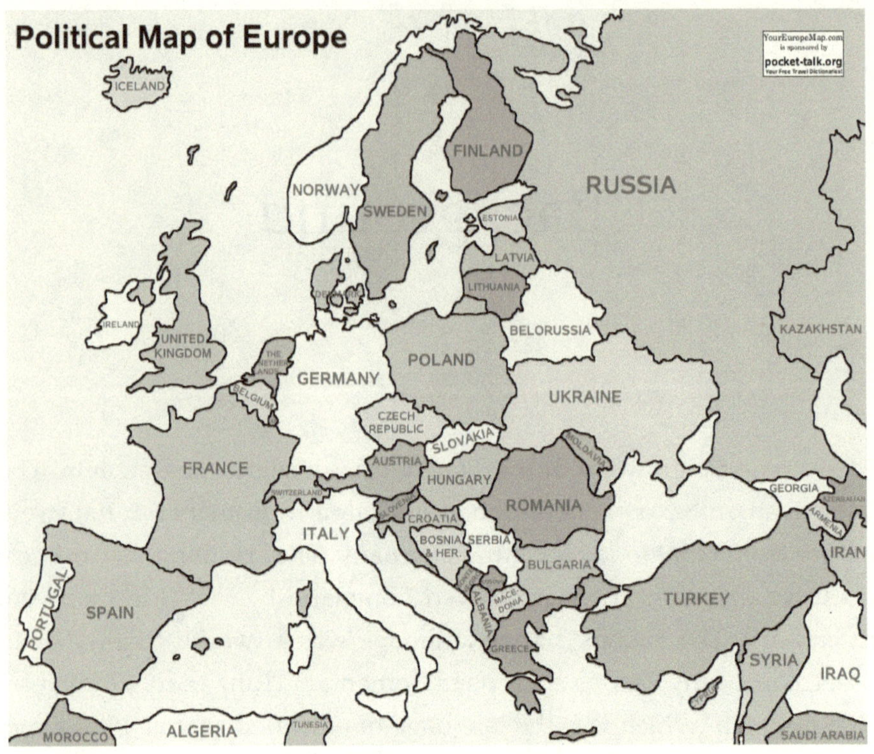

Map from http://youreuropemap.com/, sponsored by http://pocket-talk.org

Transylvania, or *Siebenbürgen* as the Transylvanian Saxons called it, is located in the Carpathian Mountains, which are in the center of Romania.

East of Romania is the Black Sea.

Nothing can stop the man with the right mental attitude from achieving his goal; nothing on earth can help the man with the wrong mental attitude.

Thomas Jefferson

Chapter 1

Life in the Old Country

WHY CAN'T SOMEBODY JUST DIE AROUND HERE?

Mom, Dad, my brother, and I miraculously survived WWII. The war had separated the family for two and a half years. We were reunited in West Germany, after our separate escapes from Communist countries.

On a warm, sunny summer day in 1947, seven-year-old Günter, my brother, was sitting on the foot-wide, brown-stained, and lacquered first-floor windowsill with his feet dangling out of the open window. It was about an hour before lunchtime, and he was very hungry. For breakfast that day, he had eaten a small, thin slice of dark bread with a thin, barely visible layer of sorghum molasses on it. He was observing people walking on the dirt road in front of the old schoolhouse where we lived and where Dad worked as a teacher. As Günter was observing some older people walk by, he turned his head toward Mom and said in German the equivalent of "Why can't somebody just die around here?" He doesn't remember Mom's response in detail, but she took it all in stride and understood what he meant. Maybe she even smiled. He didn't know it at the time, but he had just given me the title of this book.

Why would my brother say such a thing? Why would Mom react in this way? The year 1947 was a year of extreme deprivation in West Germany. There was a severe shortage of food. The average caloric intake for adults was about 1,080 calories per day.[1] According to the Mayo Clinic, a forty-year-old, five-foot, ten-inch, 150-pound active man requires 2,350 calories per day.[2]

Millions of people were starving. Some people, especially children, were dying. Since they produced their own food, the farmers in our village ate well. Refugees like my family, on the other hand, never had enough to eat.

The local Lutheran pastor in our village was old and sickly. He would occasionally ask my dad, who had studied at a Lutheran seminary, to officiate at funerals. After a death, the body was washed and placed in the coldest room of the house or a cold hallway. The funeral would usually take place about three days after death.

The local farmers in the village of Ohrenbach, where we lived, would provide food for those who traveled to the funeral, and there would be a big feast. Travelers often had long, slow journeys by farm wagon or on foot. During the winter those journeys were undertaken by horse-drawn sleighs.

For officiating at the funeral, Dad was paid in sacks of food that amounted to a substantial "carry-out order." This was the only time we had enough to eat, so for us children, funerals had a special place in our hearts.

LOVE AT FIRST SIGHT

On a nice, warm day in 1938, there was an outdoor festival in Bistritz, the Transylvanian part of Romania. Mom was eighteen years old, and some young men tricked her into walking across an elevated walkway to go see something on the other side.

Mom and Dad's wedding picture

Unbeknownst to Mom, this was the walkway for a beautiful legs contest. Much to her surprise, she was informed that she had won the contest she did not know she had entered. One person in the crowd of interested young observers was Dad. As he saw her walking, he commented to a friend, "I'm going to marry that girl!" My father was a very determined man, and my naïve mom was no match. I have no idea how long the engagement was, but Dad spoke with her father and asked for her hand. In June 1939 Gustav and Helene (Mom and Dad) were married in the Bistritz Lutheran Church, the same church where Mom, Günter, and I were baptized. My poor mother had no idea what to expect on the wedding night because her own mother had never talked to her about this topic. We can assume things worked out since my brother was born nine months later.

METTERSDORF

Günter and Mom

When my brother, Günter, was born in 1940, Dad was teaching in Senndorf. In 1942 he began teaching in Mettersdorf.[3] Mettersdorf was a small farming town about six miles north of Bistritz. The teaching job came with a house, some farmland, a small vineyard, and woods for which Dad had hunting rights. In Romania in those days, teaching was a prestigious and well-paid position. At the time, almost no women worked outside the home. I was born in 1943.

Gerhard, Mom, and Günter

Dad grew up on a small farm at the outskirts of Bistritz, but Mom, who grew up in Bistriz, was a city girl. Her life changed a great deal when she married. During the first four years of WWII, Dad continued to teach but was often gone for military training. Not only did Mom have two children to take care of, she also managed the farm whenever Dad was away. Mom had a maid and they shared various farm duties including milking the cows. My brother and I always refered to Mom and Dad as Mutti and Vati.

As the teacher's wife, she had additional responsibilities, one of which was teaching a home economics course to the girls in the school.

Although he was quite young, my brother remembers Mettersdorf rather well.

Mettersdorf—in my brother's words:

> This was strictly a farming village. In the summers, when sunrise was early, farmers were in the fields by four in the morning. Some farmers had simple outdoor summer kitchens in the field with just a roof and a stove with stovepipe. No roads or walkways were paved. Mettersdorf was one step removed from feudal times.
>
> I recall seeing both Mom and the maid milking four or five cows. We had one horse, five or six pigs, dozens of hens, and one rooster. The buildings were stone and mortar. The walls, by today's standards, were very thick. The farm's property was relatively small, although the barn/stable was not. All acreage was located a substantial distance outside of the village. Roofs were covered with either clay shingles or thatched. No one had indoor plumbing. We had an inside toilet, which was connected to an underground "sump," which was periodically cleaned out—not via a pump but with buckets lowered into the sump by hand. We did have a well-fed (cold water only) hand pump located in the kitchen. This was a big deal when compared to having the pump in the middle of the farmyard.
>
> All stoves and ovens were wood fired. No coal. The village had no electricity and indoor lighting was via "Coleman-esque" lanterns. Our radio, the only one in the vil-

lage, was powered by a lead-acid battery. I don't recall seeing newspapers in the village, though I saw several in Otata's (Grandpa's) barber shop in Bistritz. News in Mettersdorf, including the order to evacuate because the Russian swine were coming to invade, was via a town crier.

When one looked out over the stable and barnyard from our house, one could see a large tower with two-meter-thick walls. Everyone smoked their own meat and stored it in the relative cool of the thick-walled tower. Every Saturday someone would unlock the tower and a member of each family would go to their supply of smoked meat hanging in their cubbyhole on hooks and cut off one week's supply of smoked meat.

All heating, cooking, and baking were with wood. Houses had one large chimney that was fed by the flue of the baking oven and the flue of the cooking stove. In the attic the chimney had two large steel doors, which, when opened, revealed steel bars from which meat was hung on hooks and smoked. Of course there were no refrigerators, so smoking and salting were the only ways to preserve meat.

Dad must have had sharecroppers farm the property that came with the job since we fed farmhands during farming season. To feed the family, our maid, and the farmhands, it was common to bake ten large round loaves of bread each day. Our baking oven was quite large and had room to bake all of the loaves at one time. The bread dough was all hand kneaded, of course. A broomstick with a flat wooden "paddle" at the end was the tool to place and retrieve the loaves. The oven was not dissimilar to current wood-fired pizza ovens in some restaurants.

We had an outside summer kitchen close to the house. It

had a simple roof and screened-in sides. The kitchen consisted of a stove with stovepipe. It got quite warm in the summers and this made cooking without air-conditioning much more pleasant.

Günter milking Wunzu

New to the realities of farm living, Mom had too much of an emotional connection with and compassion for animals. For example, one sow had one too many piglets and the runt could not ever get to a tit to be fed. My mom concocted some kind of formula and bottle-fed the piglet. This piglet was named Wunzu and had a special relationship with my mom, even when she was a 400-pound sow.

Kids do cute things. My brother was no exception. He had seen the milkmaid and Mom milk the cows. Being an observant and industrious little guy, he decided one day to milk Wunzu. Fortunately, we have a picture of the act.

The Religious Pig

As the teacher's wife, Mom was the second-ranked lady in the town despite her young age (she married at nineteen). The minister's wife was number one. This meant Mom always sat in the front pew at church beside the minister's wife. One hot summer Sunday, Mom was in church, in her assigned seat as usual. The doors and windows were open. Mom heard some faint giggling in the back but paid it no mind. But the giggling came closer and closer. Finally she turned to see what was going on: Wunzu was moving up the center aisle to sit right beside Mom's pew. While turning many shades of red, Mom got up and escorted Wunzu out of church.

Chicken Droppings

Little children put lots of stuff in their mouths. Kids in Romania on small farms were no different. When my brother was very young, he found a deposit left by a chicken (not an egg) and stuck it in his mouth. Naturally, the sticky substance was awful. Mom tried her best to clean it out of his mouth while he was crying. I never made that error, but I am sure I taste-tested plenty of other things.

Günter's more detailed explanation of his encounter with chicken droppings and the long-term benefit of having once eaten them:

> The chicken dropping incident took place in our kitchen in late winter or early spring. The hen had hatched chicks. Mutti (Mom), in order to prevent the brood from freezing, kept them in an enclosure next to the baking oven. Only after the hen hopped out of the pen did she leave a deposit for my enjoyment.
>
> There is a side benefit to having eaten chicken droppings: when I listen to politicians, I immediately recognize if they are being factual or if I'm about to enjoy my childhood delicacy again.

Wilma the Horse

Living on a farm, Mom had to learn how to drive a horse-pulled carriage. She would often take Günter, and then later me, to visit her parents who lived about six miles away. This was all good except for the horse, Wilma. Great horse. There was only one problem: if Wilma saw another horse or carriage ahead of her, she had to run to be in front. This meant that occasionally a nice trot down a country road would turn into a race. Wilma had missed her calling. She should have been a racehorse.

Bird in Hand

Below is an event that includes Wilma—in my brother's words:

> Mutti and Vati and I (you weren't born yet) were on our way from Mettersdorf to Bistritz to visit the grandparents.

It was winter—winters in Transylvania were very cold—and Wilma was pulling the sleigh. I recall everyone was bundled up in a white-and-red thick wool blanket.

As we were gliding through a forest (sleigh riding is very quiet and the only noises heard are the muffled sounds of the horse's hooves and the not-so-muffled sounds of the horse's farts), I heard a songbird. Vati stopped the sleigh under the tree, pulled out his wolf-protection rifle, aimed at the twig the songbird was perched on, and fired one round. The stunned bird fell from its perch; Vati caught it in his hand and handed it to me. After a few minutes of my stroking the critter, it started to move and flew off into the woods.

Songbirds

We called our maternal grandfather Otata (Grandpa). Otata and Omama (Grandma) lived in Bistritz. Otata had a hobby of catching songbirds and keeping them in cages and then releasing them. He used some sort of glue, which he applied to tree branches to trap the tiny creatures.

Doing Business with Romani (Gypsies)

There was and still is a sizable Romani population in Romania. In those days there was a rule of thumb: if a Romani sold you a horse, you waited two or three days to pay for the horse. This avoided the unpleasant surprise that the docile horse you purchased became a wild and unruly animal after drugs wore off.

Dad used to do a great deal of hunting. He would often give the animal he had shot to the Romani. They would skin it, keep the meat, and return the pelt to Vati in exchange for the meat. Pelts were sold for money, and Mom wore a very stylish fox pelt around her neck when it was cold.

The Hunter

Dad's passion was hunting. Dad's salary in Mettersdorf was supplemented by in-kind income of house, barn, vineyard, a bit of farmland, a small garden, and hunting rights. Of those, he appreciated the hunting rights the most.

In my brother's words:

> Vati (Dad) was quite the hunter and during the fall and winter went into the woods almost every day prior to leaving for his teaching assignment. Such days typically started with a shot of schnapps (to ward off the cold) and a bite of dark bread.

Mom told me Dad had enormous difficulty getting up in the morning, except when it was a hunting day. On days he was to go hunting, he always got up at four-thirty without difficulty.

Dad hunted all kinds of animals successfully. Once he killed a bear that was attacking a hunting buddy. However, he never bagged a wolf. There was a large gray wolf population in Transylvania. He told me wolves were very smart. Whenever he set up camp waiting to kill a wolf and it had snowed during the night, he would wake up the next morning and see wolf tracks. The wolf tracks always made a circle around his camp. The wolves knew humans were dangerous and never got too close.

Hunting for one's meat was just another huge change for Mom. Up to the time she married, meat always came from the butcher. Now she had to learn to dress and cook what her husband shot. Almost always the Romani kept the meat, sparing Mom the unpleasant task.

–NOTES–

1. http://en.wikipedia.org/wiki/Morgenthau_Plan.
2. http://www.mayoclinic.org/calorie-calculator/ITT-20084939.
3. Mettersdorf is called Dumitra in Romanian.

Chapter 2

Hope for the Future: War Intervenes

WORLD WAR II BEGINS

On September 1, 1939, Germany invaded Poland from the west. That marked the beginning of WWII. On September 17, 1939, the Soviet Union invaded Poland from the east. The situation was hopeless for the Polish military and its people. Brave horse-mounted soldiers against tanks and airplanes was not a fair fight. The Poles no longer ruled their country. Poland was the victim of two despotic leaders of two powerful countries. Prior to the German invasion, Hitler and Stalin had signed a nonaggression pact. The pact also contained a secret agreement as to how the Soviets and Germans would divide up Eastern Europe.

Mom and Dad had a good life in rural Romania. Dad loved teaching. He also enjoyed farming and especially hunting, his favorite pastime. Mom was very close to and loyal to her family. She had made great progress adapting to being a farmwife and the wife of a teacher. She visited her parents several times per week, children in tow. Their future looked bright.

Teaching—Interrupted

Dad was a born teacher. He loved teaching, loved his students, and expected to stay in education for the rest of his life. He taught school from 1936 to May 1944. His teaching was interrupted several times by required military service for a total of two years and one month on active duty (see the appendix, 12–13). While the war was raging in much of Europe, our life had not changed much. There were no shortages of food and other necessities. We lived in peace, but concern about the war never left my parents for long.

Hello Romanian Army

Dad was conscripted into active duty in the Romanian Mountain Troops in October 1937. His training included mountain artillery, intelligence, grenade launcher, and sapper. In November 1938, he was discharged as a low-ranking noncommissioned officer and resumed teaching. The cool picture of him in uniform on his army horse is from that time.

Dad in the Romanian Mountain Troops

War clouds were looming and the Romanian army was mobilized. Dad was called up on March 16, 1939, for duty on the Hungarian border and was discharged two months later. On September 6, 1939, five days after Germany invaded Poland, Dad was called up for officers' training. In July 1940 he was promoted to second lieutenant in the Romanian army reserve infantry company (see the appendix, 12). The political machinations surrounding the war will be left to the history books. All that needs to be said now is that Romania became an ally of Nazi Germany.

Goodbye Romania, Hello Hungary

An agreement between Hungary and Germany on August 30, 1940, called for North Transylvania to become part of Hungary. This agreement was referred to as the Second Vienna Award, (*Wiener Schiedsspruch* in German).[1] This explains why my brother, who was born before August 30, 1940, was born in Romania, and since I was born in 1943, my birthplace was Hungary. We were born in the same town, in the same hospital, but in different countries.

Hello Hungarian Army

Since Bistritz is located in North Transylvania, Dad—now a Hungarian citizen—was discharged from the Romanian army in September 1940. In 1941 he was drafted into the Hungarian army and required to complete a five-month officers' training course at a military college. While still teaching, he had two short-term training tours and in 1943 and was promoted to lieutenant in the reserves. In June 1944 he reported for active military duty and in August was sent to the front to fight the Russians (see the appendix, 12).

Doing the Right Thing

My father maintained a friendship with a former Jewish classmate, Mr. Massler. Massler owned one of the more reputable stores in Bistritz. Much like the Nazi Germans, the anti-Semitic Hungarian government persecuted Jews. Eventually it became illegal for all Hungarians to do business with Jews. To enforce the decree, a list of "Jew lovers" caught doing business with Jews was nailed to the courthouse door. Enforcement of the law was left up to freelancing young Nazi and fascist Hungarian thugs to harass and brutalize "Jew lovers" and their families.

As a loyal Hungarian army officer and good citizen, Dad was expected to follow the law. Dad chose to defy this law and secretly continued to do business with Mr. Massler. Since Dad did not serve continuously in the military until June 1944, he had plenty of opportunity to do business with his friend. Dad would not go into the store to do business; instead, he would occasionally see Massler on the street and exchange pleasantries. This did not arouse suspicion. After all, it was not against the law to talk to a Jew. If anyone was within hearing distance, the listener would hear innocuous chitchat like "How are the wife and kids?" But if nobody was close enough to hear, Dad would give Massler a verbal list of all the supplies he needed for the farm. Later Massler would surreptitiously deliver the ordered goods. In this way, Dad helped Massler to continue to feed his family and operate his business.

Foreshadowing of "Glories of War"

Early in the war, Bistritz residents celebrated the departure of new recruits being sent off to war with music, flowers, and speeches. The young men traveled in cargo cars that had wood plank floors with large sliding doors on each side. Mom told me of a group of girls who were very excited to see their heroes leave for war. After the long ceremony, the train departed and proceeded at low speed. Knowing the train track made a long half circle before heading in its desired direction, the girls decided to get on their bikes and pedal in a straight line to get to the next crossing so they could again wave to the soldiers. When the train passed the girls, the railcar doors were wide open and as many men as could fit in the doors were relieving themselves. Real war is neither glorious nor romantic.

Last Time Together

This picture was taken not long before Dad was called up and began training for combat against the Russians in late May 1944. It was the last time we were together as a family until late September 1946. The youthful hope for peace and a happy family life was shattered and replaced with hunger, danger, fear, worry, and separation.

Last family picture before two and a half years of separation

FLEEING THE HOMELAND

The Russians Are Coming

Dad was on the front with his Hungarian infantry unit, fighting against the Russians. Mom had remained at the Mettersdorf farm when Dad left for the front. In September 1944 the town crier brought the news that the Russian army had broken through the front lines and would soon invade Bistritz and Mettersdorf. Mom, who was 24, had only a short period of time to decide if she should leave with my brother and me ahead of the Soviet army or take her chances by staying and hoping the enemy would treat civilians well. The Russian army had a horrible reputation for brutality against noncombatants, especially women.

One of Mom's older sisters, Medi, had married a German engineer and had been living in Germany since before the war. Medi had two children the same age as my brother and me. Mom did not want to gamble that the Russian soldiers would treat us well and decided we would flee to her sister's house in Weimar, Germany. Mother-in-law Käthe decided to flee with us.

The Train Trip

A Red Cross train for wounded and sick German soldiers was being prepared for departure. Its destination was Vienna, Austria, part of the Third Reich. Some refugees were also allowed on the train, with young women and children given priority. Once Mom had made her decision, she packed a suitcase and loaded up my baby carriage. The baby carriage had cream-colored balloon tires, a spring suspension, and a folding sunshade. In addition to clothes, she packed a ten-pound box of cream of wheat, six cloth diapers, and some jewelry, which she intended to sell.

Hidden very well was a small semiautomatic pistol Dad had given her for protection. That pistol saved my life. The jewelry was stolen later at a refugee camp. The last things she packed were family pictures and all the letters Dad had written to her since he had gone. My four-and-a-half-year-old brother carried a rucksack containing his clothes. Just before Mom left our house in Mettersdorf, she put Dad's favorite watch on top of a folded handkerchief on the nightstand and left some food for him. Those last two acts were in the hope that he might survive being overrun by the Russian army and make it home safely. She then hitched up Wilma for the six-mile carriage ride to her parent's house in Bistritz.

Once in Bistritz, Mom took care of the necessary paperwork to authorize her, my brother, me, and her mother-in-law, Käthe, to board the train (see the appendix, 14). She then briefly stopped by her sister Gredi's house to ask for a few baby clothes for me. Even though her sister did not need those clothes anymore because her children were older, Gredi refused. In the end, the entire family, including Gredi and her family, had to flee their homes and homeland forever.

A couple of days after we had arrived in Bitstriz, the three of us were taking a walk with me in the baby carriage. As we were returning to her parents' house, Mom saw her father in the distance, waving for us to hurry. He told her that she had thirty minutes to get on the train. There was just enough time to notify Käthe, grab the suitcase, load the baby carriage, put on the rucksack, say hurried goodbyes, and board the train.

The train was pulled by a steam engine. The railcars had white crosses on the top and red crosses on the sides. They were cattle cars with large sliding doors on both sides. The rough, wood plank floor was covered with straw, which was soon inhabited by a large population of head lice. There were no toilet facilities, no seats, and no heat—it was cold at night. So many people were assigned to each car that there was not enough room to for everybody to lie down at one time. Prior to boarding, I had suffered a long time from a bad skin rash that made me miserable. Mom was worried that in the filthy conditions my rash would get worse. Instead, my rash disappeared. It turns out I'm allergic to laundry soap.

The officer's assignment was to safely deliver the wounded soldiers to Vienna where they could be treated. Leaving the wounded soldiers at the mercy of an advancing Russian army was not an option. The engineer of the hospital evacuation train was an ethnic Romanian who did not want to leave his homeland and refused to drive the train. The officer put a pistol to the head of the engineer and changed his mind. I hope the engineer eventually made it back home safely.

The distance from Bistritz to Vienna is only 500 miles; however, it took three weeks to reach Vienna. Because of concern for sabotaged tracks, the train always ran very slowly. Even at slow speed, such a trip would normally take only a few days. Bombed-out bridges and damaged tracks further slowed progress. The train also stopped frequently to wait for clearance to move on because trains directly involved in the war effort had priority.

The military occasionally passed out a can of meat, but it had to be shared. The refugees had to provide most of their own food. Before boarding the train, Mom had borrowed 150 Pengö (Hungarian currency). Occasionally the train stopped at some of the towns and villages where she and the others could purchase food. The large box of cream of wheat Mom had packed supplemented our diet and that of a number of other people. At one train station, Mom stole a large lantern, which she and many other people used as a stove. Mom had to set up a cooking schedule to eliminate conflicts. She was ashamed that she resorted to stealing, but she would do anything to help her children survive.

A Slap in the Face Can Strengthen Moral Character

At one point during the three-week trip, Mom was freshening up at a train station. She was washing her upper body with a washcloth. Conditions were quite crowded with an entire trainload of people at the station, but people tried to get some privacy as best as they could. She was washing behind a sheet when a man stuck his head through an opening to take a peek. When Mom realized he was there and watching, she slapped him as hard as she could. He probably saw stars. He never had a desire for a second look. I suspect she packed quite a wallop, considering she had recently been milking cows and doing other physically hard work on the farm.

Added Misery

Among the refugees were two nurses who were caring for twenty-eight orphans, all babies. All twenty-eight caught chickenpox at the same time. There was lots of screaming and crying. A young man on the train had a two-or three-week-old baby girl and a two-year-old boy. The father, whose wife had died, begged for someone to take his children. But nobody could take on the additional responsibility. On a day with good weather, while the train was stopped, his son was sitting on a box by the open sliding door. The train lurched forward and the boy fell out. He was run over by the train and lost both legs. The boy's body was left at the next town.

Air Raids

The train was attacked numerous times from the air. In those days we worried about airplanes only in good weather. If the planes could not see the train, everyone was safe. There were airplane spotters, located at or near the engine. If a plane or planes were spotted, the engineer would immediately be notified, make an emergency stop, and blow the train whistle.

My brother recalls the following:

> Much of the time the train moved slowly enough that an athletic person could jump off and on the train. No bombs were dropped, only machine gun and cannon fire. There were also quite a few false alarms. I recall single-engine airplanes strafing the train, which was empty of passengers because everyone had run into the fields.

Some handled the stress of air raids better than others. Mom told me about one woman she knew well, who panicked every time there was an air raid. She would run away from the train in panic each time and abandon her children. Mom insisted I never tell anyone the name of the woman. She considered the woman's actions a great shame.

Nearly Losing a Son

One day when the train was stopped for an extended period of time, Mom decided to wash my diapers. One neat thing about steam engines is that there is a spigot at the engine to dispense boiling-hot water. Mom left my brother with Käthe, her mother-in-law, in our assigned car. Mom took me along and walked to the steam engine with a bucket to wash my diapers. While Mom and I were at the steam engine, the air raid whistle sounded and everyone began to run into the surrounding fields. Mom grabbed me and ran to the railcar where my brother had been. He was gone, which was good. But two babies, who had been abandoned by their panicked mother, were in the car. She grabbed me and the two other children and ran away from the train.

When the raid was over and the all clear sounded, everyone returned to the train to resume the journey. The train was ready to depart, but my brother was not in our railcar. Mom frantically called for him and searched for him, but he was missing. Mom talked in desperation with the German officer in charge of the train and explained that her son was missing. He assured her that the train would not leave until they found her son. Mom told me many years later, "He probably had children of his own and had compassion on us." Mom quickly organized a search party of a long line of people to comb the surrounding area. It took two and a half hours of searching until my brother was found. Mom said that when we found Günter, there were no dry eyes among the soldiers and civilians because of the great joy that he had been reunited with his mother.

My brother's recollections of the train trip:

> We shared this car with wounded German soldiers on their way back to Germany. These guys were very kind to us. (I suspect because we spoke German and looked German.) I recall one of the Germans carving a toy rifle out of a piece of wood, which I used, much to Mutti's (Mom's) chagrin, to shoot at an airplane during one of the several raids we experienced on our journey from and to hell.
>
> One day the train had stopped to allow all a chance to pee, stretch their legs, cook, and take care of personal hygiene.
>
> Mutti (Mom) had gone to the front of the train to get hot water—I believe she took you with her. Long story short, the warning whistle sounded, and everyone ran like hell to hide in the fields adjoining the tracks. A woman, we

called her Sumsebrumse, took me by the hand and we both took off running. When the "all clear" sounded, Sumsebrumse was so panicked that she couldn't move. The spray of .50-caliber bullets coupled with the sound of thousand-horsepower airplane engines can scare the be-jeebers out of some people. I recall the smell of urine and poop. It was hers. I tried pulling away, but the crazy lady held me with a death grip and wouldn't let go. A search party, which Mutti had arranged, found us hiding in a ditch. I sometimes wonder about my fate had Mutti not been such a fighting lioness.

In the case of this particular air raid, the train had stopped—I don't know why, but trains often stopped to fill up with water, fill up with coal, or inspect suspicious-looking track. As usual, the locomotive engineer sounded "air raid" via a predetermined number of whistles from the locomotive's steam vessel (the "all clear" was via a similar code), and everyone immediately dropped everything and ran like hell.

I recall the field as being large and flat and having been harvested, and there was no place to hide among rows of plants. Hedgerows, ditches, trees—anything that would hide a person from the pilot's eyes—were what everyone instinctively ran toward. And yes, I could hear the search party as it approached and I eventually broke free.

You and I played games such as "louse races." To have a louse race, you need three things: a piece of paper, a pencil, and some lice. With the pencil, one would draw a small circle in the middle of the paper and then a large circle at the paper's perimeter. Then each player places a louse in the small circle and the race is on. The winning

> louse was declared as it crossed the outer circle. I recall that these lice came in two colors. Most were black or dark brown, but sometimes a lighter-colored one could be seen competing for the honor of "Best Louse." You and I also had several German Wehrmacht (German army) buddies (injured German soldiers), who played with us and taught us games, including the infamous game of louse racing. Mutti liked the way these soldiers treated us.
>
> Then there's the story of the shy little girl who found privacy to do "her business" under one of the railcars. As she was crawling out, the car moved and cut off her leg between the knee and ankle. She died (bled out) within a few hours. More than seventy years later I still have dreams about that one. I did over time forget the little girl's name. She had blonde pigtails.
>
> We knew a few of the people we fled with and became friends-in-misery with many. Sumsebrumse and the mother of the dead girl (the one who lost her leg) come to mind.

In spite of many air attacks, no one was killed or injured from the attacks.

Unbeknownst to her at the time, by boarding the train Mom was leaving her homeland forever. The train trip was the beginning of a journey that would eventually take us to the part of Germany which our ancestors had left eight hundred years before (see the appendix, 41). She also did not know that an even longer trip, to America, was in our future.

–NOTES–

1. http://en.wikipedia.org/wiki/Second_Vienna_Award.

Chapter 3

Living in the Third Reich

THE REFUGEE CAMP

Refugee Camp, Herzogenburg, Austria

After three weeks the train arrived at its destination, Vienna, Austria. Mom, mother-in-law Käthe, my brother and I were now officially in the Third Reich under the control of the Nazis. Toward the end of the war, millions of refugees fleeing the advancing Soviet army streamed into Germany and Austria, which had allied with Germany in 1938.[1] The system used by the government officials to handle the refugees was well organized, but the camps were not equipped to handle so many people.

We were required to remain in Vienna for two days to complete refugee processing paperwork. We then traveled by train to Herzogenburg, Austria, to a cloister (nunnery) that was used as a refugee camp. Our possessions were in two suitcases (Mom's and Käthe's) and my baby carriage. We lived at the refugee camp from early October 1944 until early February 1945.

The nunnery was a dark, dismal building with thick stone walls and no heat. We lived in a small room housing a total of nineteen people. The room had four sets of triple bunks on each side with a pathway between bunks. The beds were placed head to toe with no space between. Families used clotheslines and sheets or whatever they had to try to provide some privacy. In some other rooms, people slept on cots and others slept on the floor. The refugees were a sorry-looking lot and everyone seemed tired. In spite of the crowded conditions, everyone was disciplined and there were no disturbances. The fact that the refugees were disciplined made conditions as good as they could be under the circumstances.

In 1988 I made cassette recordings of my mom talking about her experiences. In my mother's words:

> At the refugee camp, I used to steal coal for heat. That way I could heat our room. You had pneumonia and I made hot compresses. How can you do that in a cold facility with no heat? Every night I would go steal coal. I had a big, beautiful coat and I used it to steal coal. I made sacks to put under the coat for holding and hiding the coal. I also filled the pockets with coal. I stole from coal cars. I had to. I came home with a bucket's worth of coal. Every night I would go out. I was so afraid.

My brother recalls:

> I remember that the nuns were none too friendly, which, considering that the visiting rabble disturbed their routine of service to the Lord, is understandable. (Yes, the sarcasm was intentional.) It was from the nuns in this hospital that I learned about the dark side of Christian compassion. There wasn't any. These ladies, with their neat habits and pursed lips, went through their routines of caring for kids, with the passion and compassion of an auto assembly worker positioning hood ornaments.

For breakfast and lunch, children received one roll and a glass of milk. Adults got coffee or tea and a slice of dark bread. For other meals, everyone ate boiled cabbage and boiled potatoes. The total caloric intake was not adequate, but it kept people alive. I had trouble digesting the food, had diarrhea, was losing weight, and continued to get weaker. At night, in the totally dark room, when she thought everyone was sleeping, mother-in-law Käthe would chew on a slab of bacon that she had secreted away. She never shared the bacon.

With so many people in such close quarters and with inadequate toilet facilities, my mother and my brother contracted diphtheria and were hospitalized. Mom was released from the hospital about five weeks later. Günter was not released because he came down with scarlet fever and then with an ear infection. In those days ear infections could be deadly. Mom traveled three hours to visit him in the hospital. It was difficult because of the ice, snow, and bombings. She was not allowed to go into his room but could look at him through the glass in a door. When he saw her, he panicked. For future visits, she would look at him only when he wasn't looking her way.

Near Death

When Mom was released from the hospital, I was starving to death. I had always been a very fussy child, crying much of the time because of intestinal issues, rashes, and other discomforts. Now I just lay there with hollow cheeks, silent and motionless. Only my eyes moved if someone came close and into my field of view.

Mom knew I was going to die unless she found a way to prepare some food that I could digest. She thought if she could buy some food and cook it in the camp kitchen, she might be able to save me. She went to the camp director and explained that I could not digest the food and was close to death. Knowing that the kitchen was not used twenty-four hours per day, she asked and then begged the Nazi refugee camp director for permission to use the kitchen to cook something for me. He refused.

Mom, the Great Negotiator

She went back to our bunk and contemplated what she should do. She looked at me a long time and took out the small semiautomatic pistol from its hiding place and tucked it into her clothing. She talked to the director again, saying her son would surely die if she was not permitted to cook something for him. The camp director refused again. Mom then pulled out the pistol, pointed it at his head, and said, *"Ich werde Sie wie einen räudigen Hund erschießen"* (I will shoot you dead like a mangy cur). She explained, "If you do not allow me to use the kitchen, my son will surely die."

Mom was an excellent negotiator. I'm sure the director looked at her and decided that this crazy woman would indeed shoot him. She then dictated a document for him to write, giving all the mothers of young children permission to use the camp kitchen when it was not in use. He then signed it, with the pistol still pointing at him. Mom left his office, pistol hidden again, and showed all the mothers what the kind camp director had given her.

In spite of Mom having an illegal pistol in Nazi Austria, there were never any repercussions. The director must have decided not to let his superiors know what had occurred under his watch. Without the illegal pistol, and my mom's resolve and courage, I would not be writing this story. The food mom cooked for me that saved my life was cream of wheat. Life for us also got a tad better because the ladies on the cooking staff got to know Mom and liked her. They began giving her extra food for my brother and me.

Mom Starts a Riot

Another incident worthy of mention occurred at the refugee camp. The food situation was not good. Bread had to be rationed. One way that authorities would "extend" bread production was to add sawdust. One day, my Mom found a sizable piece of wood in her slice of bread. She became angry, stood up, and walked to the window. She showed the other refugees the piece of wood and threw it and the slice of bread out the window. Soon a near riot started, with all the women yelling loudly and throwing their bread out of the windows too. The quality of the bread improved after this incident. There was probably still sawdust in it, but much less. I guess one could say all the refugees were disciplined and did not create disturbances, except for Mom.

It was not only illness and the lack of food that made this time difficult but also the fear. Fear of tomorrow. Fear of bombings. Fear of Russian brutality.

WEIMAR, GERMANY—WARTIME

Leaving Herzogenburg Refugee Camp and Traveling to Weimar, Germany

In early February 1945, after I had regained some strength, we resumed our trip to Weimar, where Mom's sister lived. My grandmother Käthe did not travel with us. Rather than stay with us at the refugee camp for four and a half months, she had left after a couple of months to stay with a friend in Cologne.

At the train station, a train reserved for soldiers was heading in the direction of Weimar. Mom asked some soldiers if they would help us get on the train. The soldiers lifted Mom, my brother, me, and Mom's suitcase up into the railcar through windows. Later an officer walked through the railcar and made us leave the train. As soon as the officer was out of sight, the soldiers lifted us right back into the railcar. Someone gave Günter and me chocolate to keep us quiet, and we were hidden from view by soldiers who were hunkered around a hot cast-iron stove mounted to the floor. The officer walked by again but did not see us.

At Augsburg we got off the train. I was sick again and was checked at a Red Cross station. We stayed there several days, and my brother and I were given some milk with bread and marmalade to eat. The people at the Red Cross in Augsburg were very kind to us.

We arrived at the Weimar train station during a bombing raid. At the train station, Mom showed Aunt Medi's address to a man and asked him for directions. He said that Medi's house was located on the outskirts of the city, walked with us a ways, and then pointed us in the general direction. The entire time we walked to Medi's house, bombs were dropping. The area of the city where Medi lived was at a higher elevation. We could see the fires and smoke from the burning houses below. Night fell as the fires were put out, and we continued to walk. It was a cloudy, moonless sky, and the city was under wartime blackout conditions, making it too dark to read street signs or house numbers.

When we reached the general area of the city we were seeking, Mom knocked on doors, but nobody answered. They were probably afraid. In those days, all windows had heavy wooden shutters covering the windows. All shutters were closed. Since nobody was opening doors, Mom stopped under street-level closed shutters, talking to Günter and me in an unnaturally loud voice. She hoped someone would hear her and realize there was a mother with young children who needed shelter. But nobody opened the shutters. We wandered aimlessly, walking through yards and over fences. Cold and beyond exhaustion, Mom was desperate and did not know which way to turn. At about midnight, she noticed the faint outline of a house in the distance and felt compelled to go to that particular house. We stopped under a shuttered window, and Mom began talking loudly again, calling us by name. The shutters opened up and her sister stuck her head out of the window and asked, "Helene, is that you?"

Mom responded, "Yes, the children and I are here."

After they hugged each other, Medi said, "Do you know who is here? Mom and Dad arrived about two weeks ago. They are sleeping." Mom and Medi decided not to wake their parents, and the three of us slept on the floor. We were thankful to have a warm and safe place to sleep that night. In the morning, Mom's parents saw us sleeping on the floor and nearly fainted. There were many tears of joy that morning.

Bomb Stuck in the Cellar Floor

We experienced many other bombing raids before the war ended. One time, while we were in Mom's sister's house, a bomb struck the house.

In Mom's words:

> Many people died in their cellars holding their children. Their lungs burst from the shock wave. We were in Me-

> di's house when a bomb landed on the house and tore through to the cellar.

In my brother's words:

> The bomb went through the roof. We were hunkered down in the cellar when the bomb suddenly came crashing in. We found it half-buried in the dirt floor. It wasn't very large, possibly eight or nine inches in diameter. One of the four fins was knocked off. Surprisingly, the three remaining fins were intact and not bent. The rear of the bomb was not teardrop shaped, but was squared off. Its color was battleship gray.

Medi's husband was an electrical engineer. He defused the bomb.

Saved Again—Mom's Sixth Sense

On a sunny Sunday afternoon in Weimar (a rare occurrence in a German winter or spring), many people were outside enjoying the warm sun in the vicinity of the city bomb shelter. In an air raid, people would funnel into the narrow shelter opening. Because of the narrow entrance, even a bomb exploding in front of the entrance would not kill too many people inside.

Suddenly our mom felt very strongly that we needed to get away from the bomb shelter immediately. She instructed my brother to run away from the bomb shelter as fast as he could. She picked me up and followed my brother. Shortly afterward the air raid siren sounded.

With the air raid siren blaring, the people around the shelter starting filing into the shelter, but for some reason there had been inadequate warning given, and bombs dropped while hundreds of people were still trying to enter the shelter. A bomb landed right among the crowd of people seeking the safety of the shelter. Mom said that hundreds were killed.

Mom's sixth sense saved us a number of times. I think of it as divine intervention, yet we were no more special than the people who were killed that day.

My brother comments:

> I recall Mutti (Mom) speaking of this (running away from the air-raid shelter), but I cannot remember the event. I should mention that nightmares about those days were something that I dreaded—the bomb shelter carnage was one of those horror dreams. It wasn't until I was fifty that those dreams went away—as did my habit of waking every two hours to "walk and check the perimeter."
>
> When it came to the actual bomber raids, some raids were far away and the sounds were dull noises. Some raids, however, came really close and the noise from those blasts hurt my ears. I recall that the earth and buildings seemed to literally jump from their resting place. Sometimes when we came out of our shelters, be it a basement or bomb shelter, or from being caught in the open, some folks as they came out were covered with dust. To me they looked like ghosts.
>
> The Brits and Americans would also drop aluminum foil in tinsel form to screw up the radar of the antiaircraft guns. You and I played with this stuff, and Mutti used it to decorate the 'Christmas tree'—which was an evergreen branch stuck into a tin can filled with dirt.
>
> My memory is fuzzy on this, but I recall that toy-like objects were also dropped from the air. These toys were actually little bombs that would explode when handled. I don't know how they were delivered or how they worked. I do recall that Mutti made a really big deal about us not touching anything that "just happened to be lying around."

Of the bombings my mother said:

> We went through hell sometimes. This constant bombing. The last weeks—day and night bombing. It was so gruesome. You saw how the refugees ran in Vietnam. We ran just like that. Like rabbits. Such things you never forget. You forget them for a while, but then it comes back. You see it again like a replay. War is unjust and the simple people suffer. Those who make war don't suffer.[2]

Christmas

My brother remembers the Christmas of 1945:

> The Christmas gift that year was part of an apple. Grandfather Josef Maurer peeled the apple with a knife. The peel was an unbroken spiral. My brother and I got to eat the peel. We also ate a little bit of the apple and ate the core. We ate the entire core, including seeds, but we did not eat the stem.

Another gift we received while living in Weimar was a paper bag containing small pieces of wood. Mutti picked up irregular shapes of wood from a carpenter's shop. They were like pieces of a puzzle, only none of the pieces fit. The edges of the pieces had been sanded so that there were no sharp edges. At the time, the gift seemed wonderful.

Our time in Weimar can be summarized as a time of fear, exhaustion, and hunger. Mom once said, "You have no idea how afraid a person can be." She also told me once that the only time she could escape the fear and all the troubles was when she slept.

Documenting the Bombing Damage

In October 2014, while doing research for this book, I met a professional photographer, Constantin Beyer, who lived in Weimar. Mr. Beyer's grandfather took photographs of all the bombing damage in Weimar during WWII. At Mr. Beyer's house I had the opportunity to look at scores of original photos of bombing damage taken by his grandfather. They were informative and sobering. I turned page after page of his grandfather's old album, looking at the devastation. I was a bit over halfway through the album when, unexpectedly, I turned to a page showing two young boys in coffins with flowers laid on their chests. I gasped and turned away. I could not continue.

Three pictures from Herr Constantin Beyer's album are shown on the following pages. In each case the photograph of the bombing is shown first and then a photo of the same location taken by Mr. Beyer in October 2014.[3]

–NOTES–

1. http://en.wikipedia.org/wiki/Anschluss.
2. https://de.wikipedia.org/wiki/Luftangriffe_auf_Weimar.
3. http://www.scrapbookpages.com/Buchenwald/Liberation0.html.

Grüner Markt with view into Obere Schloßgasse
By permission of Constantin Beyer Lichtbilder@ConstantinBeyer.de

View from Ferdinand-Freiligrath-Straße at the Jakobstraße intersection
By permission of Constantin Beyer Lichtbilder@ConstantinBeyer.de

St. Peter und Paul Church
By permission of Constantin Beyer Lichtbilder@ConstantinBeyer.de

Chapter 4

Living in Occupied Germany

AMERICAN OCCUPATION

The War is Over

On May 7, 1945, Germany signed an unconditional surrender. May 8, 1945, was Victory in Europe (VE) Day and WWII in Europe was history. For Mom, my brother, and me the war ended on April 12, 1945, when Weimar was occupied by the victorious American army and the Buchenwald concentration camp was liberated.

Liberation of the Buchenwald Concentration Camp

The notorious Buchenwald concentration camp was located about five miles from Weimar. Although the camp was not an extermination camp, tens of thousands of prisoners died there due to harsh conditions. Buchenwald prisoners were slave laborers at a nearby armaments factory and a quarry. In addition to the horror of being slave laborers and subject to mistreatment, the prisoners also suffered from Allied bombing raids meant to destroy the factory. An air raid in August 1944 killed 388 prisoners and wounded two thousand at the factory.[1]

The camp was liberated on April 11, 1945, by four soldiers in the Sixth Armored Division of the US Third Army, commanded by General George S. Patton. Just before the Americans arrived, the camp had already been taken over by the Communist prisoners, who had killed some of the guards and forced the rest to flee into the nearby woods. Pfc. James Hoyt was driving the M8 armored vehicle which brought Capt. Frederic Keffer, Tech. Sgt. Herbert Gottschalk, and Sgt. Harry Ward to the Buchenwald camp that day.

> Keffer and Gottschalk, who spoke German, entered the camp through a hole in an electric barbed wire fence. Hoyt and Ward initially stayed at the vehicle. . . . Keffer said the prisoners, through an underground system, had already taken control of the camp. The four soldiers notified division command to get medical help and food to the prisoners as soon as possible.[2]
>
> The Americans found twenty thousand people in the camp, four thousand of them Jews.[3]

American Entry into Weimar—First Occupation Army

On the morning of April 12, 1945, when Patton's Eighth Infantry Division arrived in Weimar, they found city streets deserted except for some of the liberated prisoners roaming around.

Most of Patton's army moved east to occupy more of Germany, leaving a remnant of American forces behind to organize control over the citizens of Weimar. All citizens had to register with American authorities. Our temporary registration and residency document (pictured below)

Deutsc **MILITARY GOVERNMENT OF GERMANY**

TEMPORARY REGISTRATION — Zeitweilige Registrierungskarte

Name Maroscher, Helene — Alter 25 Age — Geschlecht weibl. Sex

Name geb. Maurer

Staendige Adresse / Permanent Address Mettersdorf/Ungarn — Beruf / Occupation Ehefrau

Jetzige Adresse / Present Address Weimar, Otto Eberhardtgartenstadt Str. 4/21

Der Inhaber dieser Karte ist als Einwohner von der Stadt Weimar vorschriftsmaessig registriert und ist es ihm oder ihr strengstens verboten, sich von diesem Platz zu entfernen. Zuwiderhandlung dieser Massnahme führt zu sofortigem Arrest. Der Inhaber dieses Scheines muss diesen Ausweis stets bei sich führen.

The holder of this card is duly registered as a resident of the town of Weimar and is prohibited from leaving the place designated. Violation of this restriction will lead to immediate arrest. Registrant will at all times have this paper on his person.

Fl. Abreisebescheinigung

Legitimations Nummer / Identity Card Number

Helene Maroscher

Unterschrift des Inhabers / Signature of Holder

(Dies ist kein Personal-Ausweis und erlaubt keine Vorrechte).
(This is not an identity document and allows no privileges).

capt. C.A.C. Name and Rank / Mil Gov Officer, U.S. Army

Weimar, d. 27.4. 1945

Dr. med. Wolff
Weimar - Schöndorf
Rosa-Luxemburg-Siedlung
Karl-Kautzky-Str. 4
18.4.46.

is in both English and German. It is dated April 27, 1945, less than two weeks before VE day, and signed by Captain Milton B. Kidd, Jr. We lived in Otto Eberhardtgartenstadt Straße 4/21 at the time.

The Americans Are Coming

I asked my mother what it was like when the Americans came. Here is what she said:

> I can't remember exactly when the Americans came. But I remember I was standing in front of the house, which was on a hill. We could look down at Weimar and Schöndorf. We saw the American tanks and trucks. It was a very moving experience. We were glad the war was over, but we lost. That is to say, not we, but the country in which we were living at the time had lost. And we did not know what would happen to us. But we were happier than if it had been the Russians. Everything was OK for a time, a couple of days. Then there was a curfew in the evenings. The Americans had let the prisoners out of Buchenwald; most of them were political prisoners, but we did not know about the political prisoners or the Jews being there. But I had been there for only two months.
>
> At least the group I had contact with, such as Aunt Medi, did not know about that. We had seen the prisoners working on streets and such. They wore striped suits as was customary at that time. The suits were gray and white. Those prisoners we saw did not look worse than we did. Anyway, they were all released. The unfortunate political prisoners tried to leave right away, but the few real criminals stayed. They went from house to house. Lots of bad things happened. There were very few men in the city. We were not allowed out for a while, but these animals went from house to house looting and raping.

> A neighbor of mine had a husband who was an engineer and was important to the war effort because he was needed to keep the power plant operational. He therefore did not go into the military. One night a gang broke into their house. The husband tried to protect them. He was shot and killed. Then they raped their fifteen-year-old daughter and his wife.

Total Breakdown of Law and Order

It was wonderful that the American army finally liberated the prisoners at Buchenwald. Those who were unjustly imprisoned tried to pick up their lives again. The Americans vacated the city each night and the police force (Nazis) had long since abandoned their posts. Most of the citizens of Weimar were women, children, and old men. There were virtually no able-bodied men to protect them from the criminals. In addition, the civilian population was not allowed to own firearms. What followed was a several-weeks-long reign of terror against the defenseless population by the criminal element of released prisoners. The entire city was at their mercy prior to the American occupation army organizing control to keep the citizens safe. Mom told me that gangs would systematically go through town at night one street at a time getting drunk, raping, and looting. She could therefore estimate what night they were likely to be on our street. Even though she was terrified, Mom developed a plan to keep us safe.

Implementing a Brilliant Plan

We lived in a duplex with a wall separating the living quarters as well as a wall separating the cellars. Mom talked with the lady next door, Frau Birkfeld, who also had two children. Frau Birkfeld's husband was in the German army and she did not know his fate. My brother remembers that an old man lived with her. Maybe it was her father. Mom explained her plan to her neighbor, who was willing to help and try to save both households.

German houses were furnished with very large, heavy wardrobes. My brother recalls that the wood was very thick. They were built to last hundreds of years. The two women and the old man tilted a wardrobe, and my brother placed sliced raw potatoes underneath the feet. It was then possible to slide the heavy furniture on the wooden floor. Eventually all doors and windows on the first floor of the entire duplex were blocked by heavy furniture.

In case the murderous gang was still able to gain entry, the plan included making a hole in the cellar wall between the two apartments. The dimly lit cellars had dirt floors separated by a rough-stone masonry wall. The old man living with Frau Birkfeld chiseled a hole into the basement wall, which my brother says was surprisingly easy. The idea was that if they gained entry into one side of the duplex, we would crawl through the hole into the cellar under the other side of the duplex. If they tried to gain entry into the other apartment, we would crawl through the hole again. A brown wooden table was placed in front of the hole in each cellar. And a heavy piece of cardboard, with a makeshift handle, was pulled up against the opening to make it even more unlikely that we would be found.

We were all quiet during the night of the attempted entry into our house. I was a sickly child and cried a lot, yet I was totally quiet as we were hiding in the basement.

In Mom's words:

> We heard noises at about midnight and we woke you all up. We took you to the cellar. You were all as quiet as church mice. We crawled through the hole into Frau Birkfeld's side. We had furniture blocking all windows and doors. They used an ax to try to break in, but they were unable to. They yelled repeatedly, *"Frau! Schnapps!"* (Woman! Liquor!) They then went to the other side of the duplex and tried to break in there too. Frau Birkfeld, her children, and we crawled through the wall into our side of the cellar. They were again unsuccessful. We were the only house not broken into.

> They would walk into a store and take whatever they wanted. The store owners and everyone else did not intervene and were quiet. They used Buchenwald as an excuse to do anything they wanted to do. It took a while for the Americans to notice what was happening, and then order was restored.

Fortunately, Mom was successful in keeping the vermin out. The other women and even young girls were not so lucky. They were defenseless with no guns, and all men of fighting age (fifteen to sixty) were either prisoners of war or dead. At that time my father was a Russian POW and could not protect us. But Mom was not defenseless; she had courage and a brain—and she still had the illegal semiautomatic pistol with her, just in case her plan did not work.

In October 2014, for the first time in sixty-eight years, I saw Frau Birkfeld's house. It still has two front doors. I did not knock on the doors and did not tell the current residents what happened there in April 1945.

Hating the Enemy

Mom did not know if our dad was still alive, and she did not have good feelings toward the American soldiers. She told me of one encounter with an American soldier: The three of us were taking a walk when an American soldier stopped us and offered us part of a chocolate bar. Chocolate was a delicacy and it represented calories, which we needed badly. Surely it was Hershey's Milk Chocolate. My mom took the chocolate, threw it on the ground, dug her heel into it and walked on. When she was telling me the story decades later, she said, "He probably just wanted to be kind. But remember: at that time, we had been repeatedly bombed by the Americans and I did not know if your dad was alive or not."

I asked Mom what the American soldiers were like in their short occupation. She said, "The Americans behaved well, but we were still afraid. We did not know what would happen to us."

First Encounter with a Black Person

My brother remembers:

> The location was Weimar and fighting had come to a halt. A convoy of US Army vehicles stopped and the Amis (German nickname for Americans) got out of their vehicles to stretch their legs. I was sitting on the steps of the house when the black man came over to where I was sitting. First he gave me either some chewing gum or chocolate—I don't recall which—and we both sat on the stoop looking each other over. This was the first black person I had seen, though Mutti told me that she had once seen a dark-skinned man from northern Africa in a circus. And yes, I did notice that the palms of his hands, fingernails, and the inside of his mouth were like mine.

That small, wordless communication made Günter realize that they shared a common humanity.

RUSSIAN OCCUPATION OF EAST GERMANY 1945–1946

Goodbye Americans, Hello Russians

Unfortunately, the American occupation army stayed in Weimar only from April 12 to early July 1945. One night the American occupation army left, and the next morning the Russian occupation army arrived. The city was now under the control of the Russian military government and all citizens had to register with the Russians (see the appendix, 16).

Simultaneously the American army also withdrew from all other East German territory they had conquered and occupied. Prior to the end of the war, the freedom of Eastern European nations had been negotiated away by President Franklin Delano Roosevelt. "Good old Joe" (i.e., the mass murderer Josef Stalin) was very happy with the deal. We had been liberated from dictatorial and cruel Nazism and were now controlled by dictatorial and cruel communism. Freedom would have to wait a while.

Many crimes against citizens were committed by the Russian soldiers. The Russians did, however, restore order among the civilians with the help of a newly created Communist German police. Buchenwald, recently liberated by the Americans, was immediately re-purposed as a prison, housing enemies of the new Communist State and criminals.

Living in "The Workers' Paradise"

We now lived in the wonderful Communist workers' paradise. How did we know that it was wonderful? Well, that is what the citizens read in the newspapers, learned in school, and heard on the radio. The press was government controlled, so there was no alternate voice. Anyone expressing any opinion against the government was jailed—or worse.

I asked Mom what it was like when the Russians came.

> We were terribly afraid. It was rather quiet. The Russians were badly dressed, with torn clothes, and so dirty one cannot imagine. They had torn-apart shoes. And many bad things happened, but nothing happened to us and those close to us. But we were very careful and used our heads.

During our time in Weimar (February 1945 to September 1946), we lived in several locations and Mom worked at various jobs, including two jobs at a time in order to support us and her parents. We once lived in a very small rented room of a house. There was just enough room for a bed, a small baby bed, one chair, and a table the size of a stool.

Her training as a nurse qualified her to work for a doctor. Each week she visited a certain number of houses and recorded health information. The job involved lots of walking.

Mom commented on this job:

> I think I covered three streets and recorded the information. I got paid once per month. The pay was two shoe

soles, one bar of soap, and a small bag of wash powder.
Otata (Mom's dad) could then sole shoes.

Through her brother-in-law, Mom also got a job at a factory. Her job was to peel potatoes and clean vegetables. At first the ladies were nasty since someone from Weimar should have been given preference for the job. After they got to know of her plight, they had a change of heart and gave her food. She had to walk three miles to work. Worried that Mom kept losing weight, Medi suggested she get another job, saying, "What will the children do if you get sick?"

Working for the Russians

Continually searching for more work, Mutti found the owner of tailor shop who needed a tailor of men's clothes. She worked at the shop using a sewing machine. Mom's parents were aging and they could not take care of me very well because I was a rather active child. By then I was much faster than my grandma and enjoyed teasing her by running away. Additionally, my grandmother was deaf, so I often tried to sneak outside the house where I could happily run around unsupervised.

The tailor then loaned Mom a sewing machine, allowing her to work at home. At that time Mom lived in a two-bedroom apartment with her parents. Having her parents live with her permitted her to live in a larger apartment. Housing, which was scarce, was controlled by the government. The apartment was an efficiency with a small kitchen.

The tailor sent Mom customers who were Russian officers wanting well-tailored uniforms. They would bring bolts of cloth to her and she would make complete uniforms. The Russian officers paid in cigarettes. In postwar occupied East Germany, cigarettes were more valuable than money. Although she did not smoke, an officer would occasionally insist that she smoke with him as he waited for her to finish a uniform. He would light her cigarette and she would take a puff without inhaling and lay the cigarette down on the ashtray and go back to sewing, making the last-minute alterations. Soon the cigarette would go out. This worked every time. The officer was not insulted by her refusal to share a smoke with him, and she had an almost good-as-new cigarette, which could be traded for all kinds of goods. Mom eventually saved two hundred cigarettes, a small fortune, which later helped us to escape the "workers' paradise" into West Germany.

In Mom's words:

> By then Mama and Tata (her parents) lived with me; otherwise I could not have gotten such a large apartment. I had to earn more and also sewed during the night since there were more mouths to feed. Mama could still cook and do other things so I could work more; Tata went from house to house cutting hair.

She's Baaack . . .

Mom's mother-in-law, Käthe, left the Herzogenburg refugee camp months before we did and traveled to Köln (Cologne), where a friend lived. A few months after the war ended, Käthe unexpectedly arrived in Weimar to find Mom. Mom was working two jobs and sewing at night to support herself, my brother, me, and her parents. Now there was one more mouth to feed. Käthe, who was fifty at the time, was satisfied with living with us and not working.

In Mom's words:

> She came from Köln to Weimar because she loved me so much (Mom giggles). She was required to work in the West so she came to us in the East. Anyway, I had just worked all night and went to bed at 6:00 a.m. Günter came running and yelling, "Grandma is here! Grandma is here!"
>
> I said, "I know Grandma is here. Now let me sleep."
>
> But he said, "But it is the fat grandma!"

> I responded, "No Günter, that grandma is in Köln."
>
> He said, "No, no, no, Grandma is here." Well, the other grandma was indeed here. She probably thought, *If I go to Lene . . . She is so stupid.*
>
> Käthe lived with us and ate with us, and she was always a good eater. And then I complained to Medi and said, "What am I going to do? I'm going to perish. It's eating me up."
>
> Medi said, "Wait, I know someone." There was a woman living downstairs who worked at the employment office. Medi told the lady about my dilemma. The lady liked me and loved you guys. Anyway, two days later, Käthe had a job in Weimar. So it got a lot better.

Able-bodied people were also required to work in occupied East Germany.

Mom is Asked Out for a Date

For fear of the occupation soldiers, Mom took great pains to assure nobody would know where she lived. In spite of the brutality of many Russians, many, especially among the officers, were decent people. Mom remembers one episode:

> I was afraid. At night when it was dark, I would go out and walk through gardens and over fences so that nobody would find out where I lived. But one of the Russians did find out. One Sunday the doorbell rang. Mrs. Luk, the owner of the apartment, answered and a Russian officer was standing there asking for me. I was scared and asked, "What can I do for you?"
>
> He answered, "Well, I'd like to take you out to dinner and a movie."

I said, "I can't. I am a mother with two children and I have a husband."

He asked, "Where is your husband?"

I responded, "I don't know yet."

"Well you can come with me then anyway."

"But I cannot do that." He came two more times and then gave up. He must have found himself another lady. (Mom chuckled when she spoke the last sentence.)

But I was so scared. How did he find out where I lived? He must have paid attention. Many things happened that were not good. For months I did not sleep well. I was the only one. Mom and Dad were old and Mom was deaf. They were incapable of protecting themselves or the family if something were to happen.

Mom with my brother and me in East Germany

Going to School

My brother attended first grade after we arrived in Weimar. What he remembers from the Nazi-controlled school was the unpleasant feeling of being considered as someone of another race. He was of a darker complexion than the other German children. Racist political indoctrination was part of the curriculum and informed the views of his fellow classmates.

Going to school as a second grader in the glorious workers' paradise of Russian-occupied Communist East Germany was no picnic either.[5] Necessary qualifications for teachers and administrators included membership in the Communist party and faithful adherence to all government policies and directives. The main emphasis was learning about the glorious socialist state and wonderful Father Stalin. That is the same Father Stalin who approved of the mass rapes perpetrated by Russian soldiers in countries conquered by the Soviet Union.

Günter's school was a nondescript gray building within walking distance. Students went to school six days per week with no school on Sunday. The classroom had three rows of student desks with attached chairs.

A large picture of Father Stalin was hanging on the front wall. When my brother looked at the picture, from anywhere in the room, the face was looking directly at him. A large slate blackboard hung in the front of the room. Each student had a personal slate board and sharpened slate pen the size of a chopstick. Each slate board was framed in wood. A small sponge for wiping the slate was attached to the frame with a string. One side of the slate had lines and the other side had no lines. The students received a good education in spite of the basic educational tools and the large dose of Communist indoctrination.

The boys wore shorts year-round. In the winter they wore thigh-high wool socks held up by a garter. Girls wore dresses. Everyone, especially the boys, had very short haircuts because of the prevalence of head lice. Due to food shortages, all the students were skinny. His teacher was average height and thin and always had a stern look on his face. He talked with his teeth clenched, and therefore had rather affected speech, but was easy to understand.

Every Monday a sharing session was conducted in which each student told the class what happened at home over the weekend. Some of the questions the teacher asked were "Did anybody visit family over the weekend? Who was there? What did the adults talk about? Did your parents go anywhere? Whom did they see?" The Communist state wanted to purge the population of people with political views not approved by the Communist government. Using children to inform on their parents was common.

My brother was too young to realize the teacher was collecting information for the secret police. But Mom and he had formed quite a bond, and he was reluctant to talk about her. Mom had also told him that we don't talk about our family. Most of the children, however, were quite eager to share. Eventually he would tell the teacher everything, but he was not enthusiastic in his sharing, and that caused him problems.

In response to my brother's reluctance to tell about all of the weekend activities of his family, the teacher would quietly come up behind him and began to slowly rub the top back of his head with a large eraser in an up-and-down motion. This continued until a long, red line, with blood seeping out, appeared on his scalp. Günter's humiliation was increased by the snickering of his fellow students. He was never afraid of the teacher but disliked him. It is common for students to "pile on" an unfortunate victim of a bully. In this case the bully was the teacher. The authority figure. The teacher's actions made Günter an outcast during lunch break and recess. And after school, the eager-to-share little Communist second graders took their cue from the teacher and beat the crap out of him every day after school.

Fish Flushing is Dangerous

One of the places we lived was a multistory apartment building. Fellow tenants included a Russian army officer and his wife. Like almost all Russians, they had never seen running water and flush toilets. To them, a porcelain sink and a porcelain toilet looked the same except for the difference in height.

Food was scarce for everyone, including the Russians. One day the officer purchased a small fish at a local market in Weimar. There was a little time till lunch, so his wife decided to keep it in one of the flush toilets the residents shared. Mom came to the communal bathroom with us and saw a dead fish floating in the toilet bowl. It never dawned on her that she was looking at someone's lunch, so she flushed it. Shortly thereafter the officer came in to retrieve his fish and realized Mom had flushed it. He pulled out his pistol and put it to her head and demanded an explanation. My brother remembers those tense moments as Mom tried, in her broken Russian, to explain why she had flushed the fish.

She Loves Me

Life was hard, but Mom did her best. A very early memory of mine is my mom feeding me little squares of buttered bread she had cut. I don't know where or when this happened, but I was very young. It is a guess that it happened in Weimar. Mom patiently fed me a little square of bread at a time, saying, "Open the barn door." I'd open my mouth and the tiny piece of bread would fly in. Sometimes, of course, the barn door would suddenly shut and the bread would crash into the closed door. I very clearly remember thinking, *She is being incredibly kind and loving toward me.* And I was thankful for the food.

Robbed at Gunpoint

Grandfather Josef (Mom's dad) was once robbed at gunpoint by a Russian soldier who took his pocket watch. To open the watch, one needed a key, so Grandfather offered the soldier the key. The soldier, apparently not understanding the kind gesture, threatened Grandfather with his pistol and left without the key and with a useless pocket watch. True to his unflappable nature, after being robbed, Grandfather came home, told the story, and was not upset.

Taking Furniture, Faucets, and Sinks Home to Russia

Russian soldiers who were scheduled to be shipped back home by train stole furniture from local citizens. They hoped to haul the furniture back home with them. But the trains were used to ship disassembled factories, not furniture. All the furniture was left outside at the train station, deteriorating in the weather and becoming worthless.

None of the Russians were familiar with running water inside a house. My brother remembers some of them ripping out faucets and sinks to take home. Was it going to be show-and-tell when they got home? Did they have any idea about the infrastructure behind running water? Or did they expect running water if they installed the faucets and sinks in their houses?

More about Russians and Americans

My brother discusses Russian and American soldiers:

> Russian soldiers were indeed a sorry-looking lot. Their uniforms were made of what looked like olive-drab-colored cotton or wool. The Russians were always dirty, their hair was ultra-short, they smelled, and their breath brought tears to the eyes. You asked about their socks . . . they somehow wrapped their feet in a long gauze-like cloth. As I remember, this rabble, both enlisted and officers, were drunk much of the time. I also recall that whenever nature called, they would relieve themselves on the spot. Compared to other armies, they were terribly mistreated, both in accommodations and rations. Soup and bread was the day-in, day-out fare. I cannot comment with regard to their soldiering expertise.
>
> I should add . . . by comparison the American soldier was well fed, had top-notch equipment, and seemed cheerful, willing to engage and share food, blankets, etc. with civilians. Indigenous people and refugees trusted the American GIs, which was the exact opposite of how they felt toward the Ruskies.

Your Daddy Will Come Back Someday

Mom would constantly remind me that I had a father. She talked about him because I had been less than a year old the last time we had seen him.

In Mom's words:

> I remember I always talked to you and your brother about Vati (Dad). (Mom cries here.) And talked about him and prayed for him. And one day I said, "Your Vati will come again." And I had you in my hands and I was talking about all kinds of stories. But you started laughing. I asked, "What is so funny about that?"
>
> You said, "My Vati has no arms and no legs." That scared me so. I thought of it as a bad omen.
>
> I asked you, "Why does Vati have no arms and no legs?"
>
> You pointed at the picture (of his head and shoulders) and said, "My Vati has no arms and no legs. He can't walk." That is when I realized that you considered the picture rather than a person as Dad. I tried to explain but that did not work. You were probably two years old at the time.

Secret Message in a Cigarette

Millions of Axis soldiers had been killed, and millions more were POWs. In the chaos following the war, no information as to the fate of these men was available. Mom sought desperately to learn her husband's fate, hoping for the best. The Soviet Union had stopped all mail service, even between two Communist countries like the DDR (East Germany) and Romania. She was also aware that if he had survived and made it home, he would have no idea what the fate of his family was and where they were.

In the hope Dad had survived and returned home, she devised a plan to get word to Dad. She learned that a Transylvanian Saxon gentleman, whom she had casually known in Romania, had received permission to travel back to Romania. She asked him if he would be willing to smuggle a small note, with her name and address on it, to Romania. He told her he would carry the secret note if she could convince him that the authorities would not find it on him.

Mom told me the story of her idea on how to successfully smuggle a secret note:

> I thought about it for weeks. I decided to wrap a tiny note inside a cigarette. (At that time all cigarettes were hand rolled.) I wrote our address in really small letters and wrote "Lene" (Mom's nickname) on a very small piece of paper and wrapped it inside a cigarette. And I made a small ink mark on the cigarette so that the man would know not to smoke that one. When the man arrived in Kronstadt (Romania), he put the note inside an envelope and mailed it to Vati's (Dad's) former address in Bistritz.

He May Not Come Back

Mom had not heard from Dad for about two years.

In Mom's words:

> Mama and Tata (her parents) always tried to prepare me for the eventuality that Vati (Dad) would not come back and kept talking to me about it. They must have talked to Aunt Medi too, because Medi started telling me the same thing.

Because the tiny note that was hidden in the cigarette did reach Dad, he finally knew his family was alive and mailed a letter to her immediately. Fortunately by then mail service was beginning to be being restored.

He Is Alive!

In Mom's words:

> Then the first letter came . . . We had moved, but it was

sent to Medi's address. Medi came running, yelling, "Lene, Lene, Lene!" I thought something had happened with Medi's children or something else terrible. And I came running down. Medi yelled, "Go back. Go back. Go back. I'm coming." I did not know what to do and ran back inside and sat down on a little box. And she said, "Imagine! You got news from Vati (Dad)." I immediately fell over on my side and lay there like I was dead.

I can remember Mama (her mother) came and shook me and said, "You silly goose. What is wrong with you? Be happy! Be happy!"

LIFE IN THE DDR—UNTIL ITS DEMISE

Life for the Average Citizen

For average citizens, living in the Soviet-controlled DDR was dismal. Contrary to official propaganda, everyone was not equal. There was a new privileged class: the bureaucrats who worked for the all-controlling government. This special class had better pay, more privileges, and better healthcare.

I Lost My Son and I Demand Answers

Medi, Mom's sister in Weimar, had a son named Gerhard. He is the one I am named after. Gerhard was killed in an industrial boiler explosion. The authorities did not investigate anything about the accident. Medi started petitioning for an investigation but was rebuffed. She was undeterred and kept pestering the authorities, demanding that they investigate the accident. However, citizens of the DDR were required to accept what the government did. Any form of criticism or dissent was punished. She was finally told to be quiet or she would be jailed. She complied. After all, she had a daughter and a husband to consider.

The one time I saw Aunt Medi after 1946 was in 1974 when my wife, our young son, and I visited West Germany. It was my first time in Europe since we had left in 1952. Since Mom and Medi were very close, I felt a special connection to Aunt Medi. She was still living in the DDR, but because she was over sixty-five, she was allowed to travel to the West.

Low-Tech Big Brother

In 2004 my wife and I toured the eastern part of Germany for several days. We stopped in the small city of Selmsdorf, saw a restaurant, and ate lunch there. Until 1989, Selmsdorf was in the Communist DDR, and the restaurant had been the Stasi (state police) headquarters. In the back of the restaurant was the old secret listening room, now made into a small museum of the "good old days." In that room the Stasi could listen in on any telephone conversation in the town, a legal activity since the DDR was a police state. The equipment was crude and similar to what the telephone operators used many years ago, in which the operator plugged in wires to connect people.

I talked to the owner of the restaurant and to a few young people at the bar, who expressed no regrets that the DDR was history. But then the owner suggested I speak to a gentleman in the restaurant who might have a different opinion of the old DDR times versus the unified and free Germany. He also said that the man was a policeman during the time of the old regime. Indeed, the man told me, politely, that life was much better in the old DDR. As we were leaving the restaurant to continue our travels, the former policeman also left the restaurant. He proceeded to get on a huge, powerful BMW motorcycle and drove off. Back in the DDR days, such a vehicle would have been impossible to own. In the DDR days, the only car anyone could buy was a smoke-spewing, twenty-six-horsepower, two-stroke-engine-powered, uncomfortable Trabant. Zero to sixty in twenty-one seconds. The standard waiting time after getting on the list to buy a Trabant was fifteen years.[6] In my opinion, what the former policeman missed from the old DDR was the power over other people, and at least in his mind, the respect shown to his position by others.

The DDR finally collapsed in 1989. When the Stasi files were examined by the unified German government (former West German government) the records showed that 20 percent of the citizens were Stasi informants. Neighbors informed on neighbors, and family members informed on family members. There were millions of files on everyday citizens. Today, of course, with all the electronic data mining, face-recognition technology, etc., a government needs fewer informants to control the people. The Stasi agents would have been envious of the capability of governments today to monitor their people.

–NOTES–

1. http://en.wikipedia.org/wiki/Buchenwald_concentration_camp; http://www.ushmm.org/wlc/en/article.php?ModuleId=10005198.
2. http://www.scrapbookpages.com/Buchenwald/Liberation0.html.
3. http://www.jewishvirtuallibrary.org/jsource/Holocaust/buchenwald.html.
4. A resident needed to be in possession of these documents at all times. Written in faded ink in the bottom-right corner of the US-issued residency permit is the date April 18, 1946. It indicated that even under the Communist East German government, the US-issued permit was still in use.
5. In 1949, Russian-occupied East Germany officially became the Deutsche Demokratische Republik (DDR)—in English the German Democratic Republic (GDR). The government was "democratic" in name only. The DDR Communist government was a vassal government under Moscow's heavy boot.
6. http://sco.wikipedia.org/wiki/Trabant; http://en.wikipedia.org/wiki/Trabant.

Chapter 5

Dad and the Russians

FIGHTING THE RUSSIANS

As mentioned earlier, starting in June 1944, Dad was on active duty with a Hungarian army combat division. The division was training in preparation for combat against the Russian army. Mom, my brother, Käthe, and I fled from Bistritz on the hospital train in September 1944. While on active duty, Dad wrote letters to Mom. His first letter was dated June 3, 1944, and his last letter was dated September 2, 1944. Dad then went to the front and Mom and Dad lost contact with each other for about two years.

Dad, with pistol and hand grenade, sleeping in a trench

Your Husband Is Dead! Oops! No, He's Not!

Just before Dad's unit went to the front, after receiving no mail from Dad for a while, Mom received a letter from Herr Ernst Otto Penteker. Herr Penteker, a Transylvanian Saxon, and Dad had been schoolmates at the Lutheran seminary and were good friends. Penteker served in Dad's unit as a noncommissioned officer. An envelope sent by Penteker contained a picture of Dad sleeping peacefully in a trench, but there was no note with the picture. Mom thought this was a picture of her dead husband in his grave. I recall Mom telling me that Penteker sent a follow-up letter about a week later with the explanation of the picture, which he had not had time to enclose when he mailed the picture in a hurry.[1]

While Dad was preparing to go to the Russian front with his unit, he was actually close enough to home to be able to go on leave. He wrote often about trying to get a couple of days off to see Mom, but he never got permission. The letters he sent were about mundane things, as well as worry about his family and finances, missing his family, and expressions of love for Mom and his children.

Dad was clearly not eager to go into combat. In a letter dated August 8, 1944, he wrote:

> I am writing in a huge rush. That is how it always is in the military, including now. Our departure (to the front) is temporarily postponed for ten days. They are "forcing" us by all necessary means to stay here and not rush to the front. And that is supposed to "offend" us. (For the full letter, see the appendix, 17.)

Yet on August 26, 1944, he indicated that his going to fight the Russians made sense because that way his family could be safe. Excerpts from his letter, translated from German, follow.

> We are ready to decamp. If it is true, it will be quite a while till we are deployed to the front. I'm lonely and thinking of you! I'm thinking about the time when we got to know each other. We have had so many happy hours together since then. But how much hardship have we undergone, especially you. And now you are alone again.
>
> I am so happy that I have you! You and our dear children give meaning and purpose to my life. You and the boys mean everything to me. Considering this, my going to the front makes sense, to stand firm out there, so that you all

> can be home, living in peace with bread to eat.
>
> How short is such a farewell. One has so much to say and yet finds no words to say it. But words are not needed in such moments, because the heart speaks. One is united in thoughts and feelings. Each one reads the other's soul, and our souls are one. (For the full letter, see the appendix, 18.)

Congratulations! Hitler Wants You to Join the Waffen-SS

Although he was in the Hungarian army preparing to fight the Russians, Dad received a draft notice from the notary of the town of Mettersdorf (which belonged to Hungary at the time) in early August 1944. He was ordered to report for induction into the Waffen-SS. On August 11, 1944, Dad wrote a letter to Mom stating the following:

> I received both of your dear letters and the solemn invitation to muster. I submitted the latter of the two to my commander and am waiting on a decision by "higher authority." (For the full letter, see the appendix, 19.)

This order had the force of law behind it. He was given an offer he could not refuse.

As the war continued, Nazi Germany needed more and more soldiers. The Nazi government decided that all male ethnic Germans of fighting age in Hungary and Romania were required to join the Waffen-SS. Since our ancestors came from Germany hundreds of years before, we were considered ethnic Germans. Citizenship did not matter; our German heritage was all that counted.[2]

What Was the Waffen-SS?

Before I continue with this story about Dad, it is important to know a few things about the Waffen-SS. Until six years ago, when I decided to write this book, I never told anyone outside my family that Dad had served in the Waffen-SS. When I discussed the history of my family, as I did when giving presentations, I would simply say that Dad was in the German army toward the end of the war. I never mentioned that he had been in the Waffen-SS to avoid conflict with anyone who might jump to wrong conclusions about what kind of a man my dad was.

Originally, the Waffen-SS was created as an armed wing of the Nazi Party. But its status changed during the war, and in combat the Waffen-SS was under the command of the regular German army (Wehrmacht). However, at the Nuremberg Trials the Waffen-SS was condemned as a criminal organization due to its connection to the Nazi Party and involvement in numerous war crimes.

Initially, the Waffen-SS was to be racially "pure," but eventually there were Waffen-SS divisions formed from many different countries, including non-German ethnic groups.

> In 1940, Hitler gave permission for the first non-German Waffen-SS formation and by the end of the war, twenty-five of the thirty-eight Waffen-SS divisions were formed from foreign volunteers or conscripts, and around 60% of Waffen-SS members were non-German.[3]

It is interesting to look at Dad's official Certification of Ancestry, which he needed in order to become an officer in both the Romanian and Hungarian armies. On the lower right of the document is printed "The bearer is Aryan and of German blood." Since both Romania and Hungary were allied with Germany, officers in those armies were required to prove their German (Aryan) ethnicity.[4] People such as ethnic Poles and Jews continued to be excluded.

Tearing Up the Waffen-SS Draft Notice

With his draft notice in hand, Dad went to his Hungarian commander and showed him the document. He told his commander that he had no desire to join the Waffen-SS. After discussing the issue with the commander, the commander's adjutant tore up the draft notice and Dad stayed with his Hungarian regiment as a lieutenant (see the appendix, 20).

With the tearing up of the draft notice, Dad avoided serving in the Waffen-SS, at least for a while. Had the order not been torn up, Dad would probably have served in the newly created 22nd SS Volunteer Calvary Division Maria Theresia.[5] The order to form the division was given on April 29, 1944. Over a period of several months, the division was formed and outfitted with equipment. I personally find the word "volunteer" in the name of the division somewhat amusing.

In Combat

In September, Dad's Hungarian regiment moved to the Russian front. What followed was a series of retrograde operations.[6] The retrograde led Dad straight through his Transylvanian homeland as the Russians advanced. It was during this extended engagement with the enemy that Herr Penteker was severely wounded on September 19, 1944, near Turda, Romania. Turda is about sixty miles, as the crow flies, southwest of Bistritz, which had already been overrun by the Russians. Mom had fled on the Red Cross train a few days before. Once Penteker was evacuated to a military hospital, Dad was the only Transylvanian Saxon in the regiment. In his affidavit, Penteker writes that while he was in the hospital, Dad wrote him of the constant retrograde and told Penteker that Penteker's promotion orders had arrived (see the appendix, 20). I find it amazing that Penteker actually received Dad's letter during the chaos of war and retrograde.

Training on German Weapons

Dad's regiment had been equipped with German weapons. Because of his knowledge of both Hungarian and German, in early November 1944 he was sent to the western part of Hungary for weapons training. There he was stationed with the replacement regiment[7] of the 8th SS Cavalry Division Florian Geyer (Waffen-SS.). His assignment was to become familiar with the weapons so he could later train soldiers in his Hungarian division. (See the appendix, 12.)

Those who were temporarily attached to the Florian Geyer division were administratively taken care of (paid, fed, and housed) by that division. This was necessary because the constant retrograde operations made it impossible to stay in contact with one's own unit. (See the appendix, 12.)

Battle of Budapest

Meanwhile, an epic battle of the German and Hungarian armies against the Russian army was taking place in Budapest, Hungary. When the Russians broke through the lines at Budapest, Dad's weapons training was terminated and he was ordered to join the defense of Budapest. While fighting at Budapest, Dad contracted hepatitis. He was evacuated to a field military hospital located in Tatabanya, Hungary, at the end of November 1944. When the field hospital had to be moved because of the Russian advance, Dad suffered a severe setback and was evacuated further to Baden, Austria.[8] That was the first time Dad had set foot in the Third Reich. (See the appendix, 12.)

Dad was severely ill from hepatitis, and the disease nearly killed him. On the other hand, contracting hepatitis also saved his life. The Russian army proved too powerful, and the encirclement of the German and Hungarian armies was imminent. Withdrawal was recommended by the German generals and would have been the best military response. Hitler, however, ordered that there be no withdrawal. On December 29, 1944, Budapest was encircled by the Russian army and the situation for the Hungarians and Germans defending Budapest was hopeless. The Florian Geyer Division suffered a fate similar to the other defenders of the city: of the thirty thousand men in the division, only eight hundred survived to become POWs. Most of the men in the division were Transylvanian Saxons who had been drafted into the Waffen-SS. The draftees did not have much of a choice but to serve. Not following Nazi orders shortened one's life dramatically.[9]

Congratulations! You Are in the Waffen-SS

In the last weeks before the total breakdown of German resistance, Dad was released from the hospital. He received orders to travel to a troop training area in Bohemia, Czechoslovakia, and find his Hungarian unit. Bohemia is the western part of the modern Czech Republic and shares a border with Germany and Austria. The distance from Baden bei Wien to a military installation near Budweis, Czech Republic, was only 130 miles.[10] When he could not rejoin his annihilated Hungarian unit, he was informed by the German commander of the agreement between Germany and Hungary: as an ethnic German from Transylvania, Dad must serve in the Waffen-SS. Given no choice but to serve as required, Dad demanded his appointment to officer at the rank he had before. The German Army High Command had previously ordered that no ethnic German, who was not a citizen of Germany, could be appointed officer without its approval. Therefore, the Waffen-SS commander sent a cable to Army High Command in Berlin requesting Dad's appointment as an officer. Because of the breakdown of communication between Berlin and units in the field as the German army was disintegrating, the orders for Dad's appointment never arrived. When the war ended, Dad was in Bohemia wearing a Waffen-SS uniform (see the appendix, 12).

An Earlier "Invitation" to Join the Waffen-SS

There was a much earlier experience in which Dad had avoided being "volunteered" into the Waffen-SS. On August 30, 1940, North Transylvania (where we lived) became part of Hungary.[11] Dad was subsequently discharged from the Romanian army and later called up by the Hungarian army in 1941.

The exact date is not clear, but early in the war some local young Saxon Nazi hotheads and Waffen-SS members were planning to force Saxon men to join the Waffen-SS. A meeting of Saxon men was scheduled in Mettersdorf. Dad always attended these meetings because he was a prominent member of the Saxon community. A friend warned Dad in advance that at the meeting Nazis would try to force him to sign induction documents. A pistol to the head is a good negotiating tool. Thanks to the advance warning, Dad talked to the local constable and asked the constable to accompany him to the meeting. Wearing his sidearm, the constable accompanied Dad. With the constable at the meeting, there was no attempt made to force Dad to join the Waffen-SS. (See the appendix, 21.)

Aftermath of the Battle of Budapest— Civilian Deaths and Mass Rape

Three months after Mom fled her homeland for fear of the Russian Army, it was demonstrated that her fear was not unfounded.

Researcher and author Krisztián Ungváry writes of atrocities committed by the victorious army:

> When the Soviets finally claimed victory, they initiated an orgy of violence, including the wholesale theft of anything they could lay their hands on, random executions and mass rape. An estimated fifty thousand women and girls were raped, although estimates vary from five thousand to two hundred thousand. Hungarian girls were kidnapped and taken to Red Army quarters, where they were imprisoned, repeatedly raped, and sometimes murdered.[12]

People were afraid of the Russians for good reason.[13] Historians believe that two million East German women and girls were raped after Soviet and Allied forces defeated Hitler's army in the spring of 1945.[14] The population of East Germany was eighteen million in 1946.[15]

WAR STORIES

Dad did not talk much about the war. It seemed to me that he did not mind talking about the war, but he was just too busy working and studying to discuss it. He was totally involved in trying to make it in our adopted country, and I was busy with my career and family. I do remember some stories from the war that he did tell me.

Saving Some Russians

Dad, exhausted

To understand this story, a short primer on firing mortars is helpful. To fire mortars accurately, one must judge distances, altitude differences, and wind. Dad had an uncanny ability to estimate those parameters. The standard procedure for shooting mortars is to judge those parameters and give instructions to the mortar operator, who adjusts the mortar per the instructions. A second soldier then drops the first mortar round down the barrel. By observing where the mortar round lands relative to the intended target, one instructs the mortar operator to adjust the settings. Based on where the second round lands, relative to the intended target, new settings are given, and the third round will hit the intended target exactly. When I was in the army, the command given for the third round was "fire for effect." "Fire for effect" is a euphemism for "destroy."

Dad with some of the soldiers in his platoon. Dad is sitting on the left, eating something. The soldier in the back left is resting a mortar round on Dad's leg.

Dad and his platoon were on high ground when they saw a small Russian unit. From his vantage point, Dad could see the Russians walking along a deep, but very narrow, rocky gorge. Dad estimated all pertinent distance, wind, altitude, and direction factors. He gave instructions to a mortar operator, and the first round was dropped into the tube. It exploded behind the column in the middle of the narrow gorge. The Russian soldiers hit the ground. Shortly thereafter, the next round landed at the front of the column, again in the middle of the gorge. The Russian soldiers knew what they were in store for. They also knew the man giving the orders knew his business. They knew the Russian equivalent to "fire for effect" was coming their way. After giving his mortar operators the third instruction, he told them to wait. They waited. The Russians, who could do nothing more than hug rocks, also waited . . . and waited. After a while, one Russian cautiously raised a white handkerchief, then another, and another. The Russians were taken prisoner with no casualties on either side, and Dad saved ammunition.[16] I hope those Russian soldiers were reunited with their families after the war and lived to tell that war story to their grandchildren.

Killing a Machine-Gun Nest

One time, Dad and his troops were pinned down by a Russian machine gun. The Russians were picking off his men. Dad had tried to take out the machine-gun nest and was close enough to be within hand grenade range, but he was taking direct fire and went down. He was not hit and played dead while the machine gun kept firing at his men. After playing dead for a while, he threw his German-style "potato-masher" hand grenade and killed the machine-gun crew.

Living to Fight Another Day

Another time, he and his men observed five Russian tanks while hidden in a cornfield. A new young officer was eager to attack the Russian tanks. Five tanks against a few ground troops is not a fair fight. Dad insisted, I suspect rather forcefully, that they stay hidden and stay alive. The young officer was quite new to fighting, very enthusiastic about killing the enemy, and therefore short on judgment. They did live to fight again some other day.

An Honorable Man and Yet a Deserter

Dad's Hungarian division was manned by Hungarians and Romanians. He was one of only two ethnic Germans. In August 1944, when Dad was just about to go into combat, Romania changed allegiance to the Allied armies.

Most Romanians in the Axis Hungarian army deserted when Romanian King Michael announced the changing of sides in a radio broadcast on August 23, 1944. King Michael, who had been a figurehead leader, led a successful coup and took over power with the help of opposition politicians. He did this in order to try to save his people from further terrible losses. Some historians say that this shortened the war by six months.[17] He negotiated an agreement with Stalin to join the Soviet Union and the other Allied armies' fight against Germany and other Axis armies. In return, Romania was promised the return of Northern Transylvania and was spared the loss of life and destruction of an invasion. Overnight, Romania became a Communist nation under the dictate of the Communist Soviet Union, continuing the fight, but fighting alongside the Soviet Union against the Germans and Hungarians.

Dad told me that after their king changed sides, some Romanian soldiers tried to kill their mostly Hungarian officers just before deserting. A Romanian soldier in Dad's heavy weapons platoon also deserted. The soldier had been Dad's orderly. At the time, in the Hungarian army, each officer had an orderly—a low-ranking enlisted man who was an assistant to the officer. This may seem odd by today's standards, but it was a different time and place. Dad and his orderly had developed a friendship. Prior to his decision to leave, the soldier had borrowed money from Dad. The night the soldier left, he counted out the money he owed Dad and left it beside Dad, who was sleeping. Dad awoke to discover the soldier missing and the loan paid.

Dad's "War" Injury

Dad's most serious war injury from fighting the Russians (starting in September 1944) was a piece of shrapnel in his forearm that he was able to remove himself.

It is ironic that Dad received little more than a scratch from enemy fire when fighting the Russians. Yet he was seriously injured in an accident which occurred because of war-related nightly blackouts. In the summer of 1943, Dad was on leave from a deployment because I was about to be born. He was riding a motorcycle with a buddy on the back. I presume they were going or coming from drinking with their friends. During the war there was always a blackout at night. Cars and motorcycles did not drive with normal headlights. Headlights had small slits to direct the beam down and dim the lights so as not to be seen by enemy airplanes. What he did not know was that since the last time he was home, railroad crossing bars had been added to make the crossings safer. That night the unlit bars were down, and he ran into the bar with his forehead. His buddy reported that after the accident Dad got up, tried to restart the motorcycle, and then collapsed. I was born a week later.

Dad had a depressed skull fracture with little chance for survival. There was no effective treatment for such a serious injury, and he lay in the hospital in Bistritz, hanging between life and death. For some time—I don't know how long—he was unconscious and noncommunicative, but he did react to some things going on around him. His mother, Käthe, would come in and throw herself on him, wailing and screaming. Each time she did this, Dad would be visibly agitated although he did not come out of his state of unconsciousness. Mom was concerned that his level of agitation was so high it might harm him. She talked to the doctor, who forbade Käthe from visiting him. This probably did not endear his mother to her daughter-in-law, with whom relations were already strained. One of Käthe's favorite things to say to Mom was "You Gypsy!" At the time, this was a terrible insult.

Dad regained consciousness and began to recover slowly. Mom, Günter, and I stayed with her parents in Bistritz during his recovery. One day, my brother walked to the hospital by himself to visit Dad. Dad asked Günter to guide him to our grandparents' house, where Mom was staying. Even though he could not see, probably because of the bandages, he wanted to visit his wife and new son. Günter was more than glad to take Dad by the hand and guide him out of the hospital and to the house. According to Mom, there was lots of excitement (not positive) when Dad showed up at the house with his head all bandaged, and being guided by his three-and-a-half-year-old son. Amazingly, Dad recovered and went back to teaching and eventually fighting the Russians. However, he was never able to wear a helmet again because wearing a helmet gave him severe headaches. The head injury also changed his personality, and not for the better. He had a hair-trigger temper afterward.

–NOTES–

1. The grenade with a handle, shown in the picture, commonly used by Axis soldiers, was called the "potato masher" by Allied troops.
2. https://en.wikipedia.org/wiki/Waffen-SS.
3. http://en.wikipedia.org/wiki/Waffen-SS_foreign_volunteers_and_conscripts.
4. The required Certification of Ancestry document provided proof that Dad was less than one-eighth Jewish. Unfortunately, that was important at the time. The Certification of Ancestry is one of the many documents my parents kept.
5. https://en.wikipedia.org/wiki/22nd_SS_Volunteer_Cavalry_Division_Maria_Theresia.
6. Retrograde refers to a retreat while still fighting to slow the enemy's advance.
7. The regiment's purpose was to replaces losses due to casualties or illness within the parent division.
8. Baden is near Vienna and is often referred to as Baden bei Wien (Baden near Vienna).
9. http://en.wikipedia.org/wiki/8th_SS_Cavalry_Division_Florian_Geyer; http://en.wikipedia.org/wiki/List_of_Waffen-SS_divisions.
10. Here is a bit of non-related information you can use in a game of trivia: the name Budweiser (the beer) comes from the city of Budweis.
11. http://en.wikipedia.org/wiki/Second_Vienna_Award.
12. http://en.wikipedia.org/wiki/Siege_of_Budapest.
13. http://en.wikipedia.org/wiki/Rape_during_the_occupation_of_Germany.

14. http://www.npr.org/templates/story/story.php?storyId=106687768.
15. http://populstat.info/Europe/germanec.htm.
16. Dad had to carefully husband his ammunition. His unit in the Hungarian army had horse-drawn wagons, and his allotment of mortar shells was two shells per mortar per week. Americans and Russians, supplied by American industry, had considerably more ammunition and mobility.
17. http://en.wikipedia.org/wiki/Romania_during_World_War_II.

Chapter 6

The War is Over

AMERICAN POW

Surrendering to the Americans

Toward the end of the war, Dad was in Bohemia, Czechoslovakia (now the Czech Republic). He and other leaders decided they would be far better off surrendering to the Americans than the Russians. The last thing he wanted was to become a POW of the Russians. They walked through the mountains toward the Americans in Germany while avoiding Czech civilians who hated the Waffen-SS. Dad, although not an officer, was the leader of a small unit of soldiers. He surrendered on or around May 4, 1945.[1] On May 4, Mom, Günter, and I were in Weimar, Germany. We were no longer being bombed and had been under American occupation for three weeks.

Many years later, Dad told me the details of his surrender to the Americans. One presumes that there were plenty of white flags as the Waffen-SS soldiers were approaching the American lines. A jeep pulled up with American officers and a driver. The Americans said, "The war is over."

The response by those who were leading the men—and Dad was one of them—was "Ja, war over" (imagine a heavy German accent here). They proceeded to negotiate the terms of surrender. Dad said that there were some young German recruits (some as young as fifteen were being drafted near the end of the war) who wanted to continue the fight and were talking about killing Americans even after surrendering. The German officers explained to the American officer the situation involving the young hotheads and proposed that officers and NCOs be allowed to retain their pistols to keep order. The American officer agreed. While holding his pistol, Dad then told the soldiers he was in charge of, "I will personally shoot you if you cause any problems." Well, that was as good a surrender as one can imagine. Dad was about as pleased as a POW can be.

Sorry, We Don't Want You—Go Surrender to the Russians

Two or three days after Dad and the others surrendered, the American officers told them that they would be turned over to the Russians. That was a dark day.

RUSSIAN POW

Congratulations! You Are Now a Russian POW

Being a POW of the Russians was a hard fate. He was at the mercy of his captors. He had no rights, the conditions he lived under were horrendous, and his cruel guards hated Germans.

Russian soldiers marched their new POWs to Budweis, Czechoslovakia. All POWs who had once been Romanian citizens were sent back to Romania. After protracted delays, Dad's month-long journey to Foscani, Romania, began. The distance from Budweis to Foscani is 810 miles and involves crossing two mountain ranges. Dad was not in good health since he still suffered from the aftereffects of hepatitis, making the arduous journey even harder.

At some point during the trip to Foscani, Dad was ordered by one of the Russian guards to hitch up two horses to a wagon. For some reason, the horses spooked and reared up. Dad and the horses tumbled head over heels down a long, steep incline. Once they landed at the bottom, Dad stood up. He was afraid he was going to get shot on the spot. But instead, the Russian guard laughed heartily over what he had just seen and took no punitive action.

Arriving at the large POW camp, the new prisoners discovered there were no dogs, cats, rats, or grass inside the barbed wire. Everything that could be eaten had already been consumed. Rations were one handful of corn kernels per day and an occasional fish head. One day, a prisoner reached through the barbed wire fence to try to pluck a blade of grass so he could eat it. Rat-tat-tat, the burst of a machine gun sounded, and the prisoner was dead. Dad once observed what happened to a dog that had strayed into the camp. The dog was grabbed by a number of POWs, literally torn apart, and eaten on the spot.

Dad suffered from dysentery and continued to weaken. He went from skinny to dangerously thin and starving. He was in serious ill health but pretended to be even sicker and weaker than he was because he knew that some of the sickest were being released. I suppose that reduced the number of bodies the guards had to bury in mass graves.

Released from Captivity

Dad had a full beard and looked like a walking skeleton. He weighed 95 lbs. and was twenty-seven at the time but appeared much older. Because of his weakened condition, he was released from Foscani on August 28, 1945. It was an emotional moment for me when I found the original Certificate of Release document in the records my parents had saved.

On the Certificate of Release, written in blue ink near the top in Cyrillic script, is "Maroscher Gustav." His birth year, 1917, is two lines below. One can also read that he was prisoner number 17223. Above his prisoner number is his release date.[2]

–NOTES–

1. http://en.wikipedia.org/wiki/End_of_World_War_II_in_Europe.
2. It is estimated that twenty thousand German citizens and ethnic Germans died at Foscani. Remains of 2,997 bodies of German soldiers were exhumed from mass graves and reburied in proper graves in a memorial cemetery. Ethnic Romanian and Hungarian POWs were also buried in mass graves. http://www.volksbund.de/kriegsgraeberstaette/focsani.html.

СПРАВКА

Н. К. О.
Войсковая Часть
Полевая Почта
— 61967 —

Бывший военнопленный

года рождения, освобожден из лагеря для военнопленных и следует по месту своего постоянного жительства

Командир В/Ч Полевой Армии

Dad's Certificate of Release from the Russian POW camp
at Foscani, Romania

Chapter 7

Dad's Struggle to Begin Again

BACK IN BISTRITZ

Back in Romania at the Old Homestead

Dad traveled the 260 miles from the Foscani POW camp back home to Bistritz, armed with his POW release document dated August 28, 1945. At the time of his release, Mom, my brother, and I were living in Weimar, East Germany. The Americans had left Weimar in mid-July 1945, and we lived in Russian-occupied Communist East Germany.

Upon his arrival in Bistritz, Dad found his mother, wife, and children gone. The only family member who had stayed was his paternal grandmother, Therese Maroscher. She lived on a small farm at the outskirts of Bistritz where Dad had grown up. The farm consisted of a house, barn, and 14.3 acres of land. Part of the land was cultivated, part was meadow, and a small part was orchard (see the appendix, 6). Therese was seventy-seven and had no intention of ever abandoning her home for any reason. Dad had lost his teaching position because all German schools had been closed by the new Communist Romanians. He could no longer live in the house in Mettersdorf and was left no choice but to live with his grandmother.

Dad thought there was a possibility that Mom might try to find her sister Medi in Weimer, Germany. However, he did not know the address. He tried unsuccessfully to find the address through the Red Cross. Mom was in Weimar, but she could not send mail to Romania because there was no mail service in or out of the Eastern European countries. Neither Mom nor Dad knew if the other had survived.

The Communist police state was firmly in power; people were being arrested and even killed without a trial. Not long after the Romanian Communists had taken over, Transylvanian Saxons of working age were arrested and transported to Soviet slave labor camps. Those arrested were packed like sardines into cattle cars without food or adequate clothing and headed to Russia or parts unknown. Considering Dad's fragile health at the time, he would not have survived the train trip to a slave labor camp.

He hid in the farm hayloft during the day and came out only at night. It would have been hard for him to blend in and not be noticed if he walked around during the day. He had bright red hair and lots of freckles. As a former teacher who occasionally preached and presided over funerals, he was well known in the small community. Although his release from captivity saved his life, his situation was perilous.

Funeral Arrangements

Two and a half months after Dad's return, Therese Maroscher died in November of 1945 (see the appendix, 22.) Dad felt obligated to give his grandmother a proper Christian burial beside her husband. He was out during daylight for the first time since his return from captivity and walked toward downtown Bistritz to make funeral arrangements. Walking in the city was risky since arbitrary arrests continued. As he walked down Holzgasse, a narrow street, he saw his Jewish friend, Mr. Massler, on the other side of the street in the distance. Dad was suddenly filled with fear.

THE PROTECTOR

True Friends—Men of Character

When he saw Massler, he did not think about their old friendship. Dad instead thought about what he heard had happened to Mr. Massler since the last time they had seen each other. Toward the end of the war, Massler and his entire family had been sent to a Nazi concentration camp. Massler and his family were released when the victorious Soviet army liberated the concentration camps. Dad's first thought was not, as we might expect, *Oh good, there is my friend Massler*. Instead his first thought was *Oh my God! He is going to turn me in!*

Dad knew that Massler and his entire family had suffered greatly at the hands of the Germans and fascist Hungarians. Considering the horrific treatment of Massler and his family, who could predict what his reaction might be upon seeing Dad? After enduring such cruelty, some people are broken, others are filled with hate, seeking revenge, and some amazingly stay true to their values. But all are changed.

When Dad saw Massler, he slowly turned away and intended to enter a store in an attempt to hide. But Massler had seen him and ran after him, yelling, "Gusti! Gusti!" (a short form of *Gustav,* Dad's name). Massler caught up with my Dad and greeted him as a true friend. Mr. Massler had not known if my dad had survived the war or not and was genuinely happy to see him. So many did not survive.

In Mom's words:

> Massler was now the Communist police chief. He was so glad to see Vati (Dad). They had a friendly and warm conversation, with Mr. Massler asking how his wife, children, and mother were doing. Mr. Massler had not forgotten.

Mr. Massler put Dad under his protection and gave him warnings whenever there were going to be arrests. The arrests were still being made at night. Thanks to Mr. Massler, Dad could safely move around town, be seen, do business, and work. Massler saved Dad from certain arrest.

Mr. Massler and my dad were men of character who had the courage to help friends in difficult and dangerous times. I have often wondered about the fate of Mr. Massler and his family. He was one of the early loyal Communists and was a useful tool for the Russian-controlled Communist government. However, once that control was fully established, minority Hungarians, Jews, Germans, and Romani were all discriminated against by the Communist Romanian government. Mr. Massler, an honorable man, probably did not fare well in the long run.

Fear on a Train

Living in Romania was difficult, even with the local police chief offering protection. At times, Dad traveled beyond Bistritz by train. For a minority, traveling outside Massler's jurisdiction was potentially dangerous. In July 1946, he was required to report to the Romanian military in Năsăud (Nussdorf in German), a twenty-five-mile train ride, and was appointed a lieutenant of the reserves. Later, his case as a former POW was reviewed, and he was released from the Romanian military (see the appendix, 12).

On that trip he found himself at risk. As Dad was riding in a passenger car, reading a newspaper, he heard a Romanian man, who was sitting with several other men, speaking rather loudly and in anger. The man was telling a story about an SOB Saxon officer who had intervened when he was disciplining one of his soldiers. As he was telling the story, Dad realized he was the officer being talked about.

Several years before, Dad had come upon the army sergeant in the act of punishing a soldier for some kind of infraction. The soldier's arms were tied behind his back. A rope was tied to his wrists and he was lifted off the ground by his arms. When Dad came upon this cruel treatment, the soldier had just been pulled up and was screaming in agony. Dad forcefully intervened and made the sergeant let the man down and admonished him for such cruel discipline.

Dad was easily recognized as a Saxon in spite of his emaciated condition. While the former sergeant continued cursing that Saxon officer and giving the details of the story, Dad hid behind the newspaper and remained undiscovered. Dad could have been beaten up by the men, or even arrested, had the former sergeant seen him.

Dad Was a Millionaire

As with many other countries in Europe, Romania faced postwar hyperinflation. The highest denomination before the war was five thousand lei (Romanian dollars). By 1947, it was five million lei.[1] Dad once sold a cow for a wheelbarrow of money. He sold it for one million lei. He also sold a goat for 250,000 lei. Dad used to enjoy telling us that he was once a millionaire.

My Family Is Alive!

Since his grandmother's death, Dad had been living alone in the farmhouse where he grew up. Thanks to Mr. Massler he could at least be out and about and find work. In January 1946, about two months after his grandmother died, Dad received the tiny piece of paper with Mom's name and address on it that had been smuggled to Romania wrapped in a cigarette. He found the note inside an envelope mailed to his address. The Saxon gentleman had kept his word, did not smoke the marked cigarette, and mailed the note as promised. Relieved and overjoyed, he immediately wrote a letter to Mom, on January 26, 1946. Fortunately mail service between countries was just beginning to be restored.

That letter arrived in Weimar, East Germany, on February 28, 1946. Mom then knew he had survived the war too. She had not heard from him since a letter he had written in September 1944 (see the appendix, 22). Mom kept all the letters and postcards she received from Dad during their time of separation. Although mail service had been restored, it was inconsistent. Some letters took months to arrive and others were lost.

In that first letter, Dad wrote, "I arrived here in good health after being released from a Russian POW camp." That was a lie, of course. He was not in good health. He also wrote, "My dearest! I have such a longing for you and I am so worried about you!" The last time he had heard from her was in August 1944. Dad did not receive his first letter from Mom until May 11, 1946. She had written him letters starting February 28, but the first letter to arrive was written March 19, 1946. The day he received the letter, he wrote her. An excerpt from his May 11, 1946, letter to Mom follows (see the appendix, 23).

> My dearest!
>
> I received your dear letter of March 19, 1946. Finally after one and a half years, a letter, yet only a letter, since we cannot be together! God grant that we will be together again. Everything is easier to bear together. Otherwise everything is as you have written, waiting and more waiting. You poor thing. I cannot support and help you during this hard time!

LETTERS

Hoping to Restart Life in Transylvania

Under Massler's protection, Dad was able to lead a relatively normal life. Although he was hoping for the best, he was fully aware that living under the Communists, especially as an ethnic German, might not be possible in the long run. At the time, the prospects for reuniting the family were grim. Travel between Communist countries was rare and was not permitted without the appropriate government-issued travel document. Dad was not permitted to leave Romania, but he was unsure of the travel restrictions placed on his wife in East Germany. However, by then her travel outside East Germany was also forbidden.

Despite those obstacles, Dad's fervent hope was to restart life in his homeland and with his family in Transylvania. He worked on and off as an electrician for a year and worked many other odd jobs. His letters to Mom testify to his hopes, his worries, some of the jobs he worked, the threatening hand of the government, his despair, and his loneliness.

Excerpts from some of Dad's letters to Mom paint a picture of his life and struggles in Transylvania.

Excerpts from a letter—May 14, 1946:

My sweetie!

Wow! What a joy! I received three letters at once from you today. I got weak in the knees. I also received a letter from my mother and one from Gerda (Berg). I will forward her postcard to Julius today. He will also be happy.

Our fate is still up in the air. With time we will know what to do. For the moment, turn to Franzi[2] regarding such questions. I'm earning enough for food, even when I help Edda[3] out. Above all, I have saved some money for us to live off of for a while should you be able to come here. The clothes I wore when I was released from Russian captivity are gradually disintegrating. In time I hope to be able to buy a suit.[4]

The main thing is that you, the children, and I are healthy; everything else we will be able to manage again.

I've cultivated Grussi's (*a nickname for Dad's grandmother, Therese*) farm and purchased a goat to be my milk supplier, a trendy practice among us Saxons. However, for now the baby goat is still drinking the milk. Should you arrive when I am not here, go to Schneider and his wife, but do this right away if you arrive! He lives on our street, number twenty.

Kissing you ardently!

Your Gusti

If only there were not this yearning . . . !

Excerpts from Letter—May 22, 1946:

I can endure everything, but worrying about you gives me

many sad and bitter hours. Not to be able to help you . . . But God willing, this separation will also end. Just so you and our boys stay healthy, everything else we will be able to manage. Therefore, please, please take care of yourself! Even if you have to sell all the clothes and other things, everything except for your health I can work for and obtain again. Please, dear, fulfill this one wish of mine! I am so anxious about you. Without you, life just has no meaning for me! And we really need to stay alive so we can raise our dear little innocent children.

My dear little one! You are writing that you are aging. With me too, fighting on the front and being a POW did not pass by without leaving its marks. But I believe with certainty if we are together again—yes, if and when! Sometimes I could bang my head against the wall when I think about the happiness, were we together! And what remains are lonely hours, closing the eyes, and dreaming, dreaming of happiness, my happiness: of you! Even now as I write this letter, I am dreaming of you. I want it! Because it is the only fulfillment of my yearning. My soul is screaming—why must this happiness bypass us? Is our cup still too full? Have we not drunk from it enough already, and always to the last bitter drop! As there is a God on this earth, this suffering must end and we be together again. (See the appendix, 24.)

Postcard—May 31, 1946:

Today I again received three letters and three postcards from you. It is amazing that you have not received a letter from me, other than the one in January!! Hopefully in between some have arrived. My dearest you! I have such longing for you, and for the children! But still, your traveling here would be premature, although the food situation here is almost the same as in peacetime. I am busily hoeing the corn, am almost done.

Everything seems so gray, always alone! Well, you can imagine my diet, considering my culinary skills. (But it would still be good for you, you poor thing.) You can count on it, when you are with me again; I will fatten you up so you can be pleasantly rounded! . . . And lastly: When?! (See the appendix, 25.)

Letter—June 23, 1946:

Recently I visited Bruno and Erna,[5] who refurbished my wardrobe. It is not a good life to be alone and so far from you, and with such uncertainty. Tomorrow it will be seven years since we were married! And we live off the beautiful hours of being together; we live off the memory how much longer? As a man, I'm tolerating it, although now this life seems gloomy, but you, my poor thing. Maybe our Lord realizes and will have mercy. I received your dear letter of May 9, 1946 . . . that you still have not received a letter from me!

I even have set aside food should you and the boys arrive, and I will manage the other difficulties I'm dealing with. I've even applied for the test to become a pastor. However, I doubt if I will be allowed (not because of my knowledge), but maybe it will work out anyway. The test is supposed to be in September.

I gave Edda two sets of clothes for the children, and shoes which I brought from Schobel Hanni. And I made a pair

> of wooden shoes for her so she has something to walk around in.
>
> Oh, how many loving words I want to write to you, but on paper they are cold words. May God grant the time of our reunion, and then in my arms you can forget all this misery. And then I can take care of you and our boys. (See the appendix, 26.)

Waning hope for reunion in Romania

While talking about a future reunion in Transylvania and beginning to make long-term plans in hopes of staying, Dad was keenly aware of the obstacles in Communist Romania. In the following letter he suggests Mom would be better off living with her oldest brother, Franzi, who lived in the American sector of Austria. Austria was divided into four occupation zones by the United States, Soviet Union, France, and United Kingdom.[6] However, crossing the guarded Communist East German border was not permitted and very dangerous.

Letter—July 10, 1946:

> Such a feeling of anxiousness and worry about you has grabbed me again. For over a month now I have had no mail from you. The last letter I received from you is from May 9, 1946. That you have not received a letter from me?
>
> All my thoughts and longing revolve around you. What will our future be? When and where will we find each other again? It is so gloomy, always so alone! If I knew you were at Franzi's, then a reunion would be easier. Of course, we would have to start over, but if we were together again, my motivation would come back again—immediately. You have it much harder with the kids, so I do not want to complain. (See the appendix, 27.)

One of Dad's jobs was hauling boards with a horse-pulled wagon. That job required traveling, but it was not a standard business trip. He spent nights with the horses and wagon out in the open.

Letter—August 14, 1946:

> When I came back again from a trip, I found another dear letter from you. I was bringing boards back from Kolibitza with a wagon. That means two days, including nights, in one long drive, hard but at least an honest day's work. I'm not earning much but I can, in addition to setting aside some money for us, also help support Edda and others a bit more.
>
> I am still hoping for a reunion here, but wait until I write. Should living in my house be disallowed, which is quite possible, I will travel to Franzi right away. But please continue to write to the old address until I tell you otherwise. Someone will send the mail to me.
>
> Your parents and my mother should also stay put. Commerce here is much like before, enough but somewhat expensive. In spite of that, we could make ends meet with my current earnings here. Only clothes are unaffordable. If it were possible someday for you and the kids to come here, it would be good if you could bring yarn with you. For twenty spools of twine (one thousand meters), one can buy a good horse.
>
> The outlook to teach again is not good. I'm actually considering not teaching in the future anymore. A coachman (like me) earns more than a teacher.
>
> Luckily I'm staying out of the serious difficulties—up to now.
>
> I came home late again tonight. I was busy looking for work. Now I am home again and alone—writing you and

> thinking about our lost happiness! Oh God, when will this being alone be over?! How gladly I want to work for you and the children to help you. My poor little dear! You should be with me again! (See the appendix, 28.)

House and Farm Confiscated by the Government

At the bottom of the above letter, Dad wrote in very small script:

> August 19, 1946. Grussi's property has been confiscated. If that is carried through, I will travel to Franzi, because then I will be homeless.
>
> G.

Although he was the legal owner of the property, the process of the government confiscating his farm and house was underway. It is also the first mention of him fleeing from Romania to the West. When Mom received this letter, she began making plans to escape to West Germany in hopes of their being reunited.

Around this time, Massler had told Dad that more and more control was being exercised from higher-up Communist authorities. Massler told Dad that eventually he would not be able to offer his protection any longer and that he would give Dad a warning when that happened. Massler finally said, "I cannot protect you anymore. If you get arrested, I will not know you." One could expect nothing fairer and kinder than that warning. Massler gave him this advice: "It is time to leave." Dad's plan to escape from Romania became a reality.

That same day, August 14, when Dad wrote to Mom, he also wrote a short letter to Günter and put it in the same envelope. My brother has that small letter framed and hanging on a wall in his living room. The translation follows.

> My dear Günter!
>
> I received your dear letter and the picture of the goat. I

> was very happy that you wrote me and drew me a picture. You are now a big boy, so be nice to your mom and to Gerhard, and when you go to school, be good and study diligently. Please write again and draw me a picture because it makes me happy.
>
> Kissing you, your daddy!

Günter had not seen his dad for two years and three months, but he remembered him well. It was hard for Mom, Dad, and Günter to be separated. I was young enough that I did not remember Dad and did not miss him.

Postcard—August 24, 1946

> My dear sweet wife!
>
> I received your dear letter of July 31, 1946, with the picture of my dear little children who cause me so much worry. As a man, one pushes these bitter hours of loneliness away, but then the longing for you and the children breaks through. To be with you! Nothing do I want more than that! That is the only emotion that determines everything. To be with you! So that you can finally rest a bit and take care of yourself, because in spite of everything we still have our lives ahead of us.
>
> Until now I stood firm here, far from you, in order to accomplish as much as possible in case you could come here. That way, if you were able to come, you and the boys would at least have enough food and a place to live. After all, it was expected that you and the kids would be able to come in a foreseeable time. I won't have to worry about the property and house soon anyway. Other things I will be able to take care of in about three weeks. So if I don't get into deep shit again, I will try to come to you via Red Cross transportation.

> Spending another winter alone here does not make sense and would be pointless. My dearest! Believe in me, as I believe in you, and remain mine!

Homeless

This was the last time Dad wrote Mom before he fled Romania to the West.

Postcard—August 28, 1946

> It is time for me to go tempt fate again. Since I have been kicked out of my house and other things are occurring, too, I will travel to Franzi or Misch in about two weeks.[7] Once there I will see what else is possible. Couldn't you possibly go to Hansi's?[8] You don't have to worry about me; I will muddle through just fine. If it is possible, my mother should write her acquaintances who are living in the USA regarding the feasibility of getting an entry permit to the USA. John Wassmer, 1347 Central Ave, Detroit, Michigan.[9] Nothing has been decided regarding that, of course, but it makes sense to do it. I long so much for all of you, for you! When I imagine our reunion, my heart is warmed. Dear sweetie! Soon!!

The time had come to leave the "workers' paradise" of Communist Romania. After Dad's property was confiscated by the government to give it to "someone more deserving," Dad was homeless.

HEADING WEST

Fleeing to Vienna

Dad fled toward the American sector of Vienna, Austria. He carried with him two suitcases, a sack of potatoes, and several kilograms of salt. Salt at the time was scarce and therefore very valuable in Romania. The potatoes were his food for the journey. He also hoped that any leftover potatoes would feed his family if we were reunited. Vienna was occupied by the United States, Russia, Britain, and France. The city was surrounded by the large Russian sector of Austria. I don't know which borders he crossed, but the likely route was crossing the Romanian-Hungarian border, traveling through Hungary, and crossing into Austria from Hungary. The only story Dad ever told me about his journey to freedom was that he often rode on top of the rounded cargo train cars at night. Some of the men traveling with him on top of the railcars would fall off as they slept. They screamed as they fell.

On September 13, 1946, Dad arrived safely in the American sector of Vienna and wrote to Mom, who was still in Weimar. In his letter he wrote that he was hoping to travel to Weimar, but if that was not possible, he would travel either to Grete Herrmann Knopp[10] or Hansi. Both lived in West Germany. He included Grete's address in the letter. It was Topplerweg 4/2, Rothenburg oT,[11] Bavaria, West Germany. On September 14, he registered with the police, which was required (see the appendix, 29).

Letter September 13, from Vienna, Austria:

> Unfortunately, I have no luggage except for two small suitcases. I could not lug more because I had to carry twenty days' worth of provisions with me for the trip. For the second time I have absolutely nothing. But all that is meaningless if we were finally together again, and I could provide for you and the kids. I simply cannot even imagine anymore that we will be together and happy again. I have such a longing for you! (See the appendix, 30.)

Letter—September 17, 1946:

> I'm still in Vienna. So far the trip has gone well. Now I am waiting for a transport with which I can travel to West Germany. I am forced by circumstances to travel to Grete's (Knopp) first and will look for nearby accommo-

> dations for us there. Then I will go to you and bring you to Rothenburg. Should it be possible, I will go directly from the refugee reception camp to you! Were it only so already! Since I do not know the circumstances there, we will have to wait and wait—God, how much longer!?
>
> Please write to Grete's address: Grete Hermann-Knopp, Rothenburg oT, Topplerweg 4/2, Mittelfranken 13a. (See the appendix, 31.)

On September 18, 1946, Dad received permission to travel to West Germany. Although Dad had made up his mind to travel to Rothenburg odT, Bavaria, Germany, he still was not sure exactly where and how he and his family were going to reunite. Dad was weighing all options. Having just arrived in Austria, he was not yet fully aware of the harsh political realities.

The borders between East and West Germany were closed and could be crossed only with great danger. However, the letter from September 17 was enough for Mom to decide to make the perilous journey across the border to Rothenburg odT, in the American sector of West Germany.

–NOTES–

1. http://www.tomchao.com/hb20.html.
2. Franzi was Mom's oldest brother, who lived in American-occupied Austria.
3. Edda was a relative.
4. In those days, suits were everyday wear.
5. Bruno and Erna were relatives.
6. http://en.wikipedia.org/wiki/Allied-occupied_Austria.
7. This signaled that Dad was heading for the American sector of Vienna, Austria, since that is where Franzi and Misch resided. Misch was married to Gredi, one of Mom's sisters.

8. Hansi was one of Mom's brothers who had been released from an Allied POW camp and was living in West Germany.
9. I was surprised to find that Dad had thought about coming to the United States as early as 1946.
10. Grete Herrmann Knopp was one of Dad's cousins who had fled Romania two years before by a wagon train of mostly cow-pulled farm wagons just ahead of the invading Russian army.
11. The official name of the city where Grete lived is Rothenburg odT. The odT stands for "above the Tauber River." In his letters, Dad refers to the Bavarian city as Rothenburg oT. In the remainder of the book, it will sometimes be referred to as "Rothenburg odT," but often simply as "Rothenburg."

Chapter 8

Fleeing From East Germany

A DANGEROUS TRIP

Making Travel Plans

Mom started making plans to flee to West Germany even before she received the September 17, 1946, letter from Dad. It was illegal and therefore dangerous to leave East Germany, but she felt strongly that her two boys needed to grow up with their father and was determined to reunite the family. She asked for and received travel permission from the Russian consulate to take a train to the Russian sector of Berlin (East Berlin) and seek work with the Russians there. Having tailored high-quality uniforms for many Russian officers surely helped her to get approval for the trip.

At that time, there was no wall separating the western part of Berlin (controlled by America, Britain, and France) and the Communist eastern half of Berlin, which was occupied by the Russians. In fact, the Berlin Wall, which eventually separated East and West Berlin, was not built by the East Germans until 1961.[1] In 1946 travel between East and West Berlin was still permitted. Mom thought that once she settled down in East Berlin and became familiar with the city and how to move about, she would be able to cross over to West Berlin. She also hoped that from West Berlin it would be possible to travel to West Germany.[2]

Tearful Goodbyes

Her plan took shape quickly; it was time to begin another journey into the unknown. Before we went to bed one night, Mom told my brother and me of her plan to leave Weimar and for us to be reunited with our father. We went to bed with our clothes on and were awakened while it was still dark. She told us that we would not see our grandparents again. Grandmother cried the whole time and kept hugging and kissing us. I always turned my head whenever she hugged and kissed me. During the lengthy goodbyes, always stoic, Grandfather left several times to go have a smoke, probably to keep his emotions in check. Mom, who was very close to her mother, cried too. The decision to leave her parents was the most difficult and painful decision of her life. The scene of Grandmother and Grandfather hugging us and sobbing haunts my brother still. He understood the gravity of the situation and knew we were leaving them behind forever. Since I was only three, I did not fully understand, but I understood the tears and sorrow.

Very early that morning, we boarded a train. Mom never saw her parents again and never talked on the phone with them. They were able to communicate through letters, but the pain of separation never left her.

Travel authorization from the Russians in hand, Mom, Käthe (her mother-in-law), Günter, and I left for Berlin in late September 1946. Train travel was difficult and slow because so many train stations, tracks, railcars, and locomotives had been destroyed or damaged by Allied bombing. Due to deteriorated and hurriedly repaired tracks, trains never moved fast. Often trains did not take a direct route to their ultimate destination and traveled mostly during daylight. There was also a shortage of coal, the fuel required for steam locomotives.

Trusting Strangers

Mom had a small map and travel papers for East Berlin. Once on the train she began to doubt her plan because she did not know anybody in the huge city.[3] After several travel days, the train stopped for the night at a dimly lit train station in a city near the border with West Germany. She suddenly decided to cross the border to the west from that train station.

In Mom's words:

> I had saved two hundred cigarettes. At that time that was a fortune. With those cigarettes I made it to the West. I paid people with cigarettes to help me and to take the train close to the West. I had a small map. I did not know what route we were traveling, but then we overnighted at a city near the border. We knew the train would not travel again that night. I think at 8:00 or 9:00 PM all trains had to stop for the night. The soldiers at the train station were watching us constantly. It was a dark night. One could not see one's hand in front of one's face. No moon. No stars. There were many tracks to cross in the direction of the border.
>
> Many people who had wanted to escape to the West had been arrested. They would talk and not keep their mouths shut and then someone would betray them. Who knows what happened to them? Only God knows.
>
> We traveled with two young German soldiers who had just been released from Russian captivity. They were quite sick. They had played with you and Günter for several days. I have always had the ability to judge the character of people, whether they are good or bad people. They had no food and no cigarettes. We had been underway for about three days and I talked to them and assessed how they felt and thought and decided they were trustworthy. On the fourth day, after we had stopped at the city close to the border, I said, "If you put my baggage on the other side of the tracks, I will give you one hundred cigarettes, a half-pound of butter, and a loaf of bread." Their eyes

> opened wide. I then said, "Now things can go bad, but we will not know each other. I don't want you to have trouble, and you don't want trouble."
>
> At first they carried the baggage across the tracks, away from the dim light of the train station. Then one came back, and later the other one. They were determining where the guard was, and then they gave me a signal that it was safe to cross the tracks to where they had left the baggage. I knew West Germany was in that direction; we crossed the tracks and walked in the direction of the West German border. I did not know which way to go—left, right, or straight ahead. I knew only not to go backward.

The two young men knew that Mom had more cigarettes, butter, and bread in her suitcase, yet they left them untouched. One can find good and honest people anywhere. I hope they did well after they got home. They had survived the unbelievable hardships of war and being Russian POWs; they had nothing, yet they were honorable men.

Exhausted and Needing Help

Mom, Käthe, my brother, and I began to walk in the dark with our luggage—which consisted of a suitcase, two backpacks, and a bundle. Günter carried a backpack. We were in a strange city where Mom hoped to cross the border into West Germany. The baby carriage was long gone. No more free rides.

We met a man walking in the opposite direction. Mom asked him where the border was and he pointed in the direction we needed to walk. But it was still a long way to the border, so Mom asked him if he would be willing to accompany us for a while so we did not get lost. He explained to her that he had to work the midnight shift at a factory and could not afford to be late. Apparently he had been a member of the SS and had to be especially careful not to do anything to draw negative attention to himself. He apologized as he left. As he was walking away, Mom called out to him, "How would you feel if your wife and children needed help and someone refused?" He kept walking.

About half an hour later, we heard footsteps of someone running toward us from behind, yelling, "Frau, Frau!"

In Mom's words:

> I was very afraid. I did not know it was the same man. I tried to go faster, but could not. I had you and Günter. Günter was tired and did not want to walk anymore, and could not walk anymore. And your grandmother (Käthe) was no help since she had a broken arm. And then he came closer and said, "I am the man you talked to." He said he had found someone to take his shift. We walked—I don't know how many miles—to the other side of the city. When we saw the train station lights below us in the distance, he said, "You are on the right path. The train station is in West Germany. On the other side of the train station is the Red Cross where your children can get something to eat."

After he left us, we continued along some country roads and walked through a wooded no-man's-land patrolled by Russian and East German soldiers. The only thing protecting us from the soldiers was the dark. Had we been caught by the Russians, Mom would have probably been raped and then arrested. Had we been caught by a squad of Communist East German soldiers, Mom would have been arrested but not raped. Being arrested meant years of incarceration for her and the possibility of Günter and me being separated. Forced adoption by strangers, with all government adoption records secret, meant the entire family would have faced permanent separation. That was a common punishment for enemies of the Communist State. Mom and my brother knew we faced one of three outcomes: imprisonment, death, or freedom. I was just aware that this was a very serious situation.

We were all exhausted. My brother says he was more tired that night than at any time since.

Mom continues:

> By the grace of God we made our way to the train station. At the station I left our suitcase and told Käthe to stay with the luggage while I walked the short distance to the Red Cross with the children. I had a washcloth and they had soap. I washed your hands. You and Günter were given rolls and milk. We then went back to the train station, where we waited till 6:00 a.m. for the train to Rothenburg. I had a blanket, and you two were sleeping on the blanket between my legs.

IN WEST GERMANY

Final Leg of the Trip to Rothenburg odT

Our family remained intact. We were now in occupied West Germany in the American sector. The most difficult and dangerous part of the journey was behind us. We were finally safe.

My mother remembers:

> Meanwhile I met a young married couple and asked them if they would help me load my suitcase and the bundle, since I had to make sure my children would get on the train safely. It was so crowded when the train was loading. I thought, *I can lose my suitcase and the bundle, but I have to take care of my children.* First I got Käthe on board and handed her you two, and then I boarded. The young couple was honest, and they loaded the suitcase and the bundle. I think the train left at about 7:00 a.m. At about noon we were in Rothenburg. Every few miles we made short pee stops, and it took a while for people to load and unload.

So that is how Mom, Käthe, my brother, and I made it to Rothenburg. Mom knew nothing about the city, had no map, and knew only the address of Grete Herrmann Knopp, who of course did not know she was about to have visitors.

Mom continues:

> We had arrived in Rothenburg. I had a small bundle on my back. In it was the pot for you to poop in. If one travels like that, what can one do? The conductor asked what was in the sack, and he looked into the sack. He laughingly asked, "Is that a cooking pot?"
>
> I was angry and said, "If you don't know the difference, sir, I feel sorry for you." (Mom was laughing as she told me this part of the story). I was tired. We were all tired. We were all tired and dirty. Your noses were running, and you were crying. He thought he could have a little fun with us but then apologized right away.
>
> Just outside the small train station a man was walking by. I talked to him and said, "I'm looking for this address. I have no idea where it is. Can you help me?"
>
> He said, "I live on the same street."
>
> I said, "Oh, that is wonderful."
>
> He said, "How can I help you?" Anyway, he guided us to the address on Topplerweg where Aunt Grete lived.

Aunt Grete (Käthe's half-sister) and her three-year-old daughter, Ingrid, were renting two rooms from a family who owned the house at Topplerweg 4.[4] We arrived in the third week of September. Grete opened the door, discovered she had unexpected guests, and took us in. Käthe found a room elsewhere in the city and lived in Rothenburg the rest of her life.

Consequences

Mom's desire to flee East Germany to reunite the family had long-term consequences. She never saw her parents again. Many years later, when we were living in America, Mom got word that her dad had died. She cried bitter tears. When her mom died, she was inconsolable. I did not understand the reason for her intense grief. As an immature teen I thought, *Well, didn't they have a long life?*

In 1973, years after her parents had died, Mom and Dad returned to West Germany for a visit for the first time since 1952. Mom saw her brothers and sisters again. All of Mom's siblings had fled to the West or been released from captivity to the West, except for her kind sister Medi. Medi had stayed in Weimar, in Communist East Germany. The last time she had seen Medi was in September of 1946. Since Medi was over sixty-five, the East German Communist government allowed Medi to travel to the West for a visit, and Mom was able to see her sister again. Younger, productive citizens were not permitted to leave the "workers' paradise" for fear they would not return.

–NOTES–

1. http://en.wikipedia.org/wiki/Berlin_Wall.
2. Perhaps Mom knew of the train and car corridor between West Berlin and West Germany. That corridor was temporarily closed by the Soviets in 1948, precipitating the Berlin Airlift. http://www.history.com/topics/cold-war/berlin-airlift; http://en.wikipedia.org/wiki/Berlin_Blockade.
3. East Berlin had a population of 1,200,000, and the combined population of East and West Berlin was 3,171,000; https://en.wikipedia.org/wiki/Berlin_population_statistics.
4. For information on how Grete and her daughter had fled Romania two years prior, see the appendix, 32.

Chapter 9

The Fate of the Transylvanian Saxons Who Stayed

The Romanian Communists, under the control of the Soviet Union, governed our Transylvanian homeland and all of Romania. Having to live under communism and fear of the Russians caused many Saxons to flee. But not all families fled; some could not flee and others decided to continue their lives as best they could. The family of my cousin, Diethard Knopp, decided to stay in Transylvania. Another cousin, Hanna Rothmann, was not given a choice. She was arrested and became a slave laborer. Diethard Knopp and Hanna Rothmann gave me their personal accounts of their lives under communism.

A TRANSYLVANIAN SAXON FAMILY AND COMMUNISM

Diethard Knopp's Story

Diethard's narrative describes what life under communism was like for him and his family from 1944 to 1977. Diethard was born in 1943. His brothers were born in 1946 and 1955. In late 1944, right after the Soviet invasion, Romania under communism was transformed so dramatically that it was as if his brothers had been born into a different world. He had a university education and was a teacher of English.

Excerpts of his story follow:

> In Romania the regime of terror installed by the Communists unfolded in two waves: from 1945 to 1965 and from 1965 to 1989. During the first one, the country was under the direct control of Moscow. It started in January 1945 with the mass deportation of more than seventy thousand ethnic Germans from Romania to forced labor in the Soviet Union, which lasted for five years.
>
> Other "glorious deeds" of this period were the 1948 government "nationalization" and the forcing of our farmers into collective farms, which took place in 1949. Flouting the most elementary human rights, the Saxon factory owners were robbed of their factories, the Saxon farmers of their soil, cattle, and machinery, and the whole ethnic German population of their church-owned schools.

Diethard's father, a lawyer, advocated for the rights of minorities living in Romania. A common punishment for those who did not submit totally to the government by continuing to practice Christianity or complaining about the abuse of human rights was to deny them the right to practice their professions.

> Father's law firm was taken away from him and he was forbidden to practice law any longer. In addition, the government systematically damaged his ability to earn money.

The state secret police (securitate) was a lawless arm of the Communist gangster-government that spied on citizens, enforced lawless decrees, and ensured the punishment of people who still believed they had human rights.

> In 1952 many ethnic German citizens were expelled from their stately urban residences. They were forced to settle in the countryside. In 1956 they were allowed to return to

their towns but not into their former homes.

The securitate staged political trials like the one against our father during his first arrest from 1963 till 1964.

They used to come late in the evening at ten. Among their procedures were house searches, cross examinations, etc. During their first "visit" I was already a student at Klausenburg University and was able to visit our father after his arrest in his jail for political prisoners at Sziget on the northern border. But the second time I witnessed it fully; I was back home again in Kronstadt by then.

Our father was sent to prison twice, first in 1963/64, and again shortly before his being expelled from the country in 1972. This was due to his political beliefs and his bravely advocating for the rights of the Transylvanian Saxons.

By that time they had begun to camouflage prisons for political detainees as psychiatric hospitals, prescribing them pills, which of course nobody took.

Non-ethnic Romanian minorities suffered the most.

Jews, Hungarians, ethnic Germans (e.g., our father in 1971) and Gypsies were often arbitrarily arrested. They (but also the Romanian elite!) were sent to jail or abroad (like our parents with their still-underage son, our youngest brother, in 1972).

The Romanian Roman Catholics were persecuted, and their one-million-strong religion was reduced to meaninglessness.

Their bishops and many priests were sent to jail, where many of them were brutally murdered. Their families were exposed to systematic persecutions.

Diethard also lost the right to practice his profession.

> From the time in the fall of 1976, when I was forbidden to teach any more at school, until we left the country at the beginning of 1977, we could hardly make ends meet, subsisting only on my teaching English privately at home.

Even without persecution, life under communism was difficult for all.

> One more word about everyday life under communism: the day usually started long before school by queuing up for a couple of liters of milk at five in the morning, followed by my wife and me alternately hunting for groceries all day.

In 1977, Diethard and his family were permitted to leave Romania and settled in West Germany. They prospered in West Germany, where he taught English. Under an agreement between West Germany and Romania, from 1978 to 1989 the West German government paid about $5,000 for each German-Romanian allowed to emigrate. The cash-strapped Communist Romanian government permitted ten to fifteen thousand of the highly educated and skilled minority to emigrate each year.[1]

LIFE OF A SLAVE LABORER: HANNA ROTHMANN

Beginning in January 1945, even before the war ended on May 8, 1945, the ethnic German population was suffering under the new Russian-controlled Communist Romanian government. Our families lost their civil rights and property, suffered under discrimination, and were arrested. Of those who were arrested, many were transported to the Soviet Union to become slave laborers. A total of seventy-five thousand men between the ages of seventeen and forty-five and women between eighteen and thirty became slave laborers in Russia. Fifteen percent of them died.[2]

Hanna Rothman's Story

In January 1945, three months after the Russian army swept through Transylvania, Hanna Rothmann, who was twenty-one at the time, was arrested by the Communist Romanian police and taken from her home in the middle of the night.

Hanna was one among many who were stuffed into cargo railcars. Hanna's railcar was jammed with 105 men and women. The trip took fourteen days, and the train's destination was Konstinanovka, Russia. The cars were unheated and became much colder as they headed north. They slept on the floor of the cars. The long ride, the cold, the terrible conditions, and an unknown future filled them all with fear. No water was supplied, and except for a few stops to eat snow, they were kept locked in the railcars.

The end of the journey was a slave labor camp next to a bombed-out factory. The barracks were unheated and each was divided into many smaller rooms. Hanna and thirty other women were extremely crowded in their room. The wooden-plank beds had no mattresses, their "pillows" were boards at a slight angle, and because the room was so overcrowded, three women shared a bed. When one turned, all had to turn. They slept with one blanket on the boards for insulation and one blanket on top. One dim electric lightbulb hung from the ceiling. There were no toilets, wash, or shower facilities provided in the barracks or anywhere else.

On the first day at the compound, they awoke to the horror they faced. In Hanna's words:

> The first night passed with grunting and groaning. We were awakened in the morning. Since no wash facilities were available, we were rubbing our hands in the snow to clean them—and then I also saw the first ethnic Romanian slave laborers. They were carrying square logs on their shoulders, two men to each log. Their heads were deeply bowed, looking neither to the left nor right. They moved

> like work animals, as if they were yoked. We were shaken. Was this the kind of work that awaited us, and would we also walk in such a lifeless manner? A guard with a rifle walked behind them. We called to them in Romanian. The guard cursed and the prisoners continued to walk apathetically as if they had heard nothing. We were horrified. Had they been there a long time?

Hanna and her companions were slaves with no rights, facing an unknown future doing back-breaking and dangerous work. They worked outside in all kinds of weather: rain, sleet, snow, bitter cold, summer heat, and in early fall, nice weather. Almost all work consisted of carrying heavy loads, chiseling bricks, and searching for and cutting pieces of sheet metal.

> It is winter 1945. It is terribly cold. The rags we wrapped around our mouth and nose to ward off the cold are frozen stiff from our breath, frozen on our cheeks. Our lips are tight and split, and in our nostrils we have ice buildup. We have been outside all day in the extreme cold, carrying loads of heavy stones with our handbarrows.
>
> As we work, we encounter a man. What does he look like? He is covered with hoarfrost. Our clothing, too, our head covering and hair underneath, are white. But we do not look so ghostlike. Or does it only seem so? After all, it is extremely cold.
>
> The man is close to us. He is also a slave laborer, but one who seems to be already broken. He walks like a marionette with stiff, frozen joints, and his face is covered with hoarfrost. But his beard—his long beard is an icicle. We are shaken. His eyes seem to notice nothing. We are very close now; he does not see us. We have now passed him. The man is walking alone through the huge compound in the opposite direction.

> What group is he with? We do not know. He seems older than we are. Maybe he has a family at home—wife and children, people who hope. For him, hope seems to have died here.
>
> We continue to carry our loads. The extreme cold takes possession of our entire bodies. We must move, move—and hour after hour—back and forth. Our feet seem like blocks of ice. The snow crunches; it is ice. Our backs hurt. The spine seems to break when we lift the loads. But it holds up and we brave the extreme cold—for now. How long can a person endure such inhumanity? And the man whom we encountered? Just don't give up.
>
> As we finally return to the compound, we hear that today it was -32°F and we were outside all day.

Rations were totally inadequate and the workload was extreme. The daily ration was a small slice of bread, a bowl of thin cabbage soup, and a soupspoon full of millet gruel.

> Today the waking up goes as usual. It seems to still be midnight. The brigadier (a civilian overseer) comes again and yells, "Go! Go! Out!" Then he sees someone on a bed on the other side of the room. In the confusion, we had not even noticed. He yells,"Go! Go! Girl! Wake up! Out!" He grabs the legs and shakes them. In horror he lets go; he had shaken a dead person. She was already rigid.
>
> She died among us and beside her sister and nobody noticed.
>
> We are ordered out again. We are despondent and dejected. What does a life mean here? Yesterday the girl was still working—and today? Her sister told us later that she had swollen legs, but was not given a doctor's excuse,

> because she did not have a fever. For days she had just dragged herself to work.
>
> It is incomprehensible. We were lying so close together on the hard board beds, touching each other, and nobody noticed what had happened. We are always so tired and exhausted when we return to camp after a day's work. When we lie down to rest, we really do not notice what is happening around us anymore.

In her time as a slave laborer, Hanna experienced the whole range of human behavior, from extreme cruelty to human kindness. The kindness some Russians showed her and her companions was often a risk to themselves.

She was released due to severe illness on September 22, 1946—one year and nine months after her arrest. Hanna and many other extremely ill passengers were loaded onto freight cars and thought they were going home to their beloved Transylvania. The trip lasted fourteen days. When the train stopped at the final destination, with them still locked inside the cattle cars, they heard German being spoken, not Romanian. They realized they were not home. They were in Germany. When registering with the authorities, they learned that Germany had been split into two countries and they were in Communist East Germany.

While in East Germany, Hanna was able to contact her mother, who still lived in Mediasch, Romania. Then both she and her mother knew the other had survived. She requested permission to travel home to Romania, but her request was denied. She felt unsafe among the Russian soldiers of the occupation army in East Germany. In the slave labor camp, the officers kept tight discipline and the women were protected from what the Russian soldiers might have done to them. But in conquered East Germany, the Russian army was undisciplined. Women were not safe. When Hanna discovered that her brother Arno was in West Germany, she decided to flee to the West.

She and a fellow former female prisoner attempted to cross the border in the deep snow. On their first attempt they were arrested and interrogated by East German police. The policeman in charge was kind and released them rather than sending them to prison and gave them information on how to avoid Russian patrols. At the edge of a forested no-man's-land, they avoided by seconds being discovered by a Russian patrol on cross-country skis. Upon arriving at a village, they were relieved to learn that they were now in West Germany. There they heard that three days earlier a married couple and their adult daughter had also arrived. A Russian patrol had discovered them, raped the women, stolen all their belongings, stripped them of all their clothes, including shoes, and then allowed them to walk the remaining miles in cold and snow to the border.

In February 1947, Hanna knocked on her Aunt Grete's door in Rothenburg. Grete took her in, just like she had taken us in the previous September. Neither of my parents had met Hanna, but in early 1947 Hanna entered our lives. Not long after she arrived in Rothenburg, out of the blue she knocked on our door in Ohrenbach. Her presence in our lives was a blessing.

–NOTES–

1. https://www.nytimes.com/1990/12/28/world/ethnic-germans-in-romania-dwindle.html.
2. http://www.siebenbuerger.de/portal/land-und-leute/siebenbuerger-sachsen/.

Chapter 10

Beginning Life in West Germany

THE REUNION IN ROTHENBURG

The medieval town of Rothenburg odT was founded in AD 1170 and is one of the most picturesque and beautiful places in Germany. It is surrounded by a wall, and originally a moat with drawbridges and gates. In modern times the gates are openings in the wall for the cobblestone streets. All new construction and renovation inside the wall are required to be in the same traditional medieval style as the rest of the city.

Das Ist Vati! (That is Daddy!)

The back of the house where Aunt Grete Herrmann lived was outside of and very close to the wall that surrounded the city. The house was located near the Galgentor (Gallows Gate). About three days after we arrived at Grete's, Mom decided to go for a walk in the city with my brother and me. Mom, Günter, and I had just left the house and turned left, and we were walking toward the gate on the sidewalk when, about fifty yards away, a gaunt, shabby man with a mustache came walking through the gate toward us.

Mom did not recognize that it was her husband, and of course neither did I. Although Dad had changed dramatically, my brother recognized his father. Günter told Mom, "*Das ist Vati!*" (That's Daddy). She insisted, "No, that is not Daddy." But my brother was convinced the man was his dad and ran to him. Well, Günter was right. It was Dad.

Who is That Stranger?

Mom hurried a bit toward the stranger so she could apologize for her son's error. After a few words of apology, there were a few awkward moments until Mom realized it was indeed her husband. A long, emotional hug followed. I was looking up at this stranger hugging my mom, and I did not like it one bit! I pushed him away and told him to go away, but that did not have the desired effect of getting him away from Mom, so I kicked him in the shin as hard as I could. I had kicked him so hard that Dad stood on one foot while holding his shin. A determined three-year-old (and I was determined) can indeed pack quite a wallop.

Dad was extremely skinny, had sunken cheeks, and had a yellow complexion. He was quite weak, still not fully recovered from hepatitis and deprivation. When Dad arrived in Rothenburg, he still had seven potatoes and four pounds of salt. I am sure those potatoes made a much-needed meal or two. A truckload of salt had been delivered to Rothenburg a few days earlier, so Dad's bag of salt was worth much less than when he had left Romania.

Superior Germans

During the time we lived in Grete's apartment, we encountered the attitude of superiority that people who were born and raised in Germany (Reichsdeutsche) felt toward the ethnic Germans from other countries.

My brother describes:

> Yes, we were living with Grete. I also recall that the people who owned the house were "typical Reichsdeutsche snobs," and I got in *big* trouble for having used the word *brunzen* (to piss) when conversing with their bitchy daughter, who was my age. The little twerp delighted in tattling on the "barbarian" (me). Specifically, the twit had been in the (only) bathroom a long time and delighted in my having to wait on her. I finally blurted out that I had to do some serious *brunzen* and if she didn't come out, I would do my *brunzen* out the window.

Rothenburg odT.
Bomb damage from the one bombing raid.
https://en.wikipedia.org/wiki/Rothenburg_ob_der_Tauber.

The War Had Reached Rothenburg odT

About 45 percent of the city had been destroyed in one bombing raid near the end of the war. At the time of our arrival in late September 1946, reconstruction had not yet begun, resulting in a housing shortage for residents and the newly arrived refugees.[1]

New Town, New Job, New House

We now lived in Rothenburg odT as refugees and stateless persons. Dad immediately registered with the police and applied for ration cards and at the employment office (see the appendix, 33–34). Dad also went to the district school administration headquarters in Rothenburg and applied for a teaching position. Within three or four days he was slated to be a teacher at a school in the village of Ohrenbach. The Ohrenbach school was in desperate need of a teacher because the current teacher was severely ill. Ohrenbach is about 7.5 miles from Rothenburg. However, Dad's past education and teaching experience were not recognized by the Regional Education Administration. He was hired as a full-time teacher's aide, not as a teacher. His salary was not enough to provide for a family of four, making our lives as refugees in a foreign country much harder. At the time, he needed and wanted the job and hoped he would be able to obtain adequate documentation and be hired as a licensed teacher in the future. Due to necessary paperwork, registering in Ohrenbach, and setting up housing, his first teaching day was October 22, 1946, a little more than three weeks after he arrived in Rothenburg.

Our new residence was the village schoolhouse. The schoolhouse was a two-story, faded, cream-colored stucco building with large, double front doors in the center with one large casement window on either side.

The doors opened into an eight-foot-wide foyer with brown ceramic tile flooring. On either side of the foyer was a door. Each door led to a separate teacher's apartment. We lived on the right side, with two rooms and a kitchen. The disabled teacher and his ailing wife lived in the apartment on the left. Students entered through the double doors, walked to the back of the foyer, and climbed a wooden stairway to the two classrooms on the second floor. Also on the second floor was a very small apartment where Frau Scholler, a widow, lived with her two young daughters.

Our three-room apartment had no furniture, no stove, no chairs, no heat, no beds, and no running water. Our water came from a hand pump well in front of the schoolhouse.

In Mom's words:

> All that we had were two worn-out suitcases loaded with badly worn clothes. After one week in Ohrenbach we were able to get some military folding cots (with stretched-canvas sleeping surface). Then we got some blankets, but even with the blankets we were too cold at night. It was already late fall and it was too cold to sleep on the cots without a mattress. We then made mattresses out of sacks of straw. We had to make the straw sacks narrow since the cots were so narrow. I was always afraid that you and your brother would fall out at night, especially since you moved around a lot in your sleep. We moved the cots against the wall and wanted to keep you from falling off the other side of the cot with chairs. But we had no chairs, so we borrowed chairs from the local farmers and put the chairs against the cot to keep you from falling off during the night.
>
> Water in the buckets was frozen in the morning. Your blankets were full of ice from where you breathed. The walls had frost on them. You can imagine how cold it was. Our biggest problem was that we did not have enough food to eat.

At the time, there was a serious food shortage, and we had to rely on government ration coupons since Dad's teaching salary did not cover our living costs of food and other necessities.

Mom comments on the ration coupons:

> Others wanted only butter or meat, but their rations were so small that they did not do well. The allowed ration was for ten grams of beef, or we could get three times as much horse meat and four times as much horse blood. We calculated the nutritional value of horse meat and horse blood and chose horse meat and blood over beef. Children up to three years old got a little more milk, but it was skimmed.

The skimmed milk was blue; however, when the farmers got to know us, they started to give us whole milk. When I asked my mom how much meat we got per person, she responded, "Maybe two ounces per person per week."

EARLY OHRENBACH
(October 1946 to mid-1948)

Spartan Living

With most of the power plants bombed out, electricity was rationed. Each community was supplied electricity at a specific time on a rotating basis. In the mornings between 7:00 and 8:00 a.m., Ohrenbach had electricity. Mom had no way of cooking food. Frau Scholler, who lived on the second floor, had a hotplate and Mom would go upstairs and cook for the day, always soup or a casserole, which we ate cold. To quote Mom, "It was a pain." After a couple of months we finally were able to buy a six-inch-diameter hotplate. The exposed spiral-wound wires were nestled in ceramic grooves and glowed like toaster wires. Several months later, Dad and Günter traveled to Ansbach to buy a stove. The trip took all day.[2] To get to Ansbach they had to leave early in the morning to take a bus to Rothenburg and then a train to Ansbach. I saw Günter and Dad walking toward the schoolhouse.

Dad was carrying the small sheet-metal stove strapped to his back.

In Mom's words:

> We tried to get a stove right away, but it took about six months till we got the little stove. It was not as big as a Coleman stove. It was about eight inches by eighteen inches. An eight-inch pan would just fit. The legs of the stove were just little stubs. Vati made metal legs and screwed them on, but the stove was always rickety and would move when I was cooking. But we were very happy to have a stove.

The stove had a tiny sheet-metal firebox that pulled out. We would fill the firebox with short, small-diameter pieces of wood. More sticks were added as necessary. That was our stove until we got a much larger wood- or coal-burning stove several years later.

We had three low-wattage bare incandescent bulbs hanging from the ceiling, one in the kitchen, one in our parents' bedroom, and one in our bedroom. Initially we had no kerosene lantern or other source of artificial light. Germany is approximately at the same latitude as Newfoundland, with long nights and short days in the winter. In that first winter, the only light in the long, dark evenings was one candle to give Dad light for planning his lessons. As time passed, electrical availability increased. By the time we left Ohrenbach in 1952, we had electricity twenty-four hours per day.

Reunited, and It Feels So Good—Sort Of

Mom was no longer the shy, young wife she had been in Romania. She had grown into an independent, fierce lioness who had endured and overcome many adversities. She had risked everything to save her children. Dad was also not the man she had married. Combat changes people. Today we call it PTSD. This change was in addition to the aftereffects of the serious head injury sustained in the motorcycle accident. The head injury had made Dad very short-tempered with his family. Because of his cultural and military background, he knew the man was the ruler of the family. His wife was subservient and the children were to follow his desires at all times, no questions asked. After more than two years of independence, the idea did not settle well with Mom. They had many serious conflicts and arguments after reuniting. Many families who had suffered similar hardships divorced. I believe this did not happen to Mom and Dad only because Mom felt she owed it to her children to have them grow up with their dad. In the process, she sacrificed much.

In Mom's words:

> If we had not liked each other so much, the war would have destroyed us. But since we liked each other, it brought us together even though we had our difficulties. We excused each other and forgave each other. I had to get used to Vati and he had to get used to me. I had been mother and father for three years and became self-reliant. Then Vati came back and it was all over. I had no more say. He was the boss and I had to go along with that. It was hard. The first year was especially difficult because I did not want to give in. I said, "Hey, what's wrong with you? I could live without you!" It (the war) changes one. Well, somebody had to give in and it was not going to be Vati.

Very early in our time in Ohrenbach, I remember arguments with lots of yelling and brutal verbal attacks by Dad. There was one time when Dad took it too far. Mom suddenly snapped. She lunged at him with animal-like fury. She was totally out of control and he had to hold her to stop the blows. Mom collapsed and sank to the floor. She collapsed mentally. She was broken. Her nose was running profusely, and there was excessive saliva flowing from her open mouth. She was sobbing and wailing. The argument was over. Dad's demeanor was instantly transformed. He was silent and had a very concerned look upon his face. His expression screamed, "My God, what have I done?"

After a couple of minutes he asked my brother and me to go outside and not talk about what happened. I remember my brother and me walking out quietly and spending a long time outside. I felt like I had to guard a deep, dark secret. I was very concerned about Mom. It took her some time to recover, and Dad was ultra-careful and caring during that time. He had seen enough in life to know this was serious. In the long run, however, that did not change how he interacted with Mom. He was a good man and a loyal husband and father, but he was not perfect.

The only time Dad's PTSD posed a physical danger to the family was when Dad was dreaming he was in a death struggle with a Russian soldier. In his dream, he was choking the Russian. In actuality, he was strangling Mom, who in desperation slapped him as hard as she could. Fortunately, he woke up and there was no tragedy.

FOOD ISSUES

Food

As kids, our lives revolved around food. There was never enough. We were always hungry. In West Germany there was even less food available after the war than during the war. The year 1946 was bad, but for most people 1947 was worse as a direct result of the implementation of the draconian Morgenthau Plan. It was a time of severe hardship during which nearly everyone in West Germany went hungry and people, especially children, were dying from malnutrition.

Thanksgiving at Christmas

Around Christmastime, in that first winter in Ohrenbach, one dark winter evening, I was hungry and concerned that we would have nothing to eat for dinner. I looked out the front window at the lit windows of the farmhouses and wondered if those people had anything to eat. For the first time since we had arrived, there was a knock on the door during the evening time. Since this was so unusual, we all went to the door as my dad opened it. The visitor was the young daughter of one of the farm families. She had a gift for us. The gift was a large pot of hot water with fat floating on top. The sausages had been removed, but the fat had calories, and flavor. We desperately needed calories. The joy I felt for the pot of water with fat is almost indescribable. The smell from the pot was glorious. What a wonderful gift. My despair and the despair my parents were trying to hide from us vanished. That desperation was replaced with joy and thankfulness. My mom probably added some flour and a potato, to make some gravy. I did not go to bed with an empty stomach as I had feared. I fell asleep with joy in my heart and an almost-full stomach.

Choking

Dad came home with very small bit of some kind of mystery meat that had been discarded by someone. Mother said it was inedible and he should not attempt to eat it. They argued, but Dad, as usual, knew best. He cooked it in a small pan of boiling water, using our newly acquired hotplate. Guessing from its appearance, I think it might have been the esophagus of a chicken or rooster. He nearly choked to death. When people are starving, they will eat what they would reject under normal circumstances.

Horse Blood and Snails

For a long time, we could not afford to purchase meat, but we did purchase horse blood using our ration coupons.

My brother recalls:

> In times of rationing we always bet on horse. Meat was *never* the main course—it was always just another ingredient. Mutti would prepare the blood in a skillet with anything else that was available—onions, potatoes, stale bread, salt, pepper, etc.—and we had "scrambled blood."
>
> We also picked greens along the side of the road and in meadows. Nettles were one of our favorites. Once these were boiled (blanched), they were prepared similar to spinach. Wild mushrooms were a delicacy.

> I recall only one item that everyone refused: snails. Mutti tried her best to prepare them, but they were full of sand and tasted awful. Maybe if we'd had loads of butter, garlic, French bread, and white wine and called them escargot, the little slime balls would have been more acceptable.
>
> It wasn't unusual to "recycle" molded bread. The recipe: Scrape off the mold, toast bread on stove top (we didn't know that GE made toasters), and spread toast with molasses. 'Twas a yummy afternoon or bedtime snack.

I never really liked horse blood, but I ate it.

Packages from America

I remember the first of several boxes of food we received from the United States.[3] The package contained various food items, one of which was the most wonderful food I had ever tasted—Spam. What glorious food! With Mom's culinary skills, we had quite a few wonderful meals from that 12 oz. can. The first package was wrapped in pieces of a durable pink fabric carefully sewn together to fit the box, becoming much-needed dish towels. Nothing was wasted.

MIRACLE HEALING

Mom's Surgery

In 1947 Mom had major surgery at a hospital in Nürnberg (Nuremberg).

The Dying Room

Mom's surgery did not go well. Mom was dying. The hospital ward had more than twenty beds, and the other recuperating patients were aware of the dying patient. The Catholic hospital had a special room reserved for people who were expected to die. In consideration for the other patients, Mom was moved to the small dying room. Shortly thereafter, the head nun talked to Mom and asked if it was OK if she prayed for and with Mom. Mom was so weak that she was able only to move her lips and say *ja* (yes). The nun then said, "Now we will make you well," and started praying for Mom. The nun checked up on Mom several times per day and prayed for her each time by kneeling beside the bed and holding my mom's hands. Mom was very weak and could only occasionally say a very weak "amen" during the prayers. Whenever Mom managed to say the barely audible "amen," the nun would say, "Good, you are praying with me." Mom was so ill that she did not know what the nun was saying in her prayers.

Two or three days later, the nun and Mom were alone in the room, praying, and the door was closed. The nun said, "There is someone else in the room."

Mom said, "Yes, I know. I can see him. I see his head." As Mom described to me later what she had seen, she told me, "First the head appeared, and then the rest of the figure slowly appeared." Once he was fully visible, Mom saw a figure wearing a cloak. As she was relating the story to me, she said, "I knew that the end was coming. But I was not afraid."

The nun simply said, "We will keep praying." The nun kept praying until my mother could no longer see the figure and the nun could no longer feel the presence of someone else in the room. Although Mom was still as weak as before, at that moment she started to think about her children, and her will to live returned.

Once Mom's will to live returned, she needed to eat to regain her strength and heal. The hospital food was unbelievably bad and there was not much of it. The nun would come and say, "What would you like to eat today?" She would somehow get the best food, cook for Mom, and feed her so she would regain her strength. Mom told me that she thought the food may have been intended for the hospital director.

For two or three days after the figure had left, the nun kept feeding my mom and praying several times per day with her. Mom said she did not know how long the nun prayed, but it seemed like hours each time. After those two or three days, someone came to take her from the dying room and returned her to the same ward in the hospital. Mom estimated that she had been in the dying room for five or six days. Mom said she would always remember the nun's kindness.

I believe the above described events show the power of prayer and a miracle of healing. Thank you, Lord.

Dad's Cooking

My only childhood memory of this event is my mom's extended absence and Dad's cooking. He made the first potato pancakes I had ever eaten. The pancakes were mashed potatoes flattened into patties and browned in a skillet. I remember thinking, *I had no idea he could cook.* They were delicious. By the way, Dad never could cook. As a matter of fact, that was the only time he ever tried.

During Mom's hospital stay, girls from the school babysat while Dad was teaching. One of them, Kathi, also did housework for us when Mom came back from the hospital. In those days there was a great deal of work to be done because nothing was mechanized or automatic. Years later Kathi wrote her to thank her for everything Mom had taught her.

Dad taught, worked on lessons, and built radios from parts scavenged from shot-down airplanes until late into the night. Dad's hard work after his teaching hours reaped important benefits. He paid the doctor who performed the operation with a liter of potato schnapps and a radio he had built. Those two items covered the cost of the doctor and the hospital bills. Schnapps and radios were much more valuable than money in postwar Germany. At the time, it was impossible to buy a radio in West Germany.

HANNA ROTHMANN KNOCKS ON OUR DOOR

Hanna Rothmann, Dad's cousin from Romania and survivor of a Russian slave labor camp, came into our lives after she escaped to West Germany. She arrived at Aunt Grete's door in Rothenburg and, like many others, was taken in. Not long thereafter, Hanna came to visit us in

Ohrenbach. She was in worse shape than we were because of the horrific deprivations from her time as a slave laborer in Russia.

In Mom's words:

> Hanna knocked on the door and said, "Lene?"
>
> I said, "Yes, who are you?"
>
> She responded, "I am your cousin." I did not know I had a cousin. I had never met her. Vati (Dad) had not met her either. She was wearing nothing other than badly worn warm-ups, like sweats. She wore heavy working shoes. Rags were wrapped around her feet instead of socks. She did not even have a bra or panties. I had only one dress, two skirts, and two sets of underwear. I shared those clothes with her until she got the right paperwork filled out so she could buy something. We got along so wonderfully, just like I got along with my sister Medi. We had such a good time. We got along so well.

Hanna stayed with us part of that year to help our family during Mom's long recovery from the aftereffects of surgery. Despite the fact that it was the most difficult postwar year due to the lack of food and other necessities, Mom said that the time Hanna lived with us was one of the happiest times in her life. Mom told me how she, Dad, and Hanna used to joke around and laugh and just enjoy life, amid great hardship. As long as my mother lived, she and Hanna stayed in close contact via letters and occasional phone calls.

Hanna talks about this period of time in her journal:

> Aunt Grete allows me to live with her and begins to fatten me up. After that terrible time, which—thank God—is over, I look pitiful. I am recovering both physically and mentally. I am no longer alone. I have much to thank Aunt Grete for.
>
> Yet, nightmares continue to follow me.
>
> In Rothenburg I have a home again. I'm helping my aunt keep

> house and then I help in the house of my cousin, Aunt Käthe's son, Gustav Maroscher, whose wife is often sick and has to go to the hospital. He has two children. My cousin is a teacher in Ohrenbach, a community not far from Rothenburg.
>
> I feel very at ease with the Maroscher family and am becoming a little bit of my former self. My life has meaning again. I am needed. I am beginning to enjoy life again.

When Mom was fully recovered, Hanna resumed her life in Rothenburg. She married Alfred Gellfart, a former POW, who lost both his homeland and his four brothers, who were killed in the war. Hanna and Alfred had two children: Klaus and Ruth.

In 2007 I went to a family reunion in Rothenburg odT and had the opportunity to talk with Hanna and her family. It was so good to talk to this wonderful lady. She had been through so much in life, yet she was one of the nicest and kindest people I have ever known. When her daughter Ruth informed me via email that her mom had died, I cried. I loved Hanna. Hanna died at the age of eighty-nine. Her daughter, Ruth, wrote that her mother was *liebenswürdig*. According to the German–English dictionary, *liebenswürdig* means "gracious, gentle, kind, loveable." She was all of that.

Mom at about twenty

WAR TAKES ITS TOLL

The war took not only its mental toll but its physical toll as well. When I look at the picture on the right, I can see in my mom's eyes that she experienced hardship and horror. War changes people. Mom was no longer the same, but she persevered.

Mom in 1946 at about twenty-six

Dad as a young teacher.

Mom once told me, "The only thing that got me through was my faith, and the fact that sleep enabled me to forget, at least for a few hours."

The war, contracting hepatitis, being a POW, and the stressful life in Romania after the war changed Dad physically and emotionally. He was not healthy when he began his life in Ohrenbach.

Dad after the war in late 1946 or 1947. He was twenty-nine.

TEACHING AGAIN

Teaching in Ohrenbach, Bavaria

When Dad started teaching in Ohrenbach, he was the only teacher for all eight grades. One classroom was for grades one through four and the other for five through eight. Dad had over one hundred students. He picked the best students and had the older, better students teach the others while he monitored their teaching.

In Mom's words:

> No wonder he did not want anything to do with you boys when he got home. It was hard, especially when you want to teach. He could have done what other teachers might do and just get by. But he was a teacher in his heart and soul, and that made it hard. In his life he accomplished more than someone who lived to be one hundred. He was very driven. He always tried the best to help his family.

Later, other teachers were added and Dad was able to personally concentrate on students in grades five through eight. One of the subjects Dad taught was horticulture. To reinforce the students' learning, he arranged for the creation of a student test garden.

Mom remembers this test garden:

> He told the parents that the students needed to learn gardening skills and that there was a need for a school garden. A farmer donated a small parcel of land the size of my back lawn (about seventy-five by thirty feet.), which became the school garden. We showed the town how to get a higher potato yield with this test garden.

Mom and Dad in the center with one of Dad's classes in Ohrenbach

The test garden worked out very well for the students, the farmers, and us. We were able to harvest some of the produce from the very prolific garden to supplement our meager diet. Prior to having access to the garden, Dad gave private music lessons for an entire year and was paid one large sack of potatoes, which helped keep us alive. Although we lived in the schoolhouse, we had no personal garden plot and owned no land. The school test garden was a blessing.

The Master Teacher

His efforts had a significant positive impact on the education of the Ohrenbach youth. He started a youth group, a brass band, an orchestra, a drama club, and a sports club. Dad could play a number of musical instruments and taught the students to play. The sports club sponsored athletic events. I remember multisport athletic events on a dedicated field just outside Ohrenbach, where athletes from the big city (Rothenburg) were invited. The atmosphere was reminiscent of a fair.

Student Activities Room

Dad needed a large room for the student club meetings, drama club practices, play performances, and orchestra practices. He persuaded one of the parents, a farmer, to donate a bottom-floor cow stable. For hundreds of years, farmers often had a large, low-ceiling room on the ground floor of their houses. The ceiling was high enough for cattle but not high enough for people. Having the cattle under the living quarters actually supplied heat through the floor in the wintertime. It was just such a room that was converted into the all-purpose student room. The transformation from cow stable into a new, large, and bright room with both a stage and seating for the audience was completed under Dad's supervision. What the men did—through brainpower and muscle power—was raise the ceiling of the room significantly, creating a high-ceiling activity room. They did it inches at a time, pausing each time to place temporary pillars under the ceiling until the ceiling was quite high. I observed the process from the open doorway. One great memory I have of this room, after its completion, was the performance of a humorous student play called *Der Poltergeist* (The Noisy Ghost). I have never laughed harder.

Dad leading the Ohrenbach school brass band, Rothenburg odT, 1948.
Note the bombed-out buildings in the background.

–NOTES–

1. How Rothenburg was saved from total destruction: http://en.wikipedia.org/wiki/Rothenburg_ob_der_Tauber.
2. The distance from Ohrenbach to Ansbach is about twenty-five miles, a forty-minute car ride today.
3. The packages were sent to us by the Fleischer family from Detroit, Michigan. The Fleischers were distant relatives. They shipped one or two more packages. Years later, when we were in the United States, Mom and Dad made contact with them and thanked them, and they became friends.

Chapter 11

Memories of Ohrenbach

MEMORIES OF A YOUNG BOY
(Early 1947 to Early 1952)

The Ohrenbach memories paint word pictures of what it was like to grow up in a farming village in the West German state of Bavaria after the war. The events are in no particular order. Günter's memories add the perspective of an older brother.

Leave Some for Me!

Having enough food was always an issue for our family. Our meals were always some kind of a casserole. Whenever anyone would take food, I would scream, "Leave some for me!" And I do mean *scream*. It was instinct. I was hungry all the time. After the Marshall Plan went into effect, I was much more reasonable at the dinner table, although our family never really had enough to get "full." At least my screams were not as shrill anymore.

One time during the "worst of times," my brother reached with his fork to take a morsel out of the dish in the center of the table. I wanted it for myself, but he got it. All I got with my fork was the back of his hand. He still has a scar to remind him of being "forked."

Keeping Warm

Eventually Mom and Dad bought a potbellied stove for their bedroom. Much later, they purchased a large, new (to us) wood-and-coal-burning kitchen stove. Then both the kitchen and their bedroom were heated. In the winter, whenever meals were being prepared, everyone gathered in the kitchen because it was the warmest room. Mom enjoyed cooking on the large stove and also used it to bake bread. Whenever Mom was about to cut a loaf, she would first turn the bread over to its flat side and make the sign of the cross on the crust with the knife as a way of giving thanks. When I was small, I slept in their bedroom, but as my brother and I got older, we slept in the large, unheated room. To stay warm my brother and I slept in the same bed, and Mom had us sleep with our heads on opposite ends.

At some point, our parents bought us regular beds with large, thick straw mattresses, and we each had our own bed. The straw mattresses were large burlap-like bags filled with straw. Straw was a great insulator and kept us quite warm. Mom and Dad had a larger bed in their bedroom, also with straw mattresses. One way my brother and I were able to keep warm was with large, hot bricks: Mom or Dad would heat two large, solid bricks on the stove, wrap them in newspaper to insulate them, and put them under the blanket at our feet as foot warmers. There were a few times the bricks were so hot that the paper would be singed and turn light brown. The hot bricks contained enough heat to warm our feet for hours and made it much easier to fall asleep in a room with ice on the walls. For the winter of 1949/50, Mom bought us beautiful down-filled blankets. They were amazingly warm, regardless of how cold the room was.

Keeping Clean

Günter remembers:

> Then there was the Saturday bath. Lots of water was pumped from the well, much wood or coal briquettes were brought to the kitchen, the stove was fired up, and the wooden bathtub was dragged out of storage. Vati bathed first . . . you were last. Sorry.

The tub was small enough to be easy for an adult to carry and a ten-year-old to sit in. The water came from the well, one bucket at a time, and then was heated one pan at a time on the stove. Mom's and Dad's "baths" consisted of standing in the tub and washing with a washcloth. Because I was always the last to bathe, I grew up thinking gray bathwater was normal. In spite of the water being gray when I got in, I must admit it actually was a much darker shade of gray by the time I finished my bath. My brother and I were major contributors to the graying of the bathwater, especially in the summers when we ran around barefoot on Ohrenbach's dirt roads, which were also populated with horse droppings and cow pies.

Repairing Shoes

My brother remembers our issues with shoes:

> Shoes were a constant maintenance headache. Since we were often forced to walk in soft mud or snow, shoes had to be cleaned every night and then dried by the stove. In the morning they were smeared with polish and shined. In such conditions shoe soles didn't last long and Father would resole our shoes with leather or rubber, depending on what was available. Both wooden and steel nails were used. Do you recall the cast iron "lasts," complete with a stand?[1] Cold, wet feet were an everyday pain in the buttocks, and cutting out shoe inserts from newspaper was a nightly ritual.

Cleaning shoes was not only a way to extend the life of shoes; it was a cultural standard to have clean, polished shoes.

The Manure Pile

A farmer's property, with house and barn, jutted up against the schoolhouse wall. His manure pile was right under the kitchen window. There were no screens on the windows, and with the manure pile directly under the kitchen window, we had more than our share of flies, gnats, bugs, and stink. Mom complained all the time, but the manure pile had been there long before we came, and the farmer was not interested in moving it.

Farmers looked at large manure piles as a measure of wealth. The more animals the farmer had, the larger the manure pile and the better off the family was. That reminds me of an authentic Nazi joke my dad had heard during the war: "A man greets another with a Nazi salute and instead of saying, 'Heil Hitler!' he says, '*So hoch*!' (So high!). When questioned about what '*so hoch*' meant, he responds, 'That is how high the manure pile is at my house.'"

Happy Toes

One memorable feature about the dirt roads was that in the summertime, if it had been a long time since the last rain, there was a thick layer of dust on the road, maybe an inch thick in places. Walking barefoot (we were always barefoot in the summer) in the dust that had been heated by the summer sun was a pleasure. How good it felt to have warm dust squeeze between my toes.

Buried Memories of War

Although I experienced the horrors of war, I have no conscious memory of WWII. I do recall the one time I encountered "war" in Ohrenbach. When we were young, children were not watched as closely by their parents as they are today. We ran around all day playing or exploring and—within certain boundaries—went anywhere we wanted to go. The term *helicopter parent* had not yet been coined. One warm summer day when I was about five, I was by myself, walking alone through a small woods. I left the woods and walked on the main road that ran by Ohrenbach. The main road was unpaved and did not have any gravel to keep down the dust.

Suddenly I saw something that can best be described as a monster from hell coming toward me at high speed, making a great deal of noise.

It was an American tank. Because of the thick layer of fine dust on the road, the tank generated a massive, impenetrable dust cloud, obliterating the world behind it. I could see only the front of the tank rumbling and screaming toward me! I knew instantaneously that what was coming toward me was a death machine. I panicked. In absolute terror I ran home to Mom, screaming, "*Der Krieg ist hier! Der Krieg ist hier*!" (War is here! War is here!). She patiently calmed me down, and then I explained what I had seen. She assured me that we were not at war and that everything was OK.

As an adult, during my own officers' basic training, I had the opportunity to stand near sixty-ton moving tanks with massive tracks, turrets, and guns, as well as to drive one. I can attest from my experiences as both a child and an adult that they are large, powerful, noisy, fear-inducing tracked vehicles.

Reflecting back on that incident, I think there were many experiences I had during the war that are not part of my conscious memory. However, they are stuck somewhere in my brain. These buried experiences have in part, for good or bad, shaped me into the person I am today.

Meeting American Soldiers

After my scary encounter with the tank, I learned that American soldiers were no longer waging war. I no longer feared military vehicles or soldiers. I learned from older and wiser boys that Americans were a good source of chocolate, something we all loved but never got to eat. I even learned how to say "chocolate" in English. This knowledge proved to be invaluable.

The main street through the village made a T intersection with the road that went past just outside Ohrenbach. Just before the T was a tree in the middle of the main road out of town. One day I was near the tree with two younger boys when we saw a tank drive past from right to left. The tank traveled fairly fast and turned left at another T intersection about a quarter mile away. That intersection was flanked by two large poplar trees, a favorite hangout for a family of crows. Seeing the tank go by was interesting, and I waited to see if any other vehicle would come along.

A few minutes later, a jeep with four American soldiers drove up. They spoke no German and we spoke no English, but their hand gestures indicated that they wanted to know if the tank had turned left or right at the end of the road. I stuck out my open hand and said in what I thought was very good English, "Chokolat?" Perhaps this was my first negotiation ever. The clever Americans pulled out a few pieces of chocolate and laid them in my open hand. I smiled, took the chocolate, pointed left, and said, "*Links*" (Left). Oh, how delicious the chocolate was! Hershey's, I am sure. Oh, the joy of knowing a foreign language! I gave each of the other two boys a little square of chocolate, and they were quite impressed with my foreign-language and negotiation skills.

I Don't Eat Pets!

Our "backyard" was a small area behind our section of the schoolhouse surrounded by a concrete wall. The enclosed area was long and narrow and paved with concrete. To the right was a small wooden shack that served as a tiny stable and a rabbit hutch. After we had lived in Ohrenbach for a few years, Dad was able to buy a goat and a rabbit. One day, the goat had a kid! I loved the little goat as a boy would love his dog. I got to walk the baby goat around town with a rope around its neck. One day the baby goat was gone and we had meat to eat. It did not take me long to figure out that I was about to eat my beloved goat. I refused to eat the meat. At first, my brother was reluctant, but he was smarter and much less attached to the little goat. His resolve to not eat the meat dissolved rather quickly, within a matter of minutes. For a period of several weeks I refused to eat meat of any kind, just in case it was my goat. As an adult, my brother told me with a sheepish grin that he kept reminding me that this might still be goat meat as a way to have more for himself. It worked.

All the Beer I Could Drink

I got all the free beer I wanted at the local guesthouse across the street from the school. The Red Stallion Guesthouse was part of the Gögelein family property. A guesthouse is a pub with a restaurant, a bar, and a few rooms for overnight guests. I had my own small beer mug and could walk up to the bar for free beer anytime. The bar was higher than I was tall, so I would reach up high and place my beer mug on the bar and the kind bartender would fill my mug. The beer was delicious. Since we really needed calories, one might say it served as liquid bread. Lest you worry too much about my young drinking habits, I estimate the tiny mug held a quarter cup when full.

All the Beer He Could Sell

My brother sold buckets of beer to GIs who would occasionally bivouac near Ohrenbach.

In my brother's words:

> In those days when folks had people over for a visit, it was not uncommon to send the kids to the local beer emporium to bring libation for the party. What I did with Gögelein went as follows: Once I learned the location of the Americans' bivouac, I would tell Gögelein that I had a "customer." He would fill a couple of buckets; I would walk into the camp and start bartering. After that, I walked out of camp with buckets full of K rations. I usually made several trips to complete my portion of the haul.
>
> By the way, bivouacs were generally in the same location outside of Ohrenbach. So whenever I saw a convoy passing by, I knew "the game was on."

My brother did not know it at the time, but he was beginning to develop his rather prodigious sales and marketing skills.

Better Than a Roller Coaster

My brother and I shared an exciting ride in the back of a big empty farm wagon that was pulled by two cows. The wagon was similar to an uncovered Conestoga wagon, the early mode of transportation for Americans heading west in the mid-to-late nineteenth century. It was a big, heavy-duty wagon with sturdy, tall sides. We had been invited to go out into the fields, and one of Gögelein's daughters was driving the wagon. Going into the fields was a big treat after usually playing in and near Ohrenbach. One of the cows had one short and deformed horn. The word was that it had been hit by shrapnel during the war.

We were moving along at a slow cow pace on a typical narrow dirt road with ditches on either side. Those ditches were often stinky, dirty, mucky places, but on this summer day they were dry with tall grass growing in them. Then an old black truck, smaller than a Ford F-150, with a tall, black covered cargo box passed us on the left rather fast (fast by Ohrenbach standards anyway). The truck was loud and came very close. Ohrenbach cows were not used to trucks on the road and they panicked. Suddenly, we were having a lot of fun bouncing in the back of the wagon being pulled by two runaway cows. Cows can move quite fast. In their panicked state, the cows pulled the wagon into the ditch on the right side of the road, and it turned over. As the wagon landed upside down, straddling the ditch, it abruptly stopped. My brother and I landed in the ditch on the tall, warm, soft grass with the wagon upside down over us. Since the sides of the wagon were about two feet tall and the ditch was a couple of feet deep, there was plenty of space for us under the upturned wagon. What fun! Miss Gögelein had jumped from the wagon as it began to overturn. She was unhurt. The cows were also unhurt, calmed down quickly, and began eating long, tender grass.

School Work Gangs

My brother explains:

> All students in all grades were expected to participate in

helping in the fields. We walked to the farm fields like students today may go from building to building on a field trip. In the spring, the classes would march out into the fields to pick potato bugs, larvae, and eggs. The bright yellow eggs were under the leaf in rows, and if you found them, the whole leaf was picked and disposed of.

In late fall the students helped harvest potatoes. They walked behind a large rake pulled by horses. The rake loosened the soil to make it easy to find the potatoes. Students would pick up the potatoes and throw them into a wagon being pulled nearby. This work was done after a frost so the green tops were dead and dry. After the potatoes were harvested, the dry green tops were collected and all placed in a large pile to be burned. Once the pile was lit, the kids would throw some potatoes on the fire. After the embers were cool, we looked for the potatoes, which were now black from being burned. But when armed with a pocketknife to cut off the burnt part, one could enjoy a good baked potato.

Runaway Horses

As impressive as runaway cows were, they were nothing compared to runaway horses. One day a driverless runaway buckboard being pulled by two crazed horses flew by. The horses' nostrils were flared, their eyes unnaturally wide and wild, manes flying. The last I saw of the horses was when they turned right at the end the street, with the buckboard tipping and running on two wheels. Who knows how long they had run or how many people had to get out of their way to avoid being run over.

The Naked Men

Once per week we got a six-page newspaper that my dad liked to read. One day in 1950 or 1951 Dad was reading the newspaper as usual when I looked over his shoulder and saw a picture that showed maybe twenty naked, slender men walking away from the photographer. Since I could see their naked butts, I thought this was funny, laughed, and asked my dad why they were walking around naked. He explained to me that they were American POWs captured by the North Koreans in the Korean War. Then I noticed the uniformed men with rifles, walking behind the naked men. My dad gently made it clear that these men were prisoners of war and that they were in a bad situation. I could tell he empathized with them. Many or all of those young men in the picture may have never made it back home.

Hare Roundup

All farmers want to keep wildlife from eating their crops, and farmers in Ohrenbach were no different. Full-grown German wild hares weigh up to 15 lbs. At the time, the hare population was large and a significant threat to crop yield. At least once per season, the local men would have hare roundups in the surrounding fields. I never participated, but I think the strategy was to have "drivers" who would make noise and herd the hares into areas where they could be shot by hunters with shotguns. Dad needed a hunting license to participate. I remember the take from one of those hunts was a large farm wagon full of hundreds of dead hares. As a participant, my father shared in the bounty and we had rabbit stew. Yum!

I was too young to go on the hare hunts. When I asked my brother if he got to go along, he responded:

> Mutti (Mom) didn't want me to go because she thought I was too young. Never mind that we'd all been participating in much more aggressive sports such as fighter-plane-onto-train strafing raids and ho-hum bombing raids, not to mention middle-of-the-night border crossings.
>
> As with almost every endeavor, nothing was wasted—including the Leporidae's fur. There were rabbit mittens, rabbit collars, rabbit earmuffs, rabbit hand muffs, rabbit slippers, rabbit hats, etc.

Fabricating radios

My father did many things to earn extra money to support his family. Three of his endeavors were giving private music lessons, making potato schnapps, and building radios. My brother recalls going with Dad to the site of a wrecked British or American single-engine plane that had been shot down. Our dad cannibalized radio parts so he could build radios for home use. He used a soldering iron heated by charcoal for wire assembly. A local cabinet maker, Herr Schweizer, made beautiful wood cabinets for the radios. The radios operated on vacuum tubes since the transistor had not yet been invented. Dad made at least three radios "from scratch," using an electrical schematic of a typical radio as a guide.

Industrial production and importation of radios was prohibited in occupied West Germany, making Dad's radios quite valuable. Before the radios were sold, we listened to radio programs. We would listen to the radio as a family. It was enjoyable and quite informative. I remember listening to repeated warnings about being careful when picking mushrooms. Many hungry people went into the woods to pick mushrooms. It seemed like every day the radio program would give a list of people who had recently died from eating the poisonous ones. I remember only the warnings and not any guidance on how to pick nonpoisonous mushrooms. I concentrated on the listing of those who had died. I am still afraid of picking mushrooms. My family did pick mushrooms at the time; I was just unaware of it.

One of the radios had a short. Nobody knew about the short except for me. There was a small screw that held one of the knobs onto a metal shaft. If your fingers were small enough, you could touch the screw and get a shock. In Germany the standard voltage is 220 volts. This was plenty of voltage to kill you if you were grounded. Fortunately, I was sitting on a wood chair on a wood floor at the time. I enjoyed the strong tingle and would occasionally touch it for fun. Nobody ever knew.

New Toy

Once living conditions had improved after the Marshall Plan was implemented, my brother received a small stationary alcohol-powered steam engine. There was a tiny metal pan for fuel under a boiler. When operating, the steam engine's one cylinder would turn a small flywheel. The whole toy had a footprint of about two and a half by six inches and was about four inches tall. It provided many hours of fun as we fired it up and watched it chug away. And one time, it provided some extra excitement: One of us had spilled some alcohol on the rough wooden floor, and the spill was burning. My brother jumped up and down, panicked, and screamed. Maybe he had seen too many houses burn during the war? I calmly walked over to where Mom kept the mop and bucket for floor cleaning and proceeded to cover the burning spot on the floor with the damp mop. End of crisis. I remember feeling pretty proud of myself since in my brother's eyes I was always the stupid little brother very worthy of teasing.

St. Nicholas Day, December 6

On December 6, kids would clean their shoes and leave them outside by the front door. Many people left cookies for St. Nicholas to eat. By morning, St. Nicholas had left candy, nuts, or fruit in the children's shoes. The first Christmas or two, we did not receive any gifts. As times got better, we were thankful for whatever we found in our shoes.

St. Nicholas would also come to visit our school on a school day close to December 6. He was a fearsome person with a leather and fur overcoat and a tall walking stick. He would come up the wooden staircase to the classrooms, pounding his thick walking stick on the stairs while making scary sounds. I was not the only young child who was totally terrified. He also carried a long switch (a long flexible branch such as a willow branch), and he would vigorously strike all "bad" boys on their bottoms. What I did not know until later was that parents told Nicholas if they wanted their sons to be switched or not. My parents spared me a public beating.

Christmas

On December 24, *das Christkind* (the Christ child) came, decorated the freshly cut tree, and brought gifts. The tree had ten or fifteen real candles. The tree and all preparations were hidden from my brother and me behind a locked door. Peeking through the keyhole to spy on the activity proved fruitless since the tree was out of sight in the closest left corner of the room.

The door to the room was opened for us when all the candles had been lit and the presents had been placed under the tree. I remember one year a branch started burning. Dad broke the branch off, carried it outside, and threw it on the snow-covered ground. We lived at about 2,500 ft. elevation in Bavaria and we always had lots of snow in the winter.

We always sang German Christmas carols on Christmas Eve. Sometimes friends would come over and Dad would play the violin.

I don't remember Christmas presents, except for one. That year my only wish was fulfilled. I had wanted a toy horse with wheels. The joy of receiving it was indescribable. The horse was about eight inches long and maybe five inches tall and cut out of a three-eighths inch board. The wooden horse was

Grades one through four in 1951. I was in the second grade at the time. The teacher, Herr Lehrer Lorenz, is upper left. I am in the second row from the top and third from the right. I am wearing a man's suitcoat altered by Mom to fit me. Courtesy of Ingrid Hatz.

hand painted, and I thought it was quite beautiful. It was glued to a small horizontal flat board with four wooden wheels about an inch in diameter. The wheels were screwed to the horizontal board, and they turned. That was the only gift I received that year, but I did not feel anything but unbounded joy.

The Gypsy Boy

Herr Vogel was my teacher for part of first grade. He was a cruel, unpleasant man with a much younger and very nice wife. One day he once took off his shirt in class to show us his war injury. He had been shot in the chest. His chest had a long depression, as if ribs were missing, and a large scar. A Gypsy boy in my first grade was regularly beaten by him. Herr Vogel would beat other boys but none as often as the Gypsy. I remember one scene where the boy was running on top of the desks from row to row in a vain effort to get away from Herr Vogel. The boy's parents obviously wanted their son to get an education, but what a hard way to do so. I was safe because of my dad's position as a teacher and principal. The brutality and the injustice did not escape me. At that time corporal punishment was the norm in Germany. It was a great excuse for cruel people who enjoyed hurting helpless students. While corporal punishment was common in the United States at that time, such excesses would not have been tolerated. Today in Germany, not only is corporal punishment outlawed, parents can be in serious legal trouble for spanking their own children.

The Best Toilet in Town

We had the best toilet in town. All other toilets I knew of were outhouses. We had an in-house outhouse, used only by the teachers' families. To reach the toilet we had to go down the short main school entrance hallway to the "in-house room." The toilet had no running water, no wash basin, and no light. At the back of the room was a wood cabinet-like structure at sitting height. The top surface had a hole to sit on. The back of the small bathroom hung out past the back wall of the building. Gravity took care of depositing the waste in a container below on ground level. Fortunately, the hole had a solid plate-like lid, which had a convenient wooden knob on top. The lid assured that our toilet did not stink too badly. The wide, flat surface with the hole in it, and even the lid, were of nice, finished wood. Now that was fancy! Whenever the waste receptacle was full, a farmer's hired hands would come to empty the container with buckets. This meant that we did not have to bother with chamber pots or go outside on cold days to take care of necessities. Even though we had the coolest toilet, toilet paper was a problem: there was none. Fortunately, we had our local small newspaper to resolve the toilet tissue issue.

We would spend hours outside in the surrounding area. But when you've got to go, you've got to go. Naturally, we did both number one and number two in the fields and woods. I remember serious conversations among us boys about which kinds of leaves were the best for wiping. Fortunately, there was no equivalent to poison ivy. We did have nettles, but those caused instant pain and welts, so we all quickly learned what to avoid.

Fertilizer

As they had done forever, local farmers used "night soil" (human waste) from the outhouses as fertilizer, an extremely unhealthy practice. We did not use it to fertilize the school's garden, but we still had to purchase vegetables from the farmers. Mom tried to take special precautions, but all of our water came from the well and was brought inside in a bucket. No matter how well Mom tried to wash the vegetables, some parasite eggs still floated on top of the water. For this reason, I never got rid of intestinal worms until I came to the United States.

Cirque du Soleil—Ohrenbach circa 1949

I was a coordinated and rather active child. Around the age of six, I observed older boys doing a really cool thing. They were "climbing a ladder" as they were transported sideways down the road. The wooden farm wagons, pulled by a cow or two, had large wooden back wheels with steel rims

Illustration by Kelly Muncy

and thick wooden spokes. The wagons were slowly driven back and forth on the dirt road in front of the schoolhouse. Unbeknownst to the driver, a boy would walk beside a rear wagon wheel at the same speed as the wagon. The boy would then jump on the spokes, grabbing a higher spoke with his hands and placing his feet on a lower spoke. Since the spokes were moving downward, what followed was very quickly grabbing spokes with alternating hands while his feet stepped up the spokes, as if racing up a ladder. When timed right, the boy was moving horizontally at the speed of the wagon, while "climbing the spokes" at the pace of about three spokes per second. Curse words would greet any "climber" if the driver noticed him, whereupon the boy would quickly jump off. After observing boys doing this for much of the summer, I thought, *I can do that too*. So when the next wagon came along, I walked beside the back wheel, jumped on, and climbed like crazy. I felt justifiably proud at my ability and jumped from the wheel after about a ten-second joyride. Unfortunately for me, my mother happened to be looking out the window at just the wrong time. She ran to the door and waited for me in front of the door until I was done with my trick. As soon as I was done, and very proud of my accomplishment, she ruined it all by yelling for me to come home. For reasons I could not understand, she was really mad at me for doing something incredibly cool. She thought it was dangerous, but I remember thinking something along the lines of *unreasonable woman!* I had to stay in for a while but got to play outside again later that day. I did comply with her demand that I never "ride a wheel" again, although I thought the request was rather ridiculous.

Eating with the Dogs

Dad had quite a volatile temper. Although I was a coordinated child, I must admit I was also unusually clumsy. Fortunately that passed—I am now an unusually clumsy adult. It was not uncommon for me to spill something at the dinner table, especially my milk. We did not have a surplus of food, so not only did I create a mess but my clumsiness also wasted food. Dad would always be very angry and yell at me for my transgression. One day Dad became so angry that he told me I had to eat on the floor under the table where dogs ate. While sobbing, I finished my meal, sitting under the table. I cannot describe in words the hurt that I felt for having to eat where dogs ate.

Lamb of Jesus

As a young boy, I received very kind, gentle, and loving religious instruction from the minister's daughter, Hannelore. The Bible stories and parables she taught stayed with me for a lifetime. It was not her fault that as a teenager I became an agnostic. Maybe the seed she planted with her instruction was a part of the reason I became a Christian as a mature adult.

My mother told me that when I was a very young boy, Hannelore occasionally came to her to tell her the latest entertaining story about her younger son. One story Mom loved to recount was Hannelore teaching a lesson about Jesus being the shepherd and us being His sheep. During the lesson Hannelore told me I was a lamb of Jesus. I said, "I am not a lamb of Jesus." She was surprised by my response and asked me why I was not a lamb of Jesus. I responded, "I am a little ram, not a lamb." Mom and Hannelore had a good laugh.

The Highest in the Church

My brother, Günter, also went to Sunday school classes. His teacher, *Pfarrer* (Pastor) Pilz, was not as nice and understanding as Hannelore. As part of the lesson one Sunday, Pfarrer Pilz asked the students, "Who is the highest in the church?"

My brother raised his hand and eagerly said, "The rooster," referring to the weather-vane rooster at the top of the church. Günter was perhaps in the fourth grade at the time. The minister must have had no sense of humor and was angry with my brother for such a disrespectful answer. Günter insisted to Mom that he tried to answer the question as best he could and did not get into trouble with her.

My brother knew precisely what he was saying and was purposely being a smart-ass. For his "fun" he was punished by the pastor, either having his fingers hit by a ruler or his butt smacked, but he does not remember which. He did tell me that he played innocent with our mom, who felt sorry for him.

Surgery without Anesthesia

After the war there were shortages of everything, including anesthetics for operations. Around 1950 my brother needed to have his tonsils out. Günter was strapped into a chair with leather straps on his arms and legs to keep him immobile. Then the surgeon did his dirty work. My brother struggled so hard because of the pain that he broke some of the straps.

A brief description of the operation in my brother's words:

> Someone (I think a nurse) tried to hold my head. I fought the son of a bitch till the bitter end. Although I understood the "why" of the surgery, I like to think of it as "theory meets reality."
>
> I broke the straps nearest my elbow. There were two straps per arm. One strap was at the wrist, the other near the elbow. There were two operations . . . removing adenoids and tonsils.
>
> The drama with all the blood, sweat, and tears was intense, and it didn't subside after the surgery, but kept on for several days.
>
> Somewhat related: I went kayak fishing today and caught

four good-sized bass . . . so what does this have to do with the adenoids and tonsils? Because I have a *long* memory about such things, I always file off the barbs of my fishing hooks.

My brother came home after his tonsillectomy, obviously in great pain. I was not happy about his suffering, but I remember thinking, *God punished him because he was so mean to me.* Like many older brothers, my brother teased me mercilessly. He knew which buttons to push and he pushed them all the time, except when a big kid was picking on me. If that happened, my tormentor would get a bloody nose.

An Amazing Cure

I remember a trip to the hospital because I was suspected of having appendicitis. My abdominal pain was severe. The doctor in the Rothenburg hospital was not eager to do surgery right away and had to "prepare" me for surgery. The preparation consisted of giving me no food and water for what I think was about three days. I had been hungry before, but I had never been so thirsty before. Being that thirsty was worse than being extremely hungry. The nurses had orders to not give me any water. I repeatedly begged a particular nurse for water. She may have violated her orders, but she gave me one or two teaspoons of cold tea. This was a drink directly from heaven. How thankful one can be for one or two teaspoons of liquid!

My situation was not getting better; the pain remained intense. I remember my parents were at my bedside and in a very serious mood. The doctor was there too. It must have been time to make a decision to do the surgery. With the serious atmosphere in the room, I began to let a long fart. The fart continued for what seemed like more than a minute. My pain was then less, but I still had pain. Several minutes later I let another fart. This one was a mere thirty seconds. Suddenly I was pain free. I was cured and got to go home! Who knows what the reason for this blockage was. I'm guessing it was related to the fact that I had intestinal worms my entire time in Ohrenbach. The poor diet probably did not help.

Dr. Drunk

I had another medical emergency: one I almost did not survive. The only doctor in Ohrenbach was a practicing alcoholic. He practiced often. One day I was running full speed on one of the dirt streets in the town when I fell. I landed with the back of my hand under my chest, skidded a bit, and scraped the skin off. There was a mixture of blood, horse manure, cow manure, dust, and who knows what else on the back of my hand. My mother took me to Dr. Häfner. I'll call him Dr. Drunk. She made the mistake of allowing me to see the doctor by myself while she sat in the waiting room. As parents, we all make mistakes that we regret, and I'm sure this was a big regret for her.

In those days the first choice for tetanus was a shot derived from horses. Every adult knew, and of course every doctor knew, that a person is good for only one horse serum shot in a lifetime. The second shot results in such a serious allergic reaction that it likely would be fatal. After cleaning the wound, he gave me a horse serum shot in my right breast without having asked my mom if I had had horse serum before. I came out of the office a short time after I had gone in, and he told her he gave me a horse serum shot. Damage done. Too late to undo. No options for treatment. By the time my mom and I walked home from the doctor's office, I noticed my right breast was as big as that of a young woman. My whole body swelled up. I could barely see because of the swelling in my face. I remember looking at my swelled-up hands. I could hardly see my fingers because my hands were so swollen. Who knows what this did to my internal organs. My father ran down to the doctor, who came and told him what they should do to help me. My desperate parents followed his instructions although they made no sense. He said to put me in a "flour bath": take our kid-sized bathing tub, fill it with water, and add lots of flour. They were to bathe me in a very thin flour paste and then not dry me off. I went back to bed covered with this paste. As it began to dry, it shrank and cracked while still stuck to my skin. The pain was excruciating. My skin, which was already painfully stretched from the swelling, was being pulled in all directions. The last thing I remember before I lost consciousness was my mother trying to relieve the extreme pain by trying to wash off the hardened crust. Parents who have experienced the loss of a child know what my parents must have gone through during those days. No medication was available to help as I lay there unconscious for days.

I was in second grade at the time and I missed the last two months of the school year. School was just upstairs, but I stayed inactive downstairs. I remember being very weak. I also missed forty-one days at the beginning of the third grade as I continued to recover (see the appendix, 36).

Decades later, Dr. Häfner committed suicide. What a tragic figure. Eventually his alcoholism destroyed him, and along the way he damaged many people. May he rest in peace.

Not an Angel

There are two times (that I'll admit to) that I was not being an angel as I was growing up.

My brother and I, like many brothers, argued a lot. I was angry with my brother over perceived injustices and nastiness. And I wanted to pay him back. One evening after an early sunset, the whole family was in the kitchen. The kitchen was a great place to be when Mom was cooking supper on the large, new wood-burning stove because the entire kitchen was warm. I noticed my brother was walking barefoot on the rough wood floor. I also saw a bottle cap. This bottle cap was made of a thicker metal than today's bottle caps. I reasoned that if I surreptitiously put the bottle cap on the hot stove and then placed it on the floor, he might step on it with his bare feet. *That would serve him right,* I thought. Thought became action, and shortly after the bottle cap was good and hot, I put it down on the floor with no one noticing. As hoped for, my brother immediately stepped on the bottle cap with his bare heel. It stuck on his heel and he hopped around on one leg, screaming in pain. Mom or Dad jumped into action and knocked the stuck bottle cap off his heel. He was still in severe pain. I had had no intention of hurting him that badly and felt terrible. I really felt guilty. But I kept quiet about my role in the "accident."

The Gögeleins had a nice, large open area, unpaved of course, in front of their barn. This area was a place where kids, almost always boys, played in good weather. One nice summer day, one of the older boys was being mean and would not let me play in some kind of a tag game. I was quite young, and my mother had been watching me play from inside the schoolhouse. She saw that I was really angry with the older boy. She wondered, *OK, what is he going to do now?* She knew I had something in mind. After a while, the chief protagonist ran close to me in hot pursuit of another boy. I quickly stuck my foot out to trip him and he fell, sliding in the dust. Before he even stopped sliding on the dirt, I triumphantly and very quickly sprinted home.

Swimming with Leeches

Our village did not have a swimming pool, but there was a fire-water reservoir, where the boys swam often and had a great time. The reservoir had deep and shallow ends, but the deepest part was not very deep and the shallow end was not too shallow. The sides of the "swimming pool" were concrete but the bottom was mud. The water had so much sediment that visibility was limited. We kept our heads mostly above water.

We were always covered with leeches after our swim. Leeches don't hurt, and if they don't feast too long, it is not a problem. We just picked them off painlessly and threw them away. We also carefully checked under our swimming trunks, which were really just our underpants.

One warm summer day I went to the "swimming hole" with my brother as usual. I got tired and decided to head on home. However, I failed to tell my brother that I was leaving. When he realized I was not around, he thought I must have gone under. He frantically searched for me for a long time. When he finally gave up and came home, he thought he'd have to tell our parents that I drowned. Needless to say, he was both glad and angry to see me.

Swimming with Beavers

In the summer we never wore shoes simply because we did not have summer shoes. We had only one pair of winter shoes. I remember getting my first pair of "not winter" shoes. They were beautiful and enabled me to run like the wind. I know because I tested them.

On the far side of the village, near the doctor's office, was a ten-foot-wide ditch, which was also a slow-flowing creek. This ditch was very interesting because a pair of beavers swam there occasionally. The ditch collected the runoff from the dirt road, which included all kinds of animal manure, not a big issue for me. I would occasionally wade in the ditch, which was deep enough that I could just barely reach the bottom. I would carefully take off my beautiful new shoes and then wade in the ditch.

My mother did not want me to wade in the ditch for obvious reasons. But her instructions to my very young mind were not quite clear enough. She told me, "Now don't take your shoes off and go wading in the ditch." I understood—or so I thought. The next time I wanted to wade in the ditch, I did not take my shoes off. Unfortunately, the shoes were made mostly of a glued cardboard-like material and they fell apart. I was devastated and cried about my destroyed shoes. Luckily, Mom was not mad at me. My parents could not afford replacement shoes, so that was the end of being the fastest kid on earth and my only summertime shoes.

Family Entertainment

Farm villages are seldom the center of exciting nightlife. Ohrenbach was no different. Some evenings Dad would hang up a sheet and show us old films with the school's film projector. Our favorite films were silent Laurel and Hardy films. In German they were called *Dick und Doof* (Fat and Dumb). I also remember a film about Pygmies in the jungles of Africa as well as a slapstick comedy about bike riding with a scythe sticking out the side of the bike at head height.

Sometimes neighbors would come over and the adults would sing. My dad had a violin, and someone would always come with an accordion. My brother and I would both watch and join in. It was great social and family time.

Homemade Toys

During our years in Ohrenbach, we could count on one hand the number of purchased toys my brother and I had. I had one small blue ball during the entire time in Ohrenbach. We compensated for this lack of playthings by making kites and paper airplanes. We had all kinds of contests as to who had the best airplane design. If there was a group of five boys flying paper airplanes, there were five boys convinced they had each made the best one.

This was not as simple as it sounds because high-quality paper was hard to come by. We used newspaper and glue made from flour and water to make kites. Many wonderful hours were spent flying kites. When that got boring, lying in the grass and watching clouds change shapes was maybe even better. Childhood imagination is a great thing.

We made wooden daggers for hunting weasels. Weasels were considered pests in farm communities. I suppose it had something to do with not wanting the chickens killed. The preferred method of hunting them was to find a weasel hole and stomp one's feet loudly. Usually there would be a stomper and a stabber. Weasels were curious critters and would stick their heads out to check on what was making the noise. As the weasel stuck its head out, it met a quick stabbing stroke with a homemade dagger, and there would be one less weasel. When I stomped the ground and stabbed a weasel all on my own, I was very proud because I was the youngest of the band of weasel-hunting boys. Although the weasel I killed was cute with its light reddish fur, I did not feel sorry for him. Weasel killing just seemed OK. When we were not hunting weasels, "fighting" with the daggers was another fun activity.

Older Boys Having Fun

One summer day, Gypsies came through town in several underpowered small trucks, some of which were three-wheeled with two-cycle engines. They parked the tiny trucks on the main street between the schoolhouse and the Gögelein's guesthouse. My brother and his friends saw this as an opportunity for some fun. When the owners of the trucks were not watching, the boys stuck potatoes in some of the tail pipes. And when I say "stuck," I mean they really pounded them quite a ways up the tailpipe. I watched what they were doing but did not participate. This was bigger boys' work, yet I found the process and the result highly interesting. We all watched from a safe distance and laughed when the trucks would not start. It took those poor men quite a while to discover the problem and clear the obstructions.

Visiting Grandma and Being Called a Dog

My brother and I would occasionally take the bus from Ohrenbach to Rothenburg to visit Grandmother Käthe for a weekend. I was used to the totally deserted streets at night in Ohrenbach. Rothenburg, on the other hand, had a few cars. It really disrupted my sleep when a car drove by on the cobblestone streets with its bright headlights.

As I mentioned, my fraternal grandmother, who was the only one of my grandparents in the West, was an unusual person. She was selfish, nice when it served her purpose, and heartless. Whenever I annoyed her, which was often, she would say, "*Du Hundeseele*!" This phrase is hard to translate but means something like "You have the soul of a dog." Now, those of us who love dogs might think that is not so bad. But it was a terribly insulting thing to say to a person in Germany.

During one of the weekends we stayed with her, she aggravated me enough that I decided to take the bus home. Right then. She made it clear that I could not do that, but I made my point by walking to the bus stop. I was determined to get on the bus and go home. Grandmother and my brother did not have much choice, so she accompanied us to the bus station and saw us off. I never did check with my brother if he was happy or not that we had left. I do recall that I did not get into trouble with my parents. I don't know how many *Du Hundeseele*s I earned that day.

Flying Geese

Many farmers kept geese for their eggs, meat, and feathers. I remember that for at least one Christmas, Mom roasted a goose. The roasted goose was delicious.

Geese are aggressive and will attack. From experience I can tell you that their bites hurt. I had to run from them many times when I was young. Fortunately, I was fast. Older boys, however, were braver than that. When a goose started going after them, they would deftly and quickly grab the goose by its long neck and swing it in a horizontal circle one or two revolutions. Upon letting the goose go, they would watch it "fly" horizontally for some distance until it crashed into the dusty ground. It was quite a scene with a goose going head over heels . . . I mean tail over beak . . . generating lots of dust when it landed and skidded to a stop. Now that made for an even madder goose, but the goose would not try to attack that boy again—at least for ten minutes.

Cider Press

One of the fun things about living a rural life long ago was seeing and maybe helping with the various activities of daily life. It was fun to watch a farmer making cider with a huge cider press constructed out of wood. The press had a large handle attached to a big wooden screw, which moved a circular wooden plate downward into a wooden barrel-shaped container. To begin the process, the apples were dumped into the container. The vertical boards of the barrel had enough space between them to allow the apple juice to flow out. A circular trough collected the cider, which then flowed into wooden buckets. The solid remains were fed to the pigs.

Puppet Theater

During the summer vacation, Günter and I did puppet shows in the entrance hallway of the school. I recall it was always cold in the hallway at the beginning of a show, but by the end, the body heat of the kids in the hallway had warmed it up. Because Günter was older, he was in charge.

In my brother's words:

> I built a U-shaped stage frame out of very thin wood slats and covered it with newspaper, which was glued on using a flour-and-water paste. The stage even had a curtain that opened and closed with each act. You, as the stage manager, were in charge of pressing the paper to the wood frame.
>
> You and I made the puppet heads out of papier-mâché, which we painted with water colors. The puppets' clothing was made of old rags and handkerchiefs, which were draped over the puppet master's index finger. The puppets were moved by strategically inserting a finger into a small cavity in the puppet's head.
>
> The plays were written, produced, and directed by your older brother, who also did all of the acting. The stage manager, who handed me the puppets, was you.
>
> The plays' subject matter was eclectic. There were the standard Grimm brothers' tales as well as some comic relief at the expense of our teachers, the minister, and the local barkeeper, Herr Gögelein. (Eat your heart out, Jon Stewart.)
>
> I'm estimating the average audience attendance was no less than twenty fawning fans. (Eat your heart out, Justin Bieber.)

A GOOD EDUCATION

Our overcrowded Ohrenbach classrooms had only desks, chairs, and a blackboard, but the education provided us with sound basics for our later years. Although I missed a year of school because of illness and be-

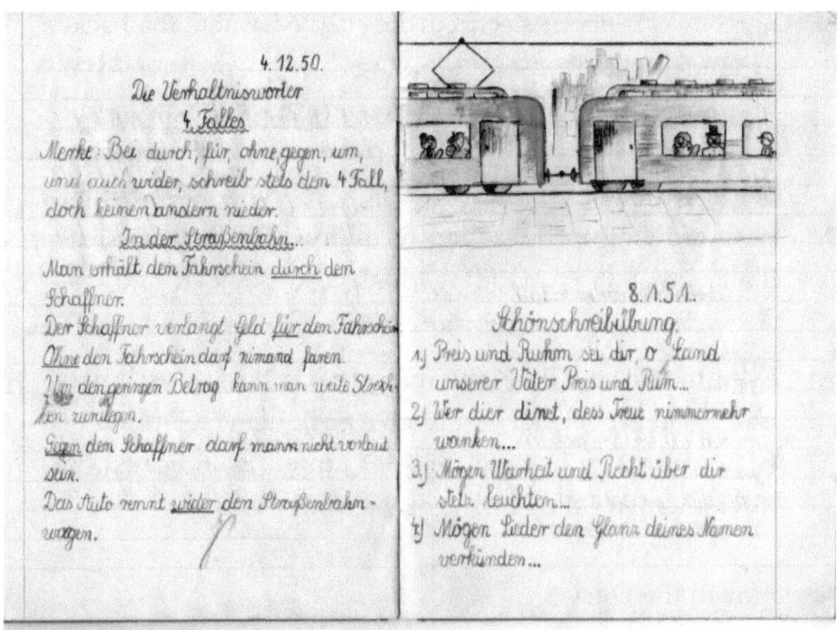

4.12.50.
Die Verhaltniswörter
4. Falles
Merke: Bei durch, für, ohne, gegen, um,
und auch wider, schreib stets den 4 Fall,
doch keinen andern nieder.
In der Straßenbahn...
Man erhält den Fahrschein durch den
Schaffner.
Der Schaffner verlangt Geld für den Fahrschein
Ohne den Fahrschein darf nimand faren.
Um den geringen Betrag kann man weite Strech-
ken zurülegen.
Gegen den Schaffner darf mann nicht vorlaut
sein.
Das Auto rennt wider den Straßenbahn-
wagen.

8.1.51.
Schönschreibübung.
1.) Preis und Ruhm sei dir, o Land
unserer Väter Preis und Rum...
2.) Wer dier dinet, dess Treue nimmermehr
wanken...
3.) Mögen Warheit und Recht über dir
stets leuchten...
4.) Mögen Lieder den Glanz deines Namen
verkünden...

Günter's fifth-grade creative writing workbook

ing in various camps prior to immigrating to the United States, I feel I received a good basic education in Ohrenbach.

We all used the same slate boards as Günter used in Weimar. I still have my wood-framed slate board and attached sponge.

My brother explains:

> The slate board was used for day-to-day classroom work because, just like a word-processing program, one's writing could be edited and deleted. Paper, not unlike a PDF document, was used as a formal and permanent record of classroom activities.

Below are my brother's comments about the two scanned pages of his schoolwork.

> The scanned picture is from my fifth-grade creative writing workbook. Although the story (on the left page of the

notebook) is about electric trolleys, please note the background of bombed-out buildings in the picture. Even though the reconstruction of Western Europe was in full swing by 1950, there were still many ruins that needed to be demolished or repaired. Note also the grass or small trees growing from the top of the ruins, which is a testament that these buildings had been bombed and destroyed many years prior to 1950.

Even though the little guy that produced the sketch had witnessed events that would give an adult a major case of PTSD, he had a healthy sense of humor as indicated by the snowman riding in one of the trolley cars.

Designs in the Dust

My brother writes:

> In preparation for Sunday morning, unless it was raining, the village women had a Saturday afternoon tradition. They swept the unpaved streets of horse apples and cow pies. Please note that was the only "trash" found on *any* street. We were all so poor that just leaving something to throw away would have been both unthinkable and a luxury. The very act of tossing a candy wrapper would have meant you actually had a candy bar! (Thus, when I hear of "wars on poverty," I hear "envy" and feel like throwing up. But I digress.) Having cleared the streets of animal droppings, the villagers would use their handmade willow-branch brooms and rearrange the dust on the streets in elaborate designs.

The dusty, unpaved streets looked clean and beautiful after the artistic sweeping.

–NOTES–

1. Lasts were shoe-shaped metal forms that guided the shoemaker as he cut the leather and shaped it before placing it on the soles. A "last with stand" had an upside-down last on a stand. "Last stands" were used to resole shoes. Dad used tiny wooden nails for shoe repair.

Chapter 12

Hell on Earth—Official Policy

THE MORGENTHAU PLAN

Devastation in the Wake of the War

WWII was the largest, deadliest, and most destructive of, and caused more suffering than, all other wars in history. Europe and much of Asia lay in ruins. All nations and peoples suffered. After the war we were living as refugees in defeated Nazi Germany. By the end of the war many German cities were destroyed, and much infrastructure and most factories were destroyed. Much of the prime-age male workforce had been killed or were in POW camps.

Nearly starving during the war is understandable. Having near-starvation rations when Mom, my brother, and I were living Communist East Germany is understandable. After my family was reunited in postwar American-occupied West Germany, we had less food than during the war and less than during our time in Communist East Germany. That was understandable, but that this deprivation lasted until the beginning of 1948 demands explanation.

Starvation, Deprivation, and further Destruction

In the postwar years of 1946 and 1947 we had less food than at any time since the war began. The year 1947 was the worst. In that year the average caloric intake for the average German adult was 1,080 calories per day. Millions of people were starving and people were dying, especially children. This desperate situation was not accidental; it was due to deliberate, purposeful action to starve the German people, including my family. This planned starvation was the result of the Morgenthau Plan, which was the official postwar foreign policy of the United States toward defeated and occupied West Germany. It sounds like the wildest of conspiracy theories. It is not.

This diabolical plan had a direct impact on me and my family. I remember the night when I looked out the window of the schoolhouse in Ohrenbach and saw the dimly lit window of the farmer's house. I wondered, *Do you suppose they have something to eat?* This did not have to be. However, part of the Morgenthau Plan was to stop all food imports into Germany, although it was widely known that historically Germany could only produce 60 percent of the food needed to feed its population. Germany had always depended on its sales of industrial goods to enable importing food.

At a young age, I felt overwhelming joy at the gift of a pot of water with glorious-smelling fat floating on top. My joy from the meager gift (by today's standards) was due to the impact of the Morgenthau Plan. One of the features of the Morgenthau Plan was to prevent the Vatican from importing food for starving German children.

For about two years a large source of animal protein intake was small quantities of horse blood. Our protein-poor diet was not supplemented adequately by plant food. We received precious little help to improve our poor diet. One of the first actions under the Morgenthau Plan was to disband the German Red Cross and prevent the International Red Cross from helping German civilians.

Under the Morgenthau Plan, the machinery in over seven hundred factories, which had not already been destroyed, was dismantled and shipped to the Soviet Union and to France to be reassembled for reuse. Factories with equipment that could not easily be disassembled were destroyed. A ban on importing radios enabled my father to build valuable radios from crashed airplanes, paying for Mom's operation and earning money to feed us. Through Dad's ingenuity, the ban on radios made up, in a small way, for food denied. But the destruction of factories assured our long-term starvation.

Stated Objective

The stated objective of the Morgenthau Plan was to make Germany into a pastoral state with no industry and no machinery, populated by pitchfork farmers. This was to make Europe safe from the militaristic Germans. Henry Morgenthau, the secretary of the Treasury, whose personal objective was revenge, had the ear of President Franklin Delano Roosevelt. Roosevelt approved of the plan. The president was asked by an American official, who was against the plan, if he wanted the German people to starve. He replied, "Why not!"[1]

President Roosevelt was quoted as telling Morgenthau,

> We have got to be tough with Germany and I mean the German people, not just the Nazis. We either have to castrate the German people or you have got to treat them in such a manner so they can't just go on reproducing people who want to continue the way they have in the past.[2]

I was included among those living in Germany who needed to be taught a lesson.

American military leadership and State Department leadership were uniformly against the Plan, but with Morgenthau whispering in his ear, Roosevelt could not be dissuaded. Secretary of State Hull was appalled by the plan and the fact that the secretary of the Treasury was dictating foreign policy. He knew 40 percent of the German population would starve to death. He also was sure the plan, which had been leaked to the press and published in September 1944, would result in last-ditch, fiercer fighting by the Germans.

Plan Approved

Joint Chiefs of Staff (JCS) order 1067, which implemented the Morgenthau Plan, was signed by President Harry Truman on May 10, 1945. That was only twenty-eight days after he assumed the presidency. Truman had served as vice president for less than three months when Roosevelt died of a massive stroke. Truman had been kept in the dark about both foreign and domestic policy by Roosevelt. He was unaware of the implications of what he had approved.[3]

Truman Begins to Grasp Implications

President Harry Truman began to be concerned about the long-range implications of the plan he had approved early in his presidency. In early 1946 he allowed relief organizations to enter Germany in order to review the food situation. In mid-1946 non-German relief organizations were permitted to help starving German children. Despite relief organizations being permitted to aid Germans and ethnic Germans living in West Germany, the situation in West Germany deteriorated further.

He selected former president Herbert Hoover, a personal friend, to ascertain the food situation in occupied West Germany. Ironically, Herbert Hoover toured the occupied country in Hermann Göring's old train coach. He wrote a number of reports critical of US occupation policy.[4]

In a report written in March 1947, Hoover stated:

> There is the illusion that the New Germany left after the annexations can be reduced to a "pastoral state." It cannot be done unless we exterminate or move twenty-five million people out of it.[5]

A Little Bit More to Eat

Hoover's presidential assignment was followed by positive action to aid the food situation for school children.

> On Hoover's initiative, a school meals program in the American and British occupation zones of Germany was begun on April 14, 1947. The program served 3.5 million children aged six through eighteen. A total of forty thou-

sand tons of American food was provided during the *Hooverspeisung* (Hoover meals)."[6]

These "Hoover lunches" were no more frequent than once per week, but since they were implemented in 1947, the year with the worst food shortage, they saved the lives of children, maybe even mine.

To receive the free lunches at the school where Dad taught and we lived, students assembled one grade at a time, holding small metal plates, in the small enclosed concrete area behind the schoolhouse. Lunch was served from a huge metal pot in which the lunch had been cooked over a wood fire. The lunches were always the same good oatmeal ladled onto our plates. Thanks to Dad's teaching position and living in the schoolhouse where the meals were distributed to the students, I stood in line for lunch even before I attended first grade. I fondly remember the free school lunches.

Americans Needlessly Killed

Prior to learning about the Morgenthau Plan in late 1944, the exhausted German military was beginning to lose their fighting spirit on the Western Front. Historians uniformly agree that, after learning of the Morgenthau Plan, the increased fighting spirit on the Western Front prolonged the war by months, significantly increasing American casualties. Because of their fear of Russians occupation, the Germans never lost the will to fight on the Eastern Front.[7]

It Was a Communist Plan Directed from Moscow

The Plan was written for Morgenthau by Harry Dexter White, who had two bosses: Henry Morgenthau Jr. and Joseph Stalin. Stalin's ultimate objective was establishing vassal Communist regimes in Western Europe, as had been done in Eastern Europe, making him the absolute ruler of a greater Soviet Union.

The first phase of the plan was to drive the West Germans to elect a Communist government through starvation and deprivation. If that failed, an invasion of an underfed, demoralized, deindustrialized, and demilitarized Germany would have been easy. Pitchforks do not stop tanks.

White was indisputably a Communist agent receiving direction from Moscow. His task was to shape the Morgenthau Plan in compliance with his foreign Soviet masters. White eventually became the assistant secretary of the Treasury under Morgenthau and collaborated with colleagues within the Treasury who were also later identified as Communists in sworn testimony.[8]

THE MARSHALL PLAN

Wiser and More Ethical Americans Prevail[9]

The Morgenthau Plan had its desired effect on the German population. In ever-increasing numbers, West Germans began to doubt there was much difference between America and Russia. In some local elections, Communist candidates won. American political leaders and military leaders who had always been opposed to the Morgenthau Plan then had more ammunition to make a strong case for rescinding it.

> Herbert Hoover's situation reports from 1947 and "A Report on Germany" also served to help change occupation policy. The Western powers' worst fear by now was that the poverty and hunger would drive the Germans to communism. . . . General Lucius Clay stated "There is no choice between being a Communist on 1,500 calories a day and a believer in democracy on a thousand.[10]

The Marshall Plan Replaces the Morgenthau Plan

In January 1947, Truman appointed retired general George Marshall as the secretary of state. In the summer of 1947, Marshall, citing national security grounds, convinced President Truman to remove JCS 1067 (the Morgenthau Plan) and replace it with JCS 1779 (the Marshall Plan). Truman signed the European Recovery Program into law on April 3, 1948. JCS 1779 was the order that allowed the Marshall Plan to be implemented.

> The Marshall Plan (officially the European Recovery Program, or ERP) was the American program to aid Europe, in which the United States gave economic support to help rebuild European economies after the end of World War II in order to prevent the spread of Soviet communism. The plan was in operation for four years beginning in April 1948. The goals of the United States were to rebuild a war-devastated region, remove trade barriers, modernize industry, and make Europe prosperous again.[11]

A High Price—Almost Wasted

In WWII, 185,000 American soldiers were killed in Europe.[12] The cost of saving Europe from Nazi tyranny was high. The West came dangerously close to losing all of Europe to the tyranny of Communism.

Thanks to a change in foreign policy, Western European countries and German industry began to rebuild. Earnings from reindustrialization gave Germany the capital to import food, invest in further economic growth, and feed its people. A revitalized Germany contributed to the economic recovery and unparalleled prosperity of postwar Europe. And most of all to a lasting peace.

Replacing the Morgenthau Plan with the Marshall Plan meant food could be imported into occupied West Germany and be distributed to desperately hungry people. In the spring of 1948, my meager diet began to improve as a direct result of the Marshall Plan. I believe the Marshall Plan captures the true spirit of Americans.

Had the Marshall Plan not been implemented, my family's escape from Communist countries would have been for naught. All of Europe would have become Communist. We would have again been under the thumb of a brutal dictatorial regime. Instead we came to the United States and experienced freedom and prosperity. (For more information please see)[13]

–NOTES–

1. http://en.wikipedia.org/wiki/Morgenthau_Plan.
2. http://en.wikipedia.org/wiki/Morgenthau_Plan.
3. http://en.wikipedia.org/wiki/Morgenthau_Plan.
4. http://en.wikipedia.org/wiki/Herbert_Hoover.
5. http://en.wikipedia.org/wiki/Herbert_Hoover.
6. http://en.wikipedia.org/wiki/Herbert_Hoover.
7. http://en.wikipedia.org/wiki/Morgenthau_Plan.
8. http://www.ihr.org/jhr/v09/v09p287_Kubek.html.
9. http://en.wikipedia.org/wiki/Marshall_Plan.
10. http://en.wikipedia.org/wiki/Morgenthau_Plan.
11. http://en.wikipedia.org/wiki/Marshall_Plan.
12. https://answers.yahoo.com/question/index;_ylt=AwrJ7KH-qFm5cOM4AmOFXNyoA;_ylu=X3oDMTEya29oZXRkBGNvb-G8DYmYxBHBvcwMxBHZ0aWQDQjY4MjFfMQRzZWMD-c3I-?qid=20080310061332AAtI2iu&p=what%20were%20the%20us%20casualties%20during%20wwII%20in%20the%20european%20theater%3F.
13. http://en.wikipedia.org/wiki/William_L._Clayton; http://www.bbc.co.uk/programmes/b01jgj0p.

Chapter 13

America, Our Best Hope

APPLYING TO COME

Hopeless Future in West Germany

Once the family was reunited in West Germany, Dad hoped to rebuild his life there and adequately support his family.

Dad immediately began his quest to secure qualified teacher status. He provided additional documentation verifying his education and experience. The difficult, time-consuming process required dealing with people in multiple languages, with authorities in Communist Romania, and with several organizations in West Germany. A key part of his documentation was a legal finding by the West German Central Department for Foreign Education Systems, confirming that "Gustav Maroscher's education, testing, and experience were equivalent to that of a native German teacher." He was further encouraged and persisted in his goal of becoming a certified teacher. (See the appendix, 5, 7, 10).

He continued working with the supportive local Rothenburg Education Office, but his status as a teacher's aide remained unchanged. Eventually he personally visited the Regional Education Administration office in Ansbach (since the Rothenburg area school system was a part of the Ansbach region) to investigate his status. There he discovered that the regional office had delayed for two years sending his documentation to the Bavarian Ministry of Education. After his documentation was finally forwarded, the Bavarian Ministry of Education ruled against him. He was rejected because the officials believed it was impossible that education at a German-speaking university outside of Germany could be equivalent to that of a German university. An unstated objection was that Dad was a Lutheran teacher in a Lutheran village located in Roman Catholic Bavaria (see the appendix, 37).

After that ruling, Dad hired a lawyer and sued the Bavarian Ministry of Education on June 8, 1951.[1] One of the many points his lawyer made in the suit was that there were other Romanian refugee teachers who were working as fully qualified teachers in West Germany. Despite the enthusiastic backing of the local Rothenburg odT Education Office, he continued to be underpaid and frustrated.

Applying to Immigrate

After two years of discrimination and being unable to provide for his family, Dad saw no hope for a successful life in West Germany. In 1948 he applied for us to immigrate to the United States. Shown to the right is the confirmation of our registration to immigrate to the United States, dated October 6, 1948. All correspondence with the US consulate in Munich was to reference the four numbers stamped on the confirmation document. These four numbers represented each of the four family members. We were now on the waiting list of people wanting to immigrate to America.

Anweisung für die Registrierung

Name des Antragstellers: [illegible] Gustav Günter
(Familienname) (Vorname) (Weitere Vornamen)

Anschrift: Ohrenbach

2206

Quota RUMANIA E-G Nr. der Registrierung: 2205

Datum der Registrierung: OCT 6 1948

(Einschließlich aller mitzuregistrierenden Personen)

2208

2207

Wir bitten Sie, unsere Dienststelle über alle Veränderungen innerhalb Ihrer Familie auf dem laufenden zu halten; dies gilt für alle Geburten oder Todesfälle in Ihrer Familie, ferner für jeglichen Aufschub Ihrer Pläne oder für einen Verzicht Ihrerseits auf Einwanderung in die Vereinigten Staaten. In Ihrer Korrespondenz mit unserer Dienststelle wollen Sie bitte die obige Nummer angeben. Sie werden benachrichtigt werden, sobald Sie an die Reihe kommen. Dokumente sollen erst an uns gesandt werden, wenn sie verlangt werden.

Das Konsulat (Gen...) der Vereinigten Staaten von Amerika in München

Confirmation of immigration registration

Rejected

We were on the waiting list, but with no assurance that we would be allowed to immigrate. One dark cloud that hung over us was that Dad might be disqualified from immigrating because of his service in the Waffen-SS.

In fact, Dad was rejected on November 4, 1951, because of his service in the Waffen-SS. Dad appealed this decision in writing on November 11, 1951, asking the US Displaced Persons Commission to investigate the documents about his Waffen-SS service to which the commission had access, and emphasized that his service was unavoidable.

In the November 11 letter, Dad explained why he hoped to come to America. What he wrote can be a reminder of why we should be proud and thankful for being Americans. Part of his appeal letter is translated below.

> The end of the war brought the Communist regime to Romania; as a result I lost my homeland and property. Here in Germany I tried through ambition, diligence, and devotion to work, to establish myself in a new home. I've worked for five years, without ceasing, in my profession. My accomplishments are recognized locally. However, the government administration has persecuted me with all forms of chicaneries to deny me the recognition of my education and professional qualification in Romania and Hungary. I am suffering terribly under the pressure of always being looked at and treated like a person of second class. Moreover, decisions reached by some Bavarian bureaucrats meant my full compensation was withheld. This has resulted in my family having to live in miserable circumstances. Because of these great difficulties, I applied to immigrate. I had the hope, no I was certain, that in your country, through hard work, to be able to establish a decent life for my family. I do not want to continue to live my life under the defamatory stamp of "refugee." Please believe me, a life where any native-born person, regardless of qualifications, is preferred over a refugee, is for me depressing and unbearable.

Reading the American Constitution

Years before Dad applied to immigrate, he read the Constitution of the United States. He also read extensively about America and had a good understanding of what America was like. He hoped for a better life for his family in the United States. Although he had enjoyed being a teacher, and was an outstanding teacher, he also dreamed of becoming an engineer, an impossibility in the West Germany of 1951. He felt that America was the land of opportunity, where one is judged not by one's background but by one's character, capability, diligence, and quality of work. Dad had had his fill of European politics, wars, and discrimination. He dreamed of his sons receiving good educations and good jobs. He did not want them to have to fight in another European war, which he felt was inevitable.

ON THE IMMIGRATION CONVEYOR

Accepted

On November 13, 1951, only nine days after Dad received the rejection letter and two days after he sent his letter of appeal, the United States Displaced Persons Commission wrote him a letter of acceptance. The reason Dad was now accepted to immigrate to the United States with his family was a change in rules, namely that some men who had served in the Waffen-SS were allowed to immigrate. Dad firmly believed that had he officially received his promotion to officer in the Waffen-SS at the end of the war, we would never have been allowed to come to the United States. Even after the rule change, applicants who had "Waffen-SS" in their files received extra scrutiny. The letter announcing the rule change and that we were again in line for coming to the United States is shown on the next page.

Following approval, much more documentation was required. Both Mom and Dad had to pass criminal background checks, and Mom needed to obtain verification that she was never a member of the Nazi party.

UNITED STATES
DISPLACED PERSONS COMMISSION
APO 407-A US ARMY
MUNICH, FUNK KASERNE BL. 1.

Date: 13 Nov 1951

TO : Herrn MAROSCHER, Gustav-Guenter, Ohrenbach 14, Krs. Rothenburg a.d.Tauber

ECN: 511 323 / Pre

ECN: Pre Sel

Your application for emigration to the United States was previously rejected because of your service with the Waffen-SS.

Due to new regulations your rejection has been rescinded and your case been put back in processing.

You will be notified as to the next steps to be taken to complete your processing.

In case you should have decided not to emigrate to the USA please notify this office at once.

cc; German Liaison Officer
IRO
Agency
Control
Dossier
file

CHARLES T. SNAVELY
Senior Officer

by : HENRI VERSTAPPEN
Chief of EGO Branch

UEBERSETZUNG

Sie wurden kuerzlich durch dieses Buero benachrichtigt, dass Ihr Antrag auf Auswanderung nach den Vereinigten Staaten wegen Ihrer Mitgliedschaft in der Waffen-SS abgelehnt wurde.

Gemaess neuer Ausfuehrungsbestimmungen wird diese Ablehnung hiermit aufgehoben und Ihr Akt kann weiterbearbeitet werden.

Von den weiteren Schritten, die Sie zu unternehmen haben um Ihre Auswanderungsangelegenheit zu vervollstaendigen werden Sie benachrichtigt werden.

Sollten Sie jedoch an einer Auswanderung nicht mehr interessiert sein, bitte benachrichtigen Sie dieses Buero sofort.

st 746

Letter of acceptance by US Displaced Persons Commision

First Step of Our Journey

Dad received notice from the US immigration authority that we were to report to the emigration camp in Munich-Karlsfeld[2] in January, 1952. On January 23, he wrote a letter to the Mittelfranken Education Department in Ansbach, West Germany, informing the office that our stay at the camp was expected to last three to four weeks. He asked for a leave of absence during our stay at the camp while his status for emigration was being evaluated. He knew there was no assurance that we would actually be successful. We could be rejected at any point in the process. He protected his teaching position until he received final approval.

Goodbye, Ohrenbach! Goodbye, Rothenburg odT!

It was finally time to take a train to begin the first steps toward immigrating to the United States. During our last night before departure, we stayed in Käthe's (Dad's mother) apartment.

Last night in Rothenburg odT.

In the picture, Mom is sitting on the left and Dad is standing close to the clock. Käthe is sitting second from the right. My brother and I are the short people. The other people are probably friends of Käthe's.

The flash for the picture was provided by a ten-by-two-inch flat pan containing magnesium powder and affixed to the end of a pole held by the photographer. The photographer lit a strip of paper and touched the powder. Poof! Big flash!

Early in the morning, in late January 1952, while it was still dark, we left for Munich by train. The "train" was a single diesel-powered red railcar, similar to a noisy streetcar. As we walked to the train station in the snow, the city looked magical with about eight inches of fluffy snow on the ground.

Not until then did Dad drop the suit against the Bavarian Education Administration. At the same time he gave up on everything German and European. He never looked back. He only looked forward—to our new life in America.

Hello, Barracks in Munich

At the emigration camp, we stayed in large rooms in former German military barracks. We were required to undergo a number of health checks for communicable diseases. One step was a smallpox vaccination. The date of my vaccination was January 28, 1952, with a follow-up check of the vaccination on February 4, 1952. I had a very painful reaction to the vaccination and developed a quarter-sized pustule with neon-green purulent drainage on my shoulder. We were also deloused a couple of times prior to sailing to America, usually by sprinkling copious amounts of DDT dust on our heads.

After the short stay at the barracks, we returned home only to receive a letter eight days later, directing us to report to the emigration camp in Munich-Freimann.

Camp Bremen-Grohn on the North Sea

Shortly after arriving at the camp in Munich, we were directed to travel to Camp Bremen-Grohn. We were on our way to Bremen, a North Sea port city from which we were to sail.

From late February to March 31, 1952, our domicile was at the outskirts of Bremen, Germany, in Camp Bremen-Grohn. The barracks housed people who had been cleared for sailing and were eager to be

My picture stapled to the smallpox vaccination certificate

booked on the next ship. These were not five-star accommodations, and our family was separated again. Men and older boys (including Günter) lived in their own barracks separate from women, girls, and young boys (me).

Mom and I lived in a room housing sixteen people of different ages and backgrounds. Two rows of bunk beds were placed very close together on opposing walls, with a space of about ten feet between the rows. The wall opposite from the only door had a window, and two incandescent lightbulbs hung from the ceiling. We had no sinks, bathrooms, or shower facilities in any of the rooms. Communal toilets were located at the end of the long halls. I never saw shower or bathing facilities. The only way we could wash was to take a sponge bath in one of the bathroom sinks or in the room for anyone who had a pan. To provide some privacy in the rooms, people would hang up bedsheets or blankets on ropes. At the time it was not all that clear that our room was for women only since at least one male visitor was there all the time. One young man in particular stayed there nearly all the time to be with his young wife.

Dad and Günter lived in a much larger room in another barracks. All barracks were large, multiple-story structures with long, dark hallways. According to my brother, the US Army barracks he stayed in during his basic training had a similar decor and ambiance. Unfortunately the barracks were not as clean or orderly as US Army barracks.

During our stay at this camp, I became ill and was admitted to a hospital. I don't remember what illness landed me there. My bed was in a hospital ward on the second floor with numerous windows on one side of the long room. The ward was big enough for about thirty beds, all filled with sick children. The beds were constructed out of metal piping with cream-colored, chipped paint. I had no idea where the hospital was relative to my barracks, which concerned me. Knowing we were to sail soon, I was afraid that the rest of my family would sail off without me. My parents had been instructed to stay away, thinking that would make me more homesick. Fortunately, about four days into my at least seven-day stay, my brother walked to the hospital and yelled my name from the street below. I got out of bed, walked to a window, and saw him. I was enormously relieved. My family had not yet sailed to America. We yelled back and forth a bit. He assured me they would not sail without me.

A Family Crying

In one of the big barracks I remember seeing a family consisting of mother, father, and two children walking down the long, dark hallway toward the exit. I was walking from the exit toward them and stopped. The parents were dressed in black, their traditional peasant clothing, and all were crying as they passed me. Later I asked Dad why they were crying, and he told me they had just been rejected and had to return to their home. He told me they were rejected because they were caught in a lie. He added that it might not have even been an important lie, but it was automatic rejection if discovered. Dad then told me that whenever he was being questioned by the immigration authorities, he always told the truth. He hid nothing.

Vetting of Refugees

As part of the vetting process, Mom, Dad, and my brother were all questioned. My brother's last interviews were at Camp Bremen-Grohn at the age of twelve. What better way to find out about Mom's and Dad's histories and what they thought than to have a matronly lady (kindly) interrogate a child who would not be cautious with his answers? I was spared such interviews. Although I was only eight, I was aware of the strict examination process.

Big Complaint

The Lutheran Relief Works Agency played a significant role in working with Lutheran families and the emigration authorities. Our stay was much longer than expected and the conditions in the camp were poor, so on March 19, 1952, my dad wrote a letter of complaint to the director of the Lutheran Relief Works Agency, Mr. Cimera.

He wrote:

> The camp is not equipped for extended stays, yet we were sent by your organization to the camp, without a verified sponsor.

Prospective immigrants could travel to the United States only with a sponsor who had committed to meeting the refugees upon their arrival, providing housing for the family, and arranging employment for the adults. In addition to the delay because we lacked a sponsor, our departure was further postponed because of my hospital stay.

Dad's letter continues:

> Families live in separate male and female barracks with many people living in the same room, the rooms are verminous, beds are unhygienic with no bed linens and with dirty blankets, and there is a constant coming and going of people since new people are constantly arriving while others are being shipped out. There are male visitors till late in the night at the women's quarters, many of whom are inconsiderate and pollute the air with cigarette smoke. These visitors also engage in other activities which decency does not allow me to report!! The amount of food the children receive is inadequate. There is an epidemic of sick children in the camp, especially those who have been here for an extended period of time and have been weakened by the inadequate diet. Every time a ship departs, countless families are kept from boarding and are put back on the waiting list because their children are sick. The camp

> hospital is constantly overcrowded.

Regarding the poor diet, my brother and I really didn't notice. We had lived through worse.

Dad continues:

> Was it necessary to pull us out of our existing, if somewhat humble, homes before all issues were settled? We blindly trusted because we were being looked after by the Church.
>
> And one more thing, based on information from your organization, I sold our bedding. Now I find out the information your organization sent me is outdated. I sold our entire bedding, including pillows and down blankets, for a ridiculously low price. Now I find out I could have shipped our bedding to the USA.

The down blankets were a huge loss because they kept my brother and me warm in our unheated room. I loved those down blankets. Mom was brokenhearted when Dad sold them. They were the only nice thing we owned in Ohrenbach.

Here are some of my brother's memories of Camp Bremen-Grohn:

> Aside from regular meals, all the children assembled in a mess hall and were given a glass of milk and a hard roll (*Brötchen*). I think the milk was a powdered milk and water mix, which I recall as being tasty.
>
> We were entertained with black-and-white Laurel and Hardy films, cartoons, and such. They were mostly in English.
>
> I don't recall going to school, though we did on occasion leave the camp and walk around the town.
>
> I also recall during one of our final interviews hearing our

> last name pronounced with an American accent by a matronly woman with graying hair. She also wore lipstick, a colored print dress, perfume, red nail polish, and what I thought was lots and lots of jewelry.

Several days before we sailed, we moved to a private room. The room was very small, but it was much nicer than the previous accommodations. Of course, no sink, kitchen, or toilet facilities were included. My parents were very pleased with the room anyway.

–NOTES–

1. On June 8, 1951, a four-page legal complaint concerning the Regional Education Administration in Ansbach was submitted to the court by Dad's lawyer, Dr. Rainer Rud Schubert. On January 14, 1952, Schubert wrote Dad a letter informing him that his suit was rejected. On January 25, eleven days after the letter was written, we were already at the Munich Resettlement Center, receiving smallpox vaccinations. We were on our way to the United States.
2. Karlsfeld is a small city, like a suburb, about ten miles from the center of Munich. Munich-Karlsfeld means it is in the Munich metropolitan area and its exact location is Karlsfeld. Munich-Karlsfed is how both the Germans and the Americans, who occupied the former German military barracks, named the military barracks facility.

Chapter 14

Coming to America

OCEAN "CRUISE"

Sailing to America—March 31, 1952

I remember when Dad came to our small room at Camp Bremen-Grohn to tell us we had been approved. He had received a standard-sized white sheet of paper with merely the outline of the United States printed in black. There were no cities or state borders indicated on this map except for the outline of the state of Ohio. In the outline of Ohio was a star with an arrow pointing at it. The arrow pointed at Columbus, Ohio. That was all we knew about the location of our new home.

Dad was told that our sponsor was the Christ Lutheran Church in Bexley, Ohio. Bexley is a small municipality within the Columbus city limits. The sponsor ensured us a place to live and jobs for my parents.

When we were about to board the ship and sail to America, Günter, Mom, and I knew very little English. Months before we were approved to immigrate, Dad had purchased a record player and a Berlitz English course on a vinyl record. Occasionally we all listened to the record; however, Dad was the only one who worked at improving his English. I remember one sentence from the course: "Here we are again in the same room." The voice on the record talked very fast with no pause between words, making the English words sound indistinct. (In English we do not really pause between words, but when speaking German, there is actually a short stop between words.) In Germany we used to say that Americans sound like they have mashed potatoes in their mouths.

The Huge Ship

A couple of days after we saw the map, we boarded the ship, with two dark brown cardboard-like suitcases with metal-reinforced rounded corners, and Dad's beloved violin in its black case. One suitcase was for Mom and me and the other for Dad and my brother. The rest of our belongings were shipped in five small crates, which were loaded ahead of time into the cargo hold of the ship. We had filled two of the wooden crates with household items. Among other items in the crates were pots, pans, and cutlery. The larger of the two crates was an eighteen-inch cube. We had very little to ship and therefore had very little with which to set up housekeeping in our new home. The other three crates contained one of the homemade radios, books, the record player, and the English language record (see the appendix, 38).

We sailed for America on March 31, 1952, on the USS *General C. C. Ballou* with over a thousand other refugees. Most would find homes in America; for others, the final destination was Canada. I know the document on the following page looks uninteresting, but to me, seeing our names on the inbound (to New York) passenger manifest is quite exciting. Because I can speak German, lived in Germany, and taught German in my second career, most people who know me think I am German. The manifest proves we were never German citizens, instead we were Romanian displaced persons. Our names are listed on lines 8, 9, 10, and 11.

Our ship, the *General Ballou,* was huge. In my adult years I thought that my perception of the size of the ship was shaped by the fact that I was only eight years old. But having researched the ship, I know it was actually the length of one and three-quarter football fields (522 feet, ten inches).

Women and small children had their quarters in the front of the ship and the men and older boys were in the back. The ship had many decks,

Form I-415
TREASURY DEPARTMENT
United States Customs Service
UNITED STATES DEPARTMENT OF JUSTICE
Immigration and Naturalization Service
(Rev. 1-5-48)

Form approved.
Budget Bureau No. 43-R079-3.

MANIFEST NO. 19

MANIFEST OF IN-BOUND PASSENGERS (ALIENS)

Class DP from Bremerhaven March 31st, 1952 (Port of embarkation)

USNS "GENERAL CC BALLOU" (Name of vessel) arriving at port of New York, 1952

Line No.	Family Name–Given Name / Destination in United States	Age (Years)	Sex (F–M)	Married or Single	Travel Doc. No. / Nationality	Number and Description of Pieces of Baggage	Head Tax Collected	This Column for Use of Master, Surgeon, and U.S. Officers
1	MADINSKI Karl c/o CWS 120 East 23rd St. New York 10, NY.	37	Ma	Md	I-1279728 Russian	3783168 (5)	No	EXEMPT
2	MADINSKI Katharina c/o CWS 120 East 23rd St. New York 10, NY.	33	F	Md	I-1279729 Russian	" "	No	
3	MADINSKI Johann c/o CWS 120 East 23rd St. New York 10. NY.	8	Ma	S	I-1279730 Russian	" "	No	
4	MADINSKI Andreas c/o CWS 120 East 23rd St. New York 10. NY.	3	Ma	S	I-1279731 Russian	" "	No	
5	MANZ Josef c/o CWS 120 East 23rd St. New York 10. NY.	43	Ma	Md	I-1279683 Russian	3783169 (6)	No	
6	MANZ Floricka c/o CWS 120 East 23rd St. New York 10. NY.	34	F	Md	I-1279684 Russian	" "	No	
7	MANZ Katharina c/o CWS 120 East 23rd St. New York 10. NY.	12	F	S	I-1279685 Russian	" "	No	
8	MAROSCHER Gustav c/o NLC LRS 145 East 32 St. New York 16, NY.	34	Md	Ma	I-1375286 Roumanian	3783170 (10)	No	4-WF
9	MAROSCHER Helene c/o NLC LRS 145 East 32 St. New York 16, NY.	31	F	Md	I-1375287 Roumanian	" "	No	
10	MAROSCHER Gerhard c/o NLC LRS 145 East 32 St. New York 16, NY.	8	Ma	S	I-1375289 Roumanian	" "	No	
11	MAROSCHER Guenter c/o NLC LRS 145 East 32 St. New York 16, NY.	11	Ma	S	I-1375288 Roumanian	" "	No	
12	MARSCHALL Adalbert c/o APIL A. Dandenburg 3905 Florence Ave. Cincinnati. Ohio	45	Ma	Md	I-1160482 Stateless	3783171 (9)	No	

and it took quite a bit of walking down metal stairways to reach our bunks. It was not a luxury cruise. The area of the ship where we stayed was a large room with a low ceiling, filled with rows and rows of cots. The sleeping surface of each cot was canvas tied to a tubular frame. Four cots were supported on either side of the round metal posts. Vertical distance between cots was about twenty-four inches. I slept on the top bunk and Mom slept below me. Beside me, on the other side of the support posts, slept another passenger. It was easy to climb up to my cot. It was like climbing the rungs of a ladder.

We were packed in the ship like sardines. Maybe we even smelled as good as sardines. I never saw any shower facilities. Frankly, as a kid I did not mind the accommodations. We had all lived in worse conditions. We did have flush toilets in the front of the ship, and they were spotless. As I recall there were perhaps two rows of fifteen toilets facing each other, rather close side by side, and totally open; there were no privacy walls to form stalls. Privacy was not a feature of this "cruise."

By permission of Russ Padden of
http://www.rpadden.com/157/AP157.htm

Needless to say, with such wonderful accommodations, we spent as much time on deck in the fresh air as possible. Mom felt strongly that it was healthy to be in the sun and fresh air. Both my brother and I were eager to be on the top deck. We did not have cameras to take pictures, but photos of the living quarters still exist. Shown in the picture are the bunks of the USS *General Ballou* filled with GIs returning from Europe in late 1945. We slept in the same bunks during our voyage.

How Much Can One Person Puke and Retch?

For much of the ten-day trip from Bremerhaven (the port of Bremen) to the port of New York, we had terrible North Atlantic storms. The first few days, Mom and I did lots of puking over the rail on the top deck. The sea air on the deck smelled better than the puke in the living quarters. My brother also vomited over the rail on the top deck whenever possible. Dad, who was sicker than the rest of us, stayed below deck until his seasickness passed. In those first few days of misery, I remember Mom having to force me to go to the bathroom. When I started feeling better, trips to the bathroom, which involved climbing many flights of metal stairs, were fun. Our bathrooms were right at the tip of the bow. When the bow of the ship accelerated upward, it was hard to walk upstairs, and then the bow would suddenly drop and one could weightlessly and quickly run up the stairs. As the bow dropped and crashed into the waves, it sounded like a giant was simultaneously hitting both sides of the ship with gigantic rubber mallets.

USS General Ballou. By permission of Russ Padden of http://www.rpadden.com/157/AP157.htm.

The waves were large enough that the front third of the deck was off limits because the waves washed over the ship. For the same reason, lower decks were off limits for nearly the entire voyage. Rhythmically the bow would rise up until you saw only sky toward the bow, and then it would come crashing down into the waves, whereupon huge waves would wash over the top deck at the bow. Early each morning, Mom and I would go up to the top deck until it was dark, going below deck only to eat and go to the bathroom. Sitting on deck provided an amazing view of an angry sea with huge waves. In addition to the front of the ship lifting and diving, the ship also rocked side to side. It rocked up at such an angle that we could see only sky and then low enough that we could look down directly at the waves. When we looked down, the waves seemed higher than the sides of the ship. I always kept a tight grip on the metal bench as I watched this wonder of nature. When we arrived in the United States, we all had good tans. Ocean cruises are that way, you know. The picture is of the USS *General Ballou* in Bremerhaven in 1952. Perhaps it was taken when we were on board. Before we sailed to America, my parents were given a postcard picture of the USS *General Ballou*. I will never forget its name!

A Grab in Time Saves . . .

When we were on the top deck, the three-foot-tall railing was the only thing that kept people from falling into the ocean. The waves continued to get worse, so the sailors strung a rope inside and above the railing on the top deck. The rope was placed at perhaps five feet from the deck. I do not recall how it was affixed, but it must have been tied to part of the boat at intervals. The weather continued to worsen. One day I was sitting by myself on the deck in my usual spot, being entertained by the waves. A boy, maybe around fourteen, was walking between me and the railing when the rhythmic rocking suddenly changed. Without warning, the ship rocked much faster and farther toward the side where we were. It seemed like someone had taken a toy ship, turned it on its side, and let everything on the deck slide off. The deck was nearly vertical and I was looking straight down into the ocean, with a death grip on my metal bench. The sudden rocking motion of the ship caused the boy's feet to leave the deck. In an instant he was falling straight down into the angry sea. At the last possible moment, he grabbed for the rope. With one hand grabbing the rope, he continued to fall vertically down toward the water. Once the slack in the rope was taken up, he was six feet beyond the rail, momentarily suspended above the water. Just as quickly, the ship righted itself and the taut rope catapulted the boy back on board. It's an event that I will never forget. If the boy was fourteen in 1952, he would be eighty-one now. If he is still alive, I am sure he has not forgotten either. Ever since this trip, I have never had the desire to take another ocean voyage.

Food, Food, and More Food

Once the seasickness subsided, we regained our appetites. For the first time in my memory, we had all we wanted to eat. The mess hall was super clean and was brightly lit. Food was served cafeteria-style. After taking an aluminum tray from one of the tray stacks, we would slide them along three stainless pipes as the American merchant marine sailors plopped food onto the tray. We had never seen so much food! It was delicious! We ate standing up and, when finished, dropped off our trays. We were not permitted to take food with us to the living quarters. Of course, I would get hungry between meals. In my case I was still feeding the intestinal parasites (worms) I had lived with for years. The worms took their share of nutrition and calories from my food. I was hungry all the time. On the ship, I wore a dark pair of pants similar to sweatpants, which had elastic at the bottom of the pant legs. I took extra rolls, opened my elastic waistband, and dropped them into my pants. Gravity worked so that the rolls ended up at the bottom of my pant legs, safely held in place by the elastic. I put so many rolls down my pant legs that the bottom of my pants bulged out and I had to walk with my feet apart. Talk about bell-bottom trousers! The sailors working in the mess hall noticed, smiled, and let me go my way. God bless Americans!

My brother remembers:

> Do you recall the first time we ate on the ship? The chow line offered so much food, you and I thought that the first meal was going to be our *only* meal. So despite strict orders that no food was allowed to be taken out of the mess, I filled my pants pockets with bread and fried chicken, only to learn that four hours later another huge meal was being served.
>
> During the sea voyage our family was again separated. After the initial sea sickness, you and I enjoyed rough seas and would "fly" up the stairs as the boat would dip into the waves.
>
> Then there's the story of how you and I hoarded food from the mess hall in our pants. We wore dark blue gym pants with elastic at the ankles—which offered plenty of room for bread and chicken legs. Once we got accustomed to being fed three times a day, I hoarded only desserts.
>
> And let's not forget Jell-O, the do-you-drink-it-or-chew-it

> food that came in unnaturally bright colors.
>
> Unlike a Carnival cruise ship, sanitation procedures on this 'US Navy liner' were courtesy of the passengers. Vati (Dad) and I had latrine duty on a rotating schedule.
>
> If I recall, the voyage lasted ten days, give or take, and unless you and I were forced to stay below deck (due to bad weather), we spent most of our daylight hours wandering and playing on the deck. I recall our Columbus hosts telling us how very "brown" we were.

Buried at Sea

I remember that a fifty-four-year-old lady died during the trip across the ocean. Her bunk was maybe twenty feet from Mom's and my bunks. She had a husband, but I do not remember children. She was buried at sea. Her body was on a board and covered with an American flag. The ceremony was dignified. The captain said a few words from a book, which I did not understand. I suppose he read some scripture from the Bible. The board was lifted at one end, and the body, which was wrapped tightly in white sheets, slid into the water. When I think about this event as an adult, I tear up. She did not make it to the United States, the "Promised Land," but she was given the honor of being covered by our flag.

Also watching the event was a group of perhaps five young men (also refugees), maybe sixteen to eighteen years old, who laughed after the ceremony and talked in a language I did not understand. I imagine they made jokes about "fish food" or something equally crass and unfeeling. I was amazed and disgusted by their callous nature.

Emergency Drill

Two or three times during the voyage, we had emergency drills. When the alarm sounded, regardless of where we were on the ship, all passengers immediately headed to their bunks, put on their life jackets, and headed off to an assigned location on the top deck. The drill ended with the crew partially lowering the lifeboats, although nobody actually boarded the boats. The trip from the top deck to the bunks was quite long. Mom's and my bunks were in the lower part of the bow of the ship, many flights of metal stairs below the deck. Although I spent a fair amount of time on the deck by myself, during all but the last drill I happened to be with Mom when the alarm sounded.

Toward the end of the ten-day voyage, we had one nice sunny day without huge waves and a violently tossing ship. This day was the only time on the ship that we were together as a family. All four of us were on a large elevated platform above the top deck, enjoying the sun and warm weather along with many other passengers.

For some reason I went down the metal stairs to the deck level. While I was on the deck alone, the alarm sounded. I immediately sprinted back to the stairs to join Mom for the long walk to our bunks. As I reached the stairs to the platform, I was met by a tide of adults coming down the stairway. Some admonished me for trying to go up the stairs as everyone was coming down. Going up the stairs quickly proved to be impossible. My initial reaction was panic. That did not last long and I headed toward the front of the ship and down many flights of metal stairs to my bunk. I was calmly putting on my life jacket when Mom showed up. End of crisis. We went up to the deck together and watched the rest of the exercise, with all passengers on the top deck in life jackets and sailors partially lowering the lifeboats on a nice sunny day.

First View of America

As always, Mom and I were up on the deck at first light. In the dawn's early light we saw the Statue of Liberty. I had no knowledge of the Statue, but still it was a clear sign that we had made it to America.

Ellis Island

The ship docked. After several hours of waiting, we walked down a long switchback gangplank. This was followed by more waiting. I remember all one thousand darkly dressed, orderly refugees waiting in lines at customs. We had our two suitcases and Dad's violin, which he had kept with him on the ship. I don't recall seeing the five wooden crates. They must have been shipped to us later and inspected by customs elsewhere.

The customs agent questioned Dad at length about his violin. Maybe he wanted to confirm that it was really Dad's. Finally the agent asked Dad to play the violin. Rather than being nervous, Dad relished this opportunity to play in front of such a large audience of scraggly-looking refugees. He enjoyed playing and soaked up the moment. All activity, including talking, stopped in the big hall while he played. When he finished, everyone applauded.

On April 12, 1952, we were registered at Ellis Island as legal aliens by the Immigration and Naturalization Service (see the appendix, 39).

OUR NEW HOME IN COLUMBUS, OHIO

Spending Money

Each refugee family was given some spending money for the trip to their new home in America. Dad received twenty dollars in spending money (twenty dollars in 1952 was equivalent to $190 in 2018). The money was to last until the first paycheck. Dad spent his first American money at Grand Central Station in New York. His first expenditure was a shoeshine for twenty-five cents. He wanted to make a good impression when we arrived in Columbus, Ohio.

We were given large signs to hang around our necks with numbers and our names on them, and we boarded the train. The signs depressed Dad, who felt we were being treated like cattle.

Train Trip

We departed at dusk, sitting in standard second-class seats, with an expected early morning arrival in Columbus, Ohio. I was amazed by the streets and highways around New York full of cars. To a boy from Ohrenbach, seeing six- and eight-lane roads of cars all with their headlights on was mind-boggling. Dad, who was always confident and willing to tackle anything to accomplish his goals, had a sad moment of reflection as we looked out the windows at the thousands of cars with headlights streaming down the roads. He said, "Everyone is driving to their home. We do not have a home." I remember discussions about how whoever was waiting for us would find us in a crowded train station. Considering how we were dressed and what we looked like, this concern seems quite funny. We just did not know how odd we looked.

As we left in the waning light, numerous TV antennas on top of private homes were silhouetted against the sky. This impressed my brother since he knew there was a TV in each of those houses. We had never seen a TV before. I was awake for long stretches of the trip. Along the way, we passed a house that was on fire. There were huge flames and the house was being consumed.

Columbus, Ohio—Union Station

Very early on April 13, 1952, Easter Sunday, we arrived at Union Station in Columbus, Ohio.[1]

We were the only passengers getting off the train that morning. We need not have worried about someone having difficulty finding us in the train station, even without the signs on our necks. We were wearing dark wool clothing, and my brother and I wore heavy boots. To assure we had good shoes in America, Dad had purchased expensive boots in Rothenburg when there was still snow on the ground. My brother and I were also wearing long brown wool socks under our dark sweatpants. The socks were held up by a garter belt under our pants. Imagine that. The thigh-length wool socks were standard clothing to ward off the cold in Ohrenbach and were worn either with our Lederhosen or under our sweatpants. That April was hotter than anything we had ever experienced in Ohrenbach.

The train station was deserted except for one woman sitting on one of the many long wooden benches in the distance. She wore a canary yellow coat and was a bit rotund. Coming from a culture in which every adult over thirty wore either black, dark brown, or dark blue, we found the color strikingly odd. Alphie Peters, the lady in the yellow coat, was there to greet us. Later I got to know Alphie as a lovely and kind person. To my almost nine-year-old mind, when I looked at Alphie in her bright yellow coat, I thought, *She looks like a very large canary*. I was amused. I was wise enough not to ever share my first impression of her, even after I learned to speak English.

Alphie Peters was the daughter of Ma and Pop Peters. She worked for Capital University in some capacity. A Capital University student had driven Alphie to the train station and then drove all of us to 806 College Avenue in Bexley, where Ma and Pop Peters lived. We were to live on Mound Street, across the street from campus, but the house was not yet ready for occupation. The Peterses were kind enough to take us into their home for three weeks until our designated residence was ready.

Big Breakfast

Alphie brought us into the Peterses' house that Easter Sunday morning. She introduced us to Pop Peters and then directed us to the kitchen, where Ma Peters was cooking breakfast. We walked into the kitchen and the kind old lady (Ma Peters) said something to us while she was cooking breakfast. I did not realize till later that she was saying good morning in German, but in a very different dialect. That morning we ate our first breakfast in America. The breakfast consisted of scrambled eggs, bacon, toast, and pancakes. Everything was delicious, but the bacon was too salty for us. We were not used to such a rich breakfast, and I did not feel good afterward. My brother vomited. Apparently our eating during our "ocean cruise" did not adequately prepare us for our first big American breakfast. We were used to toast and jam spread so thin that not all the holes in the bread were filled. We did not have enough jam to just slap it on and spread a layer over the toast with lots of butter.

Picture in The Capital Chimes, April 24, 1952

Our Sponsor

The morning of our arrival, we attended the church service at our sponsoring church, Christ Lutheran. We stood at the front of the church and were introduced. Thinking back, I realize there were no shower facilities on the train, in New York, on the ship, in the out-processing camps we stayed at for three months, in Rothenburg, or in Ohrenbach. I'm sure we did take a bath in the week we left Ohrenbach, months before. From that last bath to Columbus, the only way we had cleaned ourselves was with a washcloth and a bowl of cold water. If we stank, the kind Christians did not let us know.

Eleven days after our arrival, on April 24, 1952, an article was published in *The Capital Chimes* newspaper about our family. My brother and I wore our Lederhosen for the picture taken by the reporter (see the appendix, 37). They were the nicer of the two pants we had. While Lederhosen were what we wore almost every day in Bavaria, except in the winter, we soon learned that this was not standard dress in the United States. Can you tell from our faces that we were happy in our new country?

Back to Work

Our sponsoring church made arrangements with Capital University for Mom and Dad to be employed and for our first residence. Dad became a janitor at the university, earning ninety-two cents per hour ($8.76 per hour in today's dollars). Mom's position as a house mother for eighteen resident coeds earned us free housing. We lived in the right side of the first floor of a two-and-a-half story duplex converted into a dormitory. From our living room area Mom had access to the student side of the first floor and the stairway to the upstairs dorm rooms. I was too young to appreciate living with eighteen coeds.

Some kind church members helped us by buying my brother and me school clothes not long after we arrived so we could dress more like the other kids. After that initial help, we were self-sufficient.

Lasting Impressions for an Almost Nine-Year-Old Boy

After arriving in Columbus, we experienced an immediate and mind-boggling increase in our standard of living. The most notable aspect of this increase was food. Food and more food! For the first time in my memory (ocean voyage excluded), I had enough to eat. I ate more than most adults. My packed school lunch was three cold-cut sandwiches each day. I even kept up that pace of eating after I got rid of the intestinal parasites. Parasite-free! Yippee! Having enough to eat made a powerful lifelong impression on me. I was, and still am, thankful to our nation and its people that we were allowed to come to the United States.

Acts of Kindness

We arrived just shy of seven years since the last American was killed by Germans during WWII. Even I, not quite nine years old, realized the remarkable kindness of the Americans.

Today the coolest toy for young boys might be an Xbox 360. In 1952 the coolest toy was a cowboy hat and a shiny toy gun with a holster. A young minister took my brother and me shopping during our first few weeks and bought us each cowboy hats and guns with holsters. The minister may not have been aware of how important and memorable the gifts were, but we remembered. The American cowboy gear brought us great joy.

Mom used to bake dozens of doughnuts every Saturday morning.

So much food! Amazing! Once our bellies were properly trained to accept large amounts of food, I think my brother and I probably each ate a dozen doughnuts every Saturday morning. Two Capital University students who wanted to improve their German stopped by every Saturday morning to talk with my parents. I suppose the doughnuts were an added incentive. The fellows noticed that Mom had open sores all over her hands and asked her what the problem was. Mom told them that she did our laundry by hand. She used Tide detergent, which was hard on her hands. These young men were not particularly well off, but they pooled their money and bought Mom an old wringer washer for fifteen dollars ($143, inflation-adjusted to 2018.) What a blessing it was for Mom to have a washing machine.

Anyone who has ever used a wringer washer knows that the rollers are potentially dangerous. If one carelessly puts one's fingers too close to the wrong side of the turning rollers, they are immediately pulled into the rollers and can't be pulled out. The fingers are followed by the hand, the forearm, and I suppose—rather painfully—the upper arm. Dad was aware of this danger and showed me how to move the lever to reverse the rollers and roll the arm out again. Sure enough, a couple of days later I was showing a curious friend of mine the new wringer washer in the basement. Of course, he stuck his hand into the pinch point. His fingers, hand, and forearm were pulled in between the rollers. I moved the lever to reverse. His forearm, hand, and fingers rolled out and were free again. No injury, no tears, just relief.

Loving Sunday School

We attended Christ Lutheran Church for a while. It was in Sunday school that I discovered one of the world's greatest foods: graham crackers! It was easy to be thrilled with Sunday school when we got milk and graham crackers each time. I understood nothing and learned nothing, but I loved Sunday school.

Not-So-Fast German Singing

After several months, we began attending a church near downtown Columbus where the services were in German. The congregation consisted of Americans of German and Transylvanian Saxon descent. Several times, the young Capital University students who came over to our house on Saturday mornings attended the German church service with us. They did this to increase their exposure to German. German Lutheran hymns were sung very slowly. Unless you have sung *"Eine feste Burg ist unser Gott"* (A Mighty Fortress Is Our God) in an old-time German Lutheran church, you cannot appreciate just how *slow* the pace of a hymn could be. I remember being amused when both of the students, whose German language knowledge was minimal, commented on how amazingly fast the Germans sang.

Several years after the "fast singing" remark by the students, I listened again to the English course record Dad had played in Ohrenbach. I listened to the same sentence, "Here we are again in the same room." To the fluent English-speaking Maroschers, that same sentence was spoken clearly and very slowly. Those two memories lay dormant for many years until I began to teach high-school German in my second career. I was a better teacher because I learned from my own experience the difficulties faced by beginning language learners.

–NOTES–

1. The train service was discontinued at Union Station on April 28, 1977. The station was later demolished.

Chapter 15

All New: Country, Customs, Language, Food, School

CULTURE SHOCK

Friendly Americans Say "Hi"

Americans are outwardly friendlier than Germans. Here in Ohio it is common to greet strangers on neighborhood streets with "hi." In Germany, strangers passing on the sidewalk make eye contact but do not greet each other. We were unaware of the "hi" greeting used by Americans. We had no car and needed to walk everywhere. The first few days, as people greeted Mom with "hi," she thought they were mocking her by saying "Heil" as in "Heil Hitler." It did not take many days for my parents to understand the friendly intent of the salutation.

Our First Visit to an American Grocery Store

I remember our first trip to an American grocery store, the A&P on Main Street near the Capital University campus. All four of us were there. A nice lady met us there to help us with the shopping—a big help since everything was strange to us. We had just moved into our house on Mound Street and we had no food in the house. The amount of food available at the grocery store was astounding. I had never seen such abundance and could not fathom so many choices. We filled a grocery cart, smaller than today's carts, full of groceries. It cost about ten dollars (ninety-five dollars in 2018 dollars). I did not know someone could actually have enough food to fill such a huge basket. While we were amazed and pleased at the amount of food, it seemed to me almost wrong to buy that much. Luckily, we had a refrigerator in the house for perishable food. Now that was amazing!

The Religious Immigrant

Dad was always studying or working. He never took downtime. To a large degree this was his nature, but he was also a thirty-five-year-old man with a family, no possessions, and no money who was starting his life over.

Dad was always engaged in learning. During lunch breaks or any other short break from his job at the university, he pulled out his German–English dictionary, trying to learn new words. One day, one of his coworkers commented to Dad that he must be very religious since he was reading the Bible all the time. Dad explained that it was not the Bible but a dictionary. Years later Dad had fun telling us how religious he was and would then tell us this story. Actually, Dad tried to have Bible readings in our backyard on Sundays, but that did not work well with sons who would have rather done almost anything else.

The Kind Immigrants

One day, a coworker and fellow janitor offered Dad a peanut butter and jelly sandwich. This coworker loved PB&J and ate one every day for lunch. We know that these sandwiches are delicacies, but to Dad's European palate they tasted awful. Dad came home to report to his wife that one of his coworkers was so poor that he had to eat these terrible sandwiches. He really felt sorry for the guy. Mom then started making one extra sandwich with cold cuts for Dad to give to his coworker every lunch.

The summer of 1952 broke heat records. Where we had lived before, in Bavaria, a hot summer day was 75°F. Mom suffered greatly from the heat. Columbus, Ohio is on the fortieth parallel, the same parallel as Madrid, Spain, or Milan, Italy.

Mom repeatedly complained to Dad how unbearably hot it was. Finally in exasperation he responded to her complaints, "I did not realize this was a tropical country!" That summer, construction workers were working behind our backyard. Mom noticed and felt sorry for them to have to work in such heat. So she made ice-cold lemonade for them every day for the duration of the job.

Pockets Full of Food

A neighboring family, the Witherspoons, lived just two houses down from us. They had a son who was a little younger and a daughter who was a little older than me. I regularly went to their house to play. Sometimes Mrs. Witherspoon would invite me to eat with them. A problem with eating there was that some of the food was very strange and hard for me to eat. Cooked spinach was the worst. I would literally choke on it; the slimy stuff just would not go down. I learned to stick it in my pocket when nobody was looking so as to not offend Mrs. Witherspoon. They also ate something similar to pizza that was strange to me. I would put that in my pocket also. Mom was very tolerant of my coming home with chewed food stuffed in my pockets. It took a while for my palate to adjust to American food.

Oops!

One time in the early months of living in Bexley, the entire Witherspoon family was giving me a WWII history lesson. I think maybe they were making sure that this former heathen Nazi got a proper WWII history lesson. We were all sitting around a low coffee table looking at a huge picture book of soldiers, battles, and generals. I had never seen a picture of General Eisenhower and did not know he was running for president. They asked if I knew who he was. I looked at his picture and thought to myself, *He has a wide mouth*. Using my best English, I pointed at the large picture of General Eisenhower and said, "He has a big mouth!"

I immediately realized this was a big oops! I did not know why, but all the Witherspoons suddenly changed their expression and even the two children stiffened up. I had no idea exactly how what I had said was wrong, but I knew I had just verbally stepped in it. I tried to quickly point at his mouth and show how wide it was. They relaxed a bit but remained wary of this little Nazi for the rest of our picture book session. To their credit, this was only a minor blip in our relationship. The whole family was kind. They moved to Elyria, Ohio, a few years later and invited me to visit them, which I did by taking the train to Elyria by myself.

In case you were wondering about my loyalty after this faux pas, rest assured that I learned who General Eisenhower was and actually listened to some of his speeches as he was running for the presidency in 1952. I really did like Ike! I was still Ike's man for the November 1956 election, and wore an "I like Ike" button.

Buying Pig Meat

Early on in the time we lived in Bexley, Mom sent my brother and me to the A&P to buy four pork chops. But how does one say *pork chops* in English? When in doubt, look it up in the German–English dictionary. So we headed off to the A&P, and my brother asked for four pieces of "pig meat." The butcher asked, "Do you mean pork chops?" My brother quickly figured out that the butcher knew his meats, and *pork* must mean *pig meat*. However, I was not convinced and insisted on four pieces of pig meat, not pork. Finally the nice butcher said, "Here are four pieces of pig meat," and we headed home with our pork chops. Those pork chops at dinner were really good! Imagine being able to buy and then eat four pork chops all in one meal!

Where Is the Fire?

Günter and I had a magical moment during our first summer in America when we saw the first fireflies in our backyard. In Germany or Romania we never saw fireflies (lightning bugs). Late one evening, my brother and I looked out and saw our backyard was filled with sparks. The sparks were numerous and moving; they would light a while and then extinguish, as sparks tend to do. We rushed out to see where the fire was. Imagine our surprise and wonder when we discovered that the "sparks" were really bugs that lit up!

Poison Ivy

In Germany and Romania there was no poison ivy. A few months after we arrived, a mean kid from the neighborhood, who was my brother's age, rubbed Günter's face, including his eyes, with poison ivy leaves. My brother did not think much about it. If it wasn't a nettle, which hurt instantly and left welts, a leaf would not hurt you—or so we thought at the time. My brother had the most awful case of poison ivy imaginable and was miserable for weeks. After my brother recovered, he gave the boy a well-deserved and thorough beating, the memory of which may have lasted a lifetime as does my brother's memory of his first case of poison ivy.

That Pesky German Punctuality

Transylvanians were infected by the same need for punctuality as Germans. Interestingly, this trait never left my parents. They acclimatized themselves very well to customs in America, yet they never managed to adjust their expectations relative to "being on time." If you were invited to a person's house for dinner at 6:00 p.m., it was impolite to be one minute late. It was polite to be exactly on time or even ten minutes early. The fact that Americans did it differently, and that we should adjust our habits, never occurred to my parents. They just marveled at the impoliteness of so many people. Still, they had many good friends whom they excused and who excused them for their odd behavior.

Dental Care

In postwar Germany, people seldom if ever went to the dentist. Dental care was a luxury most could not afford. Because of our improving financial situation, I visited a dentist for the first time when I was thirteen. It took a number of visits to fill my thirty-two cavities. My brother's teeth were healthier: he had only twenty-three cavities.

Cultural Adjustments

My brother recalls an issue with the use of telephones:

> In the first years Mutti suffered severe culture shock. I recall when a girl from my sixth-grade class called the house. There was one phone for us and twenty students. She saw me sitting on the steps and heard me speaking in English; she lashed out and slapped my face. She simply could not comprehend using appliances that were common in the US. In her world only doctors used telephones. There was one phone at the Ohrenbach Post Office—it was for emergency use only.

I also remember my first telephone experience. I got a call from a girl. A call for me? A call from a girl? I felt very uncomfortable talking on the phone. This must have been a few months after our arrival since my English was good enough to actually converse. The call did not last long. Maybe Mom did not know about the call. I did not get slapped.

My brother recalls that transportation was also different:

> No one we knew had either a phone or car. In Ohrenbach we owned one (used!) bicycle that Vati, Mutti, and I shared. Lorenz (the teacher) owned a small one-cylinder, two-stroke NSU motorcycle.[1] There was one tractor shared between Ohrenbach and Scheckenbach (the next village). Personal transportation was limited to walking, biking, riding in a cow-powered wagon, or biking to the bus stop, which was a mile or so outside Ohrenbach.
>
> Ah, those were heady times.

Under the Marshall Plan the economy was picking up. Our old bicycle, Herr Lorenz's small motorcycle, and the tractor were purchased not long before we left. Prior to that, the doctor's motorcycle (probably 50cc) was the only non-animal powered means of transportation.

Surprise! Relatives!

Surprisingly, we discovered relatives in Columbus: the Albert and Mathilde Maroscher family, who had fled from Lechnitz, Romania, in the same *Treck* as Grete Herrmann Knopp (see the appendix, 32).[2] The family was already living in Columbus when we arrived. How strange that we should find Maroschers in the same city in the United States! Their children were Bruno, Udo, Albert (known as Abi), and Elfriede. Those Maroschers attended the same German Lutheran church that we did during our first year in Columbus. Albert's grandfather and my dad's grandfather were brothers.

After fleeing from Romania in September 1944, the Albert Maroscher family settled in the small Bavarian village of Malching. Both our family and the Albert Maroscher family lived fairly close to each other in Bavaria, but we did not know of each other's location or fate. Toward the end of WWII and for the next couple of years, millions of people were fleeing for their safety and for freedom. More often than not, all contact among surviving relatives and friends was lost for years.

Albert's sister, Hermine Bissett, was an American citizen and lived in German Village near downtown Columbus. She and her husband sponsored the Albert Maroscher family, enabling them to immigrate to the United States in 1949. They flew to Columbus, Ohio, from Frankfurt, Germany, via Shannon, Ireland, then Gander, Newfoundland, and finally New York City. Very few people took transatlantic flights in 1949. Udo still has his American Airlines ticket as a keepsake.

I asked Udo what his dad did in the old country and later in the US:

> My father's original trade was leatherworking, but then he decided to become a vintner. When we left Romania there was, as I have heard, a huge quantity of wine left in the cellar. There were stories told that the invading Russians drank their fill and then machine-gunned the barrels. Here in the US he had a mom-and-pop-type carryout

with some groceries and meats and he also did some investing in real estate.

Albert and Mathilde Maroscher lost their eldest son in the service of his country. On April 15, 1968, Albert George (Abi) Maroscher, a major in the army, was killed in Vietnam. His funeral was held in the German-speaking church in Columbus.

We also discovered another Gustav Maroscher, a chef at the Neil House, an upscale restaurant in downtown Columbus. His wife's name was Anna. They had no children.

More Relatives

Rudolf Maroscher, son of an immigrant to the US in the early 1900s, living with his family near Salem, Ohio, discovered that there was a Maroscher family they had not known about. We were that family.

Rudolf Maroscher, our cousin, made contact with Dad when I was about fifteen and drove to Columbus to visit us. I remember sitting in the backyard at 906 West Eleventh Avenue one summer day when Rudolf visited us. When Rudolf, known as Rudy, arrived, I was stunned. He looked like a cross between me and my dad. The two gentlemen sat in the backyard and talked for quite a while. I sat there and listened. I remember Dad telling Rudolf, "Rudy, Americans have had it so good so long, they have forgotten what hard work is. If you apply yourself and work hard, you can accomplish anything you want to do." I always thought that the discussion in our backyard might have helped Rudy to become a successful small business owner. After Dad died, Rudy and his wife, Barb, were kind enough to invite Mom and my family to their Maroscher reunions.

Four years after we arrived in the United States, Mom's youngest brother, Helmut Maurer, who had been a POW of the British, came to America with his wife Lilli and son Frank. They stayed with us for about three weeks until Helmut began working as a jeweler in Cincinnati. Later, sons Peter and Paul were born as Americans.

GOING TO SCHOOL

Montrose Elementary

On Monday, April 14, 1952, the day after we arrived, we registered for school. Our first day of school was the following day. We attended Montrose Elementary School in Bexley, Ohio. My brother started in sixth grade and I was in third grade. By then I had lost one year of school due to my long illness in Ohrenbach and lack of schooling in the immigration processing camps.

During the first few days at school, our clothes were the same dark blue sweatpants and sweatshirts we had worn on the ship. Not long thereafter, we wore new jeans and T-shirts (the weather was already hot) like all the rest of the kids.

I knew no English. My teacher, Louise Planson, was very kind to me, as were most other students. The lessons, the children, and the activities seemed very childish and not particularly rigorous. Although I had missed so much school, I felt I was ahead in my education compared to my new classmates. In Ohrenbach we had learned how to write cursive with fountain pens in our test booklets and now we used crayons and pencils.

Kids communicate even if they don't speak the same language, and so I picked up spoken English quickly in school and by playing in our Bexley neighborhood. My teacher was willing to spend maybe twenty minutes each day after school teaching me to read. She would move her finger below the words she was reading out loud. German is a phonetic language. Words are pronounced exactly as they are written. I remember thinking how strange it was that one could not predict how a word is said by looking at the letters. The oddest of all was the silent letter *e* at the end of many words. How strange. I reasoned that if Americans can learn this, so can I. Thank you, Ms. Planson—you were kind and got me off to a good start.

I remember having to do math problems without understanding English. When doing word problems, I could see the numbers, but the terminology (*multiply, subtract,* etc.) meant nothing to me, let alone the English sentences in which they were used. I knew it was a math problem, so I would do "math." Using the numbers I saw in the word problems, I'd multiply two numbers, then subtract the next number, and then add the fourth number. I figured by doing this the teacher would know that I understood math.

No Bilingual Education

From day one, I attended the same classes as all the other students. Being fully integrated into the classes, along with the after-school English help I received, maximized my chances of becoming an educated and productive American.

Teacher's Tears

One day when I was in fourth grade at Montrose, several classes walked out with their teachers to the flagpole in front of the school. It was a warm, bright, blue-sky day and each class stood with its teacher. The separate classes formed a broken circle around the American flag mounted on a tall flagpole. We (me included) recited the Pledge of Allegiance with our hands over our hearts, squinting because of the bright sun. I noticed the teacher of the class just to the left of my class turn her head to the right and look at me. We made eye contact. She began crying softly. I wondered what she was crying about and thought she was being unnecessarily emotional. As an adult, I thought that maybe she had an inkling of how my life had changed and how blessed I was to be in America.

My Brother's Impression of School in America

> My impressions of junior high school (seventh through ninth grade) and high school (tenth through twelfth grade) follow.
>
> Had I been given the translation of such terms as *multiplier, dividend, sum, fraction,* etc., math classes would have been a lot easier on me. Heck, how was I to know that an

x between two numbers meant that it was a multiplication problem? Spoken English seemed easy enough, but non-phonetic spelling was rough. I learned to write only as an adult after being transferred to Pittsburgh after a promotion. Daily activity reports, product performance evaluations, and reporting on the competition's activities—although a pain in the butt—forced me to write, and to carry a dictionary in my suitcase.

As to getting along with others my age in school . . . it was mostly an act. I found many—not all, but many—of my friends to be childish twits. Reason? They were leading insulated and sheltered lives. They weren't necessarily stupid or lazy—it's just that no one challenged them or made demands on them. Billy Banks, a black kid and fellow paperboy, was an exception and a rock-hard realist, and sadly also a violent sociopath. More about Billy later.

Having spent some considerable time in real bomb shelters and running from real airplanes strafing real civilians with real machine-gun fire, the whole notion of "duck and cover" in American classrooms seemed goofy. Even as a kid, I knew damn well that surviving an atomic blast by crawling under a desk was a macabre and calculated feel-good exercise—but since it made everyone feel good, I played along. Other than you, our parents, and the refugees we left behind, everyone I associated with, prior to getting a "real" job, seemed to be sleepwalking through life.

Only in the wonderful competition of the capitalist workplace, where work and reward are not subverted by sicko autocrats, did I start feeling comfortable in my own skin. Keep in mind that our generation of children had little time for play. In the old country, and continuing on this side of the pond, I was an accomplished water boy, wood gatherer/hauler, wood and kindling chopper, goat herder, babysitter, vegetable gardener, rabbit farmer, goat milker, goat-butter maker, wood gatherer, fire maker/tender, puppet-show producer, paperboy, grass mower, cafeteria dishwasher, house painter, etc., etc. Not to mention bartering with the occupational army and trading buckets of beer (from Gögelein's tavern) for field rations and cigarettes.

About Mr. Banks. Billy challenged me to a knife fight (I was thirteen and he was fifteen going on forty-five), and had it not been for Joel Schneider, the newspaper distribution manager, I might be writing this from jail, or not writing at all. Turns out that sometime later, Billy broke into a home, robbed and murdered an elderly woman, and was eventually and purposefully electrocuted in the old Ohio Penitentiary. Billy's booty? An old black-and-white TV.

The Big Fight

I was involved in only one fight in elementary school. The fight occurred during the first few weeks after I had started school, when I spoke no English. In the old country I had occasionally traded punches with kids, but there was never an attempt to hurt anybody. Those were not real fights. I preferred talking to fighting.

I was a skinny little kid, and one day a slightly taller but much wider, heavier, and stronger boy started picking on me. I could not communicate with him at all. I was totally nonaggressive and did not want a confrontation. He began to punch me and I half-heartedly defended myself. This quickly degenerated into a wrestling match where I was on my back with him on top. The aggressor was punching as I was trying to defend myself. He began to grab and control my arms; I could hardly move. He then put his large hand on my mouth and nose, and I could not breathe. I remember thinking, *Boy, these Americans fight dirty*. Shortly after that thought, when I still could not breathe, I panicked. I have no clue how I got out from under him. The next thing I knew was that I was the one on top and I was pounding his face with the ferocity and pace of a flyweight fighter. There was lots of commotion around us, which I did not notice until a frantic female teacher pulled me off the boy. Then I noticed that there were several distressed female teachers around us, at least one of whom was still screaming. I also noticed, with some satisfaction, that my opponent's face, shirt, and hands were covered with blood, all of it his. It is surprising how much blood can flow from a properly pummeled nose. He was wailing as a teacher led him away from the scene of the fight. His feeling of superiority, meanness, and desire to dominate someone had disappeared.

The amazing thing is that I never got into trouble. Maybe some kids or teachers had seen that the big bully was the aggressor and I was only the finisher. Then I suppose it is hard to discipline and talk to a kid who can't understand what you are saying. By the way, the boy never bothered me again, nor did anyone else. We always played nice.

Ich Bin Verloren (I Am Lost)

In proper German, "I am lost" would be "*Ich habe mich verlaufen,*" but I remember exactly what I said that day.

During the first three weeks of school, my brother would wait for me until I finished with my after-school English reading lesson. We would then walk home together. I'm sure he was required to do this so I would not get lost. One day I told him that he did not need to walk me home anymore because I knew the way. After all, I wanted to be independent. By then we were living in our new house on Mound Street.

I walked alone, took a wrong turn, and got lost. I had no idea where I was. I could not speak English and could not ask for help. I was walking aimlessly down the sidewalks of Bexley, crying quietly. After what seemed like a long time, a girl who was in my class saw me and started talking to me. I had no idea what she was saying, so all I said was "*Ich bin verloren.*" I said it a few times for emphasis. My classmate got her mom, but communication did not go any better with her. I did not know the new address yet, but then I remembered the address of Mr. and Mrs. Peters's house. In her wisdom Mom had asked me to memorize that address. I told my classmate's mom the old address and the nice lady drove me to the Peterses', for which I was thankful. No more tears—I knew how to get to our new house, which was only three blocks away. When I arrived at home, Mom was on her hands and knees, washing the floor with a rag. I could not believe it. I had just been through hell and back, and she hadn't even noticed that I was missing. I never got lost again.

Beep! Beep!

By the beginning of fourth grade I had learned more English. One day I was helping move some chairs in the classroom. I do not recall why we had several teachers in the room or why we needed to move the chairs, but I do remember my interaction with one of the teachers. I was carrying a chair and a teacher was blocking the aisle while looking the other way. I should have said, "Excuse me," but I had not learned that yet. Instead I did what cars do and said, "Beep! Beep!" in a friendly tone. The visiting teacher was instantly offended, turned around quickly, and began to correct—or more like berate—me. I was clueless as to why she was so upset. My "Beep! Beep!" had been very polite. I just looked at her silently with big eyes. My expression must have said something like, "What is going on?" Another teacher in the room intervened on my behalf and explained, in words I did not understand, the probable reason for my offense. That got me off the hook.

The Dull Boy

I was not a stellar student in junior high or high school. I was disorganized and lazy. Yet I thought I might be smart but was not quite sure. To help me evaluate my intelligence, I wanted to know my IQ score. When I was in the ninth grade, I found out my eighth-grade IQ test results with the help of a friend who worked in the school office.

I was devastated. The IQ number was so low that I was shocked. I immediately went to a library to read about IQs. I found a table with the IQ number ranges divided into different categories. I recall there was a level called "idiot" and the next higher level was "dull." Those terms are probably not used anymore. My God, I found out I was "dull," just one level above *idiot*! I was depressed for three weeks and felt really stupid.

Then I had a talk with myself. I said, "You thought you were pretty smart before you found out your IQ score. Well, ignore the score. You are pretty smart in spite of your grades." Problem fixed. This experience turned out to be very important when I digested it as an adult. I realized the reasons why I had done so poorly were my language and cultural handicaps.

I actually remember the eighth-grade IQ test. One group of questions consisted of two-dimensional drawings where the test asked, "If you cut out these shapes and fold the pieces together, what three-dimensional shape would it make?" Cinch! Easy! Another group of questions tested reasoning using family relationships, for example "If so-and-so is your uncle, and he has a child, what relation is that child to you?" No clue! I had no extended family that I interacted with. We never spoke in those terms. I remembered only one of my grandmothers and I didn't know any of my aunts and uncles abroad. I also didn't know English terms such as *niece*, *nephew*, etc. On that part of the test I resorted to randomly choosing *a*, *b*, *c*, or *d*. This made me realize the issues faced by minorities when they take IQ or similarly culturally biased tests. They can be a poor measure of inherent capability.

Shortly after deciding I was probably smart, I had a valuable experience: I was in a nearly empty classroom with three girls working on algebra problems. There was no teacher in the room and I was the only other student. They were the "in" girls. They were good-looking. They wore really nice clothes. Everybody liked them. I was the outsider. They paid about as much attention to me as if I were a chair in the room. They were talking about and discussing a difficult algebra problem they could not solve. I could hear them very well from the other side of the classroom and even though I had not seen the problem, I understood how to solve it. I walked over to them and explained how to solve the problem. Then they understood too. The three girls then stared at me silently, with their mouths open. Their expression communicated, "How can it be that you, the dummy, know how to solve this problem?" It felt pretty good as I sat back down in my corner. And that's when I decided, "Yeah, I'm not dull."

Unfortunately, this realization still did not make me a good student. I did no homework and received poor grades. Yet I paid attention in class and was respectful. I had particular difficulty with English even though I loved writing short stories, especially science-fiction stories. Writing something for which I could pick the subject was pure joy. I would vividly "live" the stories as I wrote them. But that joy faded as soon as the graded stories were handed back to me. The teachers, who meant well, had "bled" all over the stories because of my writing errors. So I stopped writing for pleasure.

In twelfth grade my difficulty with English sentence structure, context, and punctuation was evident in the one-page story I showed my new girlfriend, Ruth. She was shocked that the entire page consisted of only one or two sentences. Today, I still claim it was one sentence whereas Ruth thinks it was two.

I think part of my problem with the English language was that I did not begin reading in English until fourth grade, and maybe I was even influenced by characteristic German writing, in which sentences tend to be very long.

I am still enrolled in an English composition course fifty-eight years later. The first few years were more intensive, but I am still learning. Ruth helped me with high-school English and continued helping in college. When I was in industry and had reports to write, she also helped me with that. Thanks, Ruth.

Yes, I married my high-school sweetheart. Great decision! We celebrated our fifty-fourth anniversary in 2018.

–NOTES–

1. "NSU Motorenwerke AG, or NSU (Neckarsulm Strickmaschinen Union or Neckarsulm Knitting Machine Union), was a German manufacturer of automobiles, motorcycles, and pedal cycles, founded in 1873. Acquired by Volkswagen Group in 1969, VW merged NSU with Auto Union, creating Audi NSU Auto Union AG, ultimately Audi." https://en.wikipedia.org/wiki/NSU_Motorenwerke; https://de.wikipedia.org/wiki/NSU_Motorenwerke.
2. Grete Herrmann Knopp had provided a room in Rothenburg for my family and the late Hanna Rothmann.

Chapter 16

Chasing the American Dream

LIVING THE DREAM

The American Dream

The American dream is achieving success on one's own merits through hard work and dedication regardless of background, race, ethnicity, religion, or station in life. In America, more than in any other nation, success is based on a person's work ethic, ability, and persistence. People who feel they are victims often build barriers to their own success by giving up because they "know" the deck is stacked against them. Humans are hard-wired to move toward what they are looking at, literally and figuratively. A person who "sees" success in the future succeeds. A person who sees barriers is hindered by those barriers. The Maroschers never fell into that trap, never modified their efforts to succeed, even when they were victims of oppressive systems in Romania and West Germany. In America, with barriers removed, they flourished. Of course, America is not perfect, but then neither is life. In America, one's own hard work, ability, and perseverance can overcome barriers that stand in the way of success.

Working Hard

Dad had tried to reestablish his life and career in Romania after the war. However, the Communist government barred him from the teaching profession, seized his property, and threatened his arrest. The draconian

Communist rule made success impossible. In West Germany he began anew. In spite of his untiring efforts, his career was blocked due to governmental bureaucratic prejudice. He failed again. He could not provide for his family.

Dad was convinced the keys to doing well in American were hard work and ability. Not many days after starting his full-time job as a janitor at the Capital University power plant, he began going door to door in the neighborhood asking if anyone had work for him. Among the odd jobs to supplement his janitor income were cleaning out garages and mowing lawns with the homeowner's push lawnmower. Later, while still employed as a janitor, he worked as a Fuller Brush salesman. Fuller Brush salesmen went from house to house showing the homemakers a selection of really cool brushes and other cleaning products. This was commission work: the more you sold, the more you earned. Dad also began selling bolts of fabric. He purchased the bolts of cloth on consignment from a marketing firm and again knocked on doors. In those days, many homemakers owned sewing machines and knew how to follow a pattern. Dad hated sales work but continued doing it to make ends meet and begin saving money. When not working, he was studying.

Studying

Dad realized he could not be a teacher in the United States without a teaching degree and English fluency. Therefore, he planned another career path. His long-term plan was to become an engineer, and he intended to attain his goal one step at a time through study and hard work. He began taking ICS courses not long after we came to the United States. ICS courses were home-study courses one took via snail mail. Students were mailed books and lessons. They studied, took tests, and mailed the tests in to be graded. This was distance learning before the internet and computers. I remember one of Dad's early courses involved taking measurements with a micrometer. Next, he began studying for a drafting job. Today that would be the equivalent of computer-aided design. Back then it meant a sharp pencil, a large sheet of paper, a T-square, and a drafting board.

Mom Worked Hard Too

My brother comments on Mom's work as a housemother:

> Mutti (Mom) earned money as a housemother for the Capital University girls who lived on the left side of our duplex as well as in the second story. She also made clothing alterations and did a lot of babysitting. Mutti could not believe that these oh-so-rich girls had a different outfit for every day of the week, not to mention that they wore makeup and smelled of expensive perfume. And everyone took a shower every day . . . imagine that!

Mom took her work as a housemother seriously. She sat down with the girls, who would bare their souls and sometimes cry about issues such as boyfriend troubles. I wonder how much of this Mom understood. At the time, I was too young to really understand what duties "housemothering" really entailed.

The new culture and new language demanded our full attention. However, life was more difficult for Mom. Mom had not wanted to leave West Germany. Moving four thousand miles farther from her dear mother, father, and sister Medi distressed her. Starting and maintaining a new household in a new country, learning a new language, and interacting with the students as a housemother presented daily challenges for her. To add to the burden, that first year she had a miscarriage requiring an emergency hysterectomy.

My brother also comments on his work while we lived in Bexley:

> Part of my work, in addition to mowing our and others' lawns (sans Briggs & Stratton) and carrying the *Columbus Dispatch,* was to shovel the coal into the automatic stoker that fed the house furnace. Little did I know that this was the beginning of my work in the coal industry.

Movin' On Up

There were a number of early milestones during the year we lived in Bexley in our university-supplied house. The first and biggest milestone was the purchase of a car six months after we arrived. Dad's first car, ever, was an old black Chevy. The opportunity to drive somewhere made the simplest of trips to church or to visit someone seem like a special occasion and was a cause for celebration. Since Mom, my brother, and I had never ridden in a car before, Dad had three rather vociferous backseat drivers "helping" him.

After our first year in America, Dad left the janitor job. Surprisingly, the president of Capital University had an issue with Dad taking another job. I don't know the president's motivation, but maybe he underestimated Dad's ability and ambition and wanted to save him problems. Dad began working for considerably more pay in a union machine shop, the Accurate Manufacturing Company, where he worked as a lathe operator (see the appendix, 40). Years before, in Bistritz during summer breaks from the university, Dad had worked as a lathe operator, acquiring machine shop skills. The workers at Accurate Manufacturing had a quota for the number of pieces produced on a lathe per eight-hour-shift. Each worker was paid extra for the number produced above the minimum. Dad wanted to earn more money and could produce twice as many as the quota. But producing more would have created problems with his co-workers, who did not want to have their quota raised. What Dad did was produce as many pieces as he could and then divide the surplus equally among the workers. By doing that, Dad and everyone else earned a little more and he remained "one of the boys."

At the end of the first year, having saved some money and with Dad earning more at Accurate Manufacturing, our family no longer needed housing provided by Capital University. I well remember the apartment search. Dad wanted to find a good neighborhood and yet be able to afford the rent. We were in the apartment with the realtor, and my brother and I were exploring the empty apartment. Günter and I were on the second floor when one of us slammed a door shut. In the empty apartment with hardwood floors, the sound reverberated loudly. Dad, Mom, and the realtor were on the first floor. At the sound of the door slamming, Dad "hit the dirt." In that moment, it had sounded to him like a mortar. Dad was quite embarrassed. Veterans who have been in combat understand. We moved into a nice two-story apartment with a basement on Kings Court near Upper Arlington, a suburb of Columbus.

When we moved from our home in Bexley to the nice apartment, Mom started working for Lazarus in their downtown department store. She rode the city bus to work every day. She made bow ties and later did alterations. Mom worked for many years to add to the family income. My brother and I also had jobs.

Not long after we moved, we began attending Holy Trinity Lutheran Church on Northwest Boulevard, which had English-only services. By attending the new church, Dad also wanted to further break the bond with the people and mindset of the old country.

Although Dad consciously embraced everything American, we continued to speak German at home. He saw value in speaking a second language and wanted Günter and me to retain our fluency in German. He also thought we would learn to speak standard, accent-free English in school and on the street, not at home. Both my brother and I benefited in our careers from our knowledge of German. In my case, it also enabled me to teach German after I retired from industry.

Dad traded the old black Chevy for a used but stylish burgundy Studebaker. The most noteworthy thing about Dad's Studebaker was that one of the front wheel axles broke as Dad was driving to work. With only three wheels, the car stopped, but the fourth wheel continued to roll down the street. Dad later traded in that Studebaker for another used Studebaker. It also had a front axle break while driving. That was his last Studebaker.

While working as a machinist, Dad continued to take ICS courses. As he advanced in his career, he also took some night classes at the Ohio

State University (OSU) to prepare himself for his future engineering career. I remember seeing trigonometry and calculus textbooks.

Dad (right) and a technician with a hydraulic tractor transmission Dad developed

Dad's first drafting job was for the Jeffrey Manufacturing Company in Columbus. He advanced in pay and position, becoming a machine designer while he continued to study in the evenings. However, he was not advancing as fast as he wanted to. Dad once told me that when he began working at a company, his supervisors always remembered his starting level. He felt this limited how far and fast he could advance by staying in that company. He changed jobs again, received more pay, and worked as a machine designer at Denison Manufacturing. Denison manufactured hydraulic pumps and hydraulic systems. At Denison he kept advancing and eventually worked in the research division. There, he developed an automatic transmission for a tractor. At the time this was quite an accomplishment. Although Dad was doing advanced engineering work, he did not yet carry the title of engineer and was not compensated as an engineer. Dad asked for a promotion to engineer and was told no. It was explained to him that he had already advanced faster than anyone ever had done before. To attain his goal more quickly, Dad applied for a job at North American Aviation and was hired as an engineer. He left Denison on good terms.

One More Step

Dad worked for the North American Aviation hydraulics division and advanced quickly. He became a lead design engineer at the Columbus division. A proud day for him was when he received his secret clearance. Considering he was an immigrant who had been in three Axis armies, this was quite an accomplishment. He commented to me, "Only in America."

Just ten years after we arrived in the United States as refugees who did not know the language (although Dad had studied English at the university in Romania), Dad was working as a well-compensated engineer with a secret clearance in the aircraft industry. We were treated like everyone else. We were judged by what we could do and not by our background.

Shooting for the Moon

North American Aviation was one of the large contractors working on America's moon shot program. Dad was one of the thousands of engineers who contributed to successfully landing men on the moon. He was extremely proud—and rightfully so. You may recall the launchpad fire in which three brave astronauts (Edward White, command pilot; Virgil "Gus" Grissom, commander; and Roger Chaffee, pilot) died. Dad, who was known as Gus at work, had worked with Gus Grissom, thought highly of him, and considered him a friend. Dad was extremely upset by the tragedy.

Even as Dad reached the level of success of working on the moon shot, he continued to study nearly every evening.

A Man with Pull

In the early 1960s, several years after starting to work at North American Aviation, Dad met a recent Jewish-Romanian immigrant who was an engineer. The gentleman was looking for a job as an engineer. Dad liked him, realized he was capable, and called his old boss at Denison to put in a good word for him. This led to an interview, and he was offered a job as an engineer. Several years later the engineer noticed that he was the only Jew at Denison. After a while he asked his boss why there were no other Jews working there. The boss said, "We don't hire Jews."

The engineer then asked, "Why did you hire me?"

The boss responded, "When we hired you, we did not know you were Jewish." The engineer kept his job. As we know, America is not perfect but continues to make progress. Were Denison still in business today, they would not have such an unwritten restriction.

Dad enjoyed telling me the above story. It is a testament to what is possible in America that in such a short period of time Dad was able to move from depending on someone to sponsor him and offer him a job to being able to help another person get a job.

Dad's good reputation also enabled my brother Günter to be hired by Denison as a draftsman. While working at Denison, my brother got his big break by being offered a marketing job, leading to a very successful career in the mining industry.

Günter must not have ruined the Maroschers' reputation since I, too, was hired while he was still working at Denison. After a summer of working in clerk-like duties, I became a junior draftsman. An old "checker," Henry Mog, reviewed all my drawings. He was in his mid-sixties and kind. At first I made many errors, and he decided to take me under his wing. He patiently corrected me and taught me. It would have been much easier to just get angry and have me fired. Instead, he stuck with me and I learned. It filled me with pride to give him error-free work after several months. Working for Denison enabled me to pay for my entire college education. Henry Mog taught me a valuable lesson about how to treat newbies regardless of where we meet them in life.

Mom was fully employed most of those years and kept house the way people with German genes keep house. Regrettably, she did not get any help from the males in the family.

Observing Mom and Dad gave me quite an education on how to succeed in America. I saw with my own eyes that hard work and applying oneself was the key to success. My parents worked harder, planned ahead more, and applied themselves more than anyone I ever knew.

Movin' On Up—Again

Mom and Dad were working hard and saving money to eventually buy a house. My brother contributed a lot to the house purchase. I contributed considerably less.

In those days a 20 percent down payment to buy a house was required before a mortgage would be approved. Saving 20 percent of the purchase price demonstrated that the prospective home owner could budget and set aside money. A church friend of my parents offered to give Dad a personal loan so he could purchase a house more quickly. Dad refused to accept the offer. The gentleman offered again, and Dad refused again. Eventually his friend wore him down and Dad accepted the offer. The friend's personal loan was $500, or 25 percent of the approximately $2,000 down payment. The loan was made on a handshake.

In October 1954, two years and six months after we came ashore in New York and eight years after Dad's Romanian farm was confiscated, we purchased our first house. It was a small, comfortable house with a small yard at 906 West Eleventh Avenue in a community called University View, located just west of what is now Lennox Town Center. It is a prime location for young families and graduate students near the OSU campus. It continues to be a desirable community. We all loved our house and were very proud of it. Dad was busy realizing the American dream. We were frugal and worked hard, never went out to eat, bought day-old bread,[1] darned socks, patched holes in clothes, repaired our own shoes, and cut our own hair. We never purchased anything that was not absolutely necessary. About three years after purchasing the house, Mom and Dad began allowing themselves one treat: once per week they shared a small soft ice-cream cone. We never felt deprived even though we saved every penny. We knew what real deprivation was.

WE ALL CONTRIBUTED

My brother's comments on working in the United States:

> Vati (Dad) was quite frugal—with *my* money. After turning over paper-route money to the family kitty, I was allowed to keep fifty cents—which of course I was expected to save.

Then one Saturday after having cut two lawns and finishing both the deliveries and collections on my paper route, I decided to buy a milkshake and Superman comic book at Coulter's Drug Store. Even though sitting at the soda fountain, having a strawberry milkshake in air-conditioned comfort while soaking up the adventures of Superman foiling bank robbers and saving Lois Lane, seemed like a great idea, our father didn't agree. When I came home sans the fifty cents, our father went ballistic and explained how the road to ruin, carousing, drunkenness, and worse, start with exactly the kind of cavalier attitude and decadence of which I had just partaken.

As for collecting money from my paper route, I showed zero tolerance for slackers, ne'er-do-wells, bums, and folks who thought that I should pay for their afternoon and Sunday newspaper. Because I worked hard for my money, collecting from these clowns became my personal crusade.

Then the couple who lived in Apartment B at 134 Northwest Boulevard moved across town, leaving my collections $1.35 in the red—oh, what to do? For less than a quarter, the city bus (they were all electric) took me across town, where I found Mr. and Mrs. Freeloader sitting in their new backyard enjoying a few Blatz beers with friends. The look on the *Schnorrers* faces (a *Schnorrer* is a freeloader/sponger/parasite/etc.) as they were shamed into coughing up the dough was worth every penny of the $1.35 they owed me. In retrospect, and given that I had a sympathetic audience, I was a chump for not having demanded the bus-fare money.

The most profitable time of year in the paper-route business was Christmas—especially with the ritzy Upper Arlington folks. The average tip was (give or take) five bucks, which approximately half of my 135 customers shelled out.

Note: Tips went up in frequency and amount in direct proportion to the time of day and temperature. The most profitable collections were on cold and snowy nights.

The most generous tip came from a nice elderly lady. In addition to the forty-five cents for the weekly collection, she handed me a whopping thirty-five dollars. This tip bought us the white-oak dining room set which replaced the hand-me-down chrome-and-Bakelite dinette.

Prior to turning sixteen, when part-time work was allowed by child labor laws, cutting grass, washing cars, and other yard and window-washing chores augmented the (tax-free) income stream. The grass-cutting business increased almost exponentially when I switched from a non-motorized push mower to a motorized mower. In winter, business slowed and earnings were confined to shoveling snow.

In retrospect, the paper routes were probably the biggest cash cows, especially after our father built a lightweight, two-wheel, spring-suspension bicycle trailer. This trailer more than doubled the carrying capacity of a basket-and-saddlebag-equipped Schwinn, meaning that two hundred Sunday papers could be carried in one haul. Mind you, such a load meant that the bike had to be pushed, but as the load got lighter, peddling came into play. I even used our dog, Duke, as the official Super Duke. Duke carried a saddlebag across his back with six Sunday papers—not an easy feat since each paper was at least one and a half inches thick.

> Because we didn't take vacations until after we bought the house and the bank account had some rainy-day money piled up, summers were very busy. When the "rich kids" went on vacation, carrying their papers made for some hard work. It wasn't uncommon on Sundays to leave the house at 4:00 a.m. and return close to noon. On such days a stop at White Castle for one glazed doughnut and one hot chocolate was allowed.
>
> Yes sirree, there was no "free lunch" at 906 Eleventh Avenue in Columbus, Ohio. But it sure beat the rotten Commie/Socialist shit-house life we left behind.
>
> Speaking of "lunches": three days after hitting the streets in Columbus, I went to work in the school cafeteria as a dishwasher, table cleaner, mop specialist, and trash carry-outer. The remuneration was a not-so-free lunch, which had to be eaten in the five minutes before class started. (I have a life-sized picture in my head of today's free-school-lunch-pussies being asked to pick up a mop or scrub brush to earn their lunch. Hell, there'd be riots in the streets, while the little darlings wondered what a mop or dishrag is.) And now I'm heading to the fridge for a glass of cheap, in-the-box merlot.

At the age of ten, I also got a paper route. I had sixty customers and delivered the papers using my bicycle. I was allowed to keep twenty-five cents per week of my profits; the rest was for the family coffers. I was such a bad manager of money that I never gave Dad any money. At first Dad thought I was cheating, but he finally decided I was honest but could not manage money. Unfortunately I tolerated people who did not pay their bills on time. The most egregious example of delinquent paying was a family who lived on Chambers Avenue. They had not paid for ten weeks and I, the dummy, never stopped delivering their paper. The man of the house always had an excuse as to why he could not pay. Thinking back,

I think the problem actually had to do with his excessive drinking. At the ten-week mark, the man died and I did not have the heart to collect from his widow, who had several young kids at home. It takes a lot of paper deliveries to make up for ten weeks of free papers.

I started making money from delivering papers as I grew older. Mowing lawns and doing odd jobs supplemented my income. In the summers I carried up to three paper routes at a time for paperboys who were on vacation. I must admit, between the two of us, my brother was the harder worker and took the most initiative. I was less driven. My brother, the born salesman, made better tips than I did. In all fairness, he also delivered papers in a more affluent neighborhood. The largest tip I ever got was five dollars at Christmas from a nice old lady. But, hey, that is still a sizable tip (about forty-five dollars today).

When I began to make money delivering papers, I allowed myself one indulgence on Sunday mornings. At about 6:00 a.m., when I finished my route, I ate a glazed doughnut and drank a cup of coffee. White Castle coffee was mighty good and cost ten cents. I miss the small ceramic White Castle coffee cups. Coffee just does not taste as good out of a Styrofoam cup or a plastic-coated paper cup.

When I was around fifteen, my brother bought a car with his own money. It was a black 1936 Chevy. On Sunday mornings I would help him with his rather large paper route. I did this not just because I was a nice brother but because I got to drive his car (the real reason). After all, who is going to check to see if the kid behind the wheel is old enough to drive or has a driver's license at 4:00 a.m. on a Sunday morning? My brother, being a prudent person, let me drive only when we were on the side streets of his route. My job was to move the car, loaded with papers, as he walked the route, dropping papers on porches. The Chevy had a vacuum shift. Only old car nuts will know what that is. In the winter, on very cold days, it took a huge amount of force to actually push the shift lever into the next gear. I am here to testify that Chevy was not chintzy with the strength of the shift lever—a good thing.

WE ARE AMERICANS

Becoming Citizens

We became citizens in March 1958, six years after landing at the port of New York. My brother was old enough to swear his own allegiance and did not become a citizen at the same time that Mom, Dad, and I became citizens. He decided to do it on his own. I remember the swearing-in ceremony where we raised our right hands and swore our allegiance to America, forgoing any other allegiance. This was really easy for us. We were sold on America. America was our country. Actually, I automatically became a citizen with my parents since I was under sixteen, but I raised my hand, too, and swore my oath. Nobody in that large room of new citizens was more serious about pledging allegiance to America than I was. Becoming an American citizen was one of the proudest moments of my life. I value my Certificate of Naturalization. I would have shown you the entire Certificate of Naturalization, but it is against the law to make copies. To be on the right side of the law, my picture on the Certificate of Naturalization is the best I can do.

Picture from my Certificate of Naturalization

Politically Aware Children

Because of our background, my brother and I were more aware of world history and current events than the other kids at our school. On March 1, 1955, there was an article in the *Columbus Dispatch* about the Maroscher family and a project called Crusade for Freedom. The Crusade for Freedom was a program to collect money to fund powerful radio stations aimed at the Communist Eastern European countries to enable the people to hear news that was not produced by their governments. Totalitarian governments control the press. My brother and I made impassioned pitches to our *Dispatch* newspaper customers, explaining the reason why it was important to provide funds for those radio stations. I was eleven and my brother was fifteen. The Cold War was on, and we were doing our part to aid freedom-seeking people. My brother and I collected more money from our paper customers than any other carriers in Columbus, which is why our family was featured in the article. The portion of the article where my brother and I are quoted is shown. The article is included in its entirety in the appendix, 40.

Josef Stalin, a paranoid and amoral psychopath, was the Communist dictator of the Soviet Union from the mid-1920s to 1953. I was almost ten years old when he died. I read the headline of Stalin's death in the *Columbus Dispatch* and was overjoyed. I knew of Stalin and some of the things he had done.[2] Having suffered in war and having lived under despotic regimes increased my brother's and my interest in history even at a young age.

Life Lessons

Paper-carrying provided me with many useful lessons. I probably needed those lessons more than most. I learned to manage money, interact with people from all walks of life, and much more. The other jobs I had were helpful in shaping me into a productive adult. Observing Mom and Dad as they planned, worked, saved, and spent wisely was probably my most valuable lesson.

His sons, because of their background, took great pride in collecting Crusade for Freedom funds as they delivered their Dispatches.

"I explained that we needed stronger stations to get through the Russian jamming," said Gerhart.

"I told my customers that their donations might prevent another war," said Guenter, who remembers hearing some similar broadcast when he was in West Germany.

Their father summed it up:

"Those people, they have no other way to know what's going on in their own countries."

Gustav, Günter, and Gerhard quoted in a March 1, 1955 article

The Dream House

As Dad advanced in responsibilities and salary in his engineering career, Mom continued to work until Dad was transferred to Tulsa, Oklahoma. They lived in Tulsa from 1963 to 1965. While they were in Tulsa, they allowed me to live in their house rent-free. Dad earned enough money by then that Mom did not need to work. Continuing to prepare for the future, Dad still studied many evenings to improve his skills.

While my parents were living in Tulsa, Mom, who had never driven a car before, secretly started taking driving lessons. She understood that Dad, who was a rather controlling old country husband, was slowly changing but would never see the need for her to drive. She did not tell him about her driving lessons until she showed him her brand-new driver's license one day. Dad was surprised, but in a good way. He decided to buy her a car, a sporty, used white Corvair.

Upon their return from Tulsa, Mom and Dad agreed that they wanted to move to a bigger, more modern house. Most people, when planning to buy a house, see a realtor and begin to look at houses in their price range and preferred location. Dad decided to play architect and began to study house construction in the United States and familiarize himself with housing code requirements. They purchased a lot in a new section of Upper Arlington. On his trusty home drafting table, Dad drew all the architectural drawings for their dream home.

After finishing all drawings per his own specifications, he was the general contractor. During the design and building phase, he continued to work at North American Aviation. If any of the subcontractors thought they could get away with not doing top-notch work for this "amateur" builder, they quickly found out that was not the case. One subcontractor had to tear down and rebuild the fireplace and chimney because it did not meet specifications. Dad had high standards and would not accept anything other than first-class work. Whoever is living at 1266 Norwell Drive today has a very well-built house.

In 1967, fifteen years after we arrived in the United States with the clothes on our backs, two cardboard suitcases, five small wooden boxes, and Dad's violin, Mom and Dad moved with great joy and excitement into their new home. By that time my brother was living in another state and I was living with my wife and finishing my engineering degree at OSU.

Dad was especially proud of his accomplishment. After all, it was he who decided to pull up stakes and immigrate to America in hopes of a better life. And it was he who had not been able to adequately support his family for many years. It filled him with great satisfaction that he had not only been able to provide for his family in America but had moved into a wonderful house in a great community. He was most impressed that a citizen could simply decide to build his own house and had the right to do it all himself without a bunch of bureaucrats intervening, interfering, and running up costs. He said, "Only in America," and felt it to the core.

Not long after they moved in, Dad bought an old lathe and began to "play" with it occasionally in the basement. He was thinking of his future retirement and hoped to open up a small machine shop.

Gustav Günter Maroscher—A Great American

Dad loved America. America was the land where he found freedom and opportunity and where his two sons could enjoy the same. He appreciated America more than many Americans who were born here. Mom and Dad wholeheartedly participated in Fourth of July activities and went to the parades. They also worked enthusiastically on the parade floats for Knolls Arlington. One of the features of his dream home was a flagpole where the flag flew every day. After Dad died, Mom continued to fly the flag until she moved to a retirement home.

Dad was proud that both of his sons served in the army. My brother served in the army reserve and I served in the regular army. The first time I saw my dad cry was when I left for Vietnam. He knew what war was like. Mom told me decades later that the moment I boarded the plane for Vietnam was the only time he ever questioned his decision to come to America.

Declaring War, Forgiving, and Finding Peace

My parents' heroic struggle bore fruit. They achieved freedom, found a new homeland they loved, and enjoyed a good standard of living. But only in fairytales do people fight life's great battles and come out unscathed. Having been through so much together, we should have been a close-knit family. In a way we were, and in a way we were not. We were loyal to each other, we loved each other, but we did not always get along.

As I was growing up, my dad and I did not have a good relationship. Our difficult relationship continued until I was in my late twenties. I don't remember how old I was when Dad started beating me, but I was fairly young. Usually the beating was inflicted with a belt. Dad would become angry and take off his belt, I'd take off running and get caught, and he'd beat me as hard as he could with his leather belt. The verbal attacks were an even bigger problem. I mentioned earlier that Dad had a quick and vicious temper with Mom, Günter, and me. It didn't take much to set him off, and he had the peculiar ability to self-escalate his anger to an amazing level. Curiously, this never happened with anyone outside the family.

At the age of ten years and nine months, I silently "declared war." After an incident of beating and verbal abuse, I was in my room brooding. On the small paper lampshade of a lamp in my room I wrote in small numerals "10¾," my age at the time. This signified to me that on that day I resolved to never submit to my dad. I would never knuckle under. I would never comply. When he screamed at me, I would resist. The "10¾" was followed by several other ages written on the lampshade until I was about twelve years old. Each time I wrote my age, it was a reaffirmation of my resolve. Although I stopped writing dates on the lampshade, the resolve of noncompliance continued for a long time. To me, submitting meant acquiescence to his accusations of my faults, shortcomings, and errors. I had a deep-seated belief that if I submitted, I would cease to exist—my soul, my innermost self, my life-spark would be extinguished. This is not a healthy attitude and I do not recommend it. Also, it does not follow the biblical teaching of "honor your father and mother."

Günter's relationship with our father was much better. He was able to avoid the beatings and verbal attacks. He was much wiser. He would never buck Dad; he never talked back. He avoided conflict and complied, or at least he indicated that he was going to comply and then did what he wanted to do anyway. He was also much more organized, not scatter-brained, and more productive. He had all the right traits to reduce potential conflict with Dad.

As I matured, I began to understand my father's behavior. His serious head injury, the effects his war experiences had on him, his upbringing without a father, and growing up without normal motherly love made him a driven, demanding father with a short temper and little emotional control. Understanding him didn't make living with him any easier, but I had a healthier outlook. I did not at the time consider that my own experiences may have had a negative impact upon me.

We sat down to family dinner every night. Until I was thirteen or fourteen, someone secretly observing the family around the dinner table would have wondered what was wrong with the younger son because he would occasionally flinch. Every time my dad reached for the casserole or the jam or whatever, I would flinch and duck away from him. It was because I was within reach of his long arms and often got slapped for infractions. I have no clue what those infractions at the table may have been, but there were plenty of them.

When I was about thirteen or maybe fourteen, I decided I'd had enough of the frequent beatings. One day Dad proceeded to beat me with the belt as usual. I stood there with Dad behind me, beating me as hard as he could across my backside. I did not yell. I did not run. I just stood there silently. After a while, he put away his belt and never beat me again, although the yelling, fits of rage, and ultra-critical behavior continued. A voice can also be a weapon.

Everyone knows teenage years are hard. It is just plain hard to grow up. I was obviously an unhappy teenager, and the state of war in our home was good for no one. When I was about fifteen, my parents decided I needed to go to a psychiatrist. I did not object. I was open to anything that might help our relationship. Although they did not mention it, they must have talked with the doctor, prior to my visit, discussing their concerns about me. I visited Dr. Nicholas alone after my parents made the arrangements for an appointment. He was an average-sized, pleasant, soft-spoken, white-haired old gentleman. After introducing himself, he sat down behind a large dark-wood desk, motioned for me to sit, and began to ask questions. I responded openly and honestly and felt neither nervous nor intimidated. In the course of the hour-long appointment, I explained that my dad and I were at each other's throats all the time, and why I thought this was the case. I explained that Dad's background, including his head injury and fighting the Russians, were the reasons for his short temper and unreasonableness.

For about three weeks after my first and only psychiatric session, there was peace in the house. Everybody was making a real effort to get along. But Dad and I had had years of conditioning in yelling and screaming, so Dad's verbal attacks and my automatic response returned eventually. We were back to normal.

Decades later, long after Dad died, my mom mentioned what Dr. Nicholas had told them after the session. He said that I was still fighting the Russians. My parents' response was, "But he never fought the Russians." They could not understand the doctor's reasoning. Although I was very young during the war, I know it had some impact on me, but Dr. Nicholas had missed a major part of the problem: how Dad was affected by the war.

After I graduated from high school, I lived at home and attended OSU. By then my brother was married and living elsewhere. Although things were a little better, Dad still directed his rages at me, and I reacted predictably. Mom, Dad, and I were all miserable.

Following my freshman year, I realized I had to leave so there could be peace at home. I rented a cheap room near campus. I continued to go to school as much as my income would allow. I explained to Mom and Dad that by moving out, everyone would be happier, and I would be living only a few minutes away. My parents reacted very negatively and emotionally. Both expressed the feeling that I was rejecting them—forever. They knew I was breaking all bonds and they would never see me again. Dad even said, "If you do this, I will never forgive you." Surprisingly, I did not take him seriously. I lightheartedly explained that I really intended to come home often and get some free meals. I also hoped to come home to do the laundry. After all, I would live only a little over a mile away, renting a room in a rooming house. Yet Dad insisted that he was never going to forgive me for this betrayal. Mom, on the other hand, resurrected a tradition from the old country which I had not known about. She sewed a small heart out of red felt and gave it to me. In the heart was some dirt from our yard, a penny, and some salt. The dirt was a reminder to never forget your home, the penny was a wish for prosperity, and the salt symbolized the hope for peace and friendship throughout life. Giving me the heart was an emotional moment, mostly for her and Dad. At the same time, Mom gave me a letter she had written to me when I "rejected" them. In the letter she wrote how they had always tried to be good parents and were sorry they had failed. She made it clear in the letter that they knew, by leaving, I was forever abandoning them. However, even during the emotional "final" goodbye, since they had not deterred me from leaving, my attitude remained lighthearted. I stated my conviction in a friendly manner that what I was doing was the best for the three of us and that I did not look upon this as any sort of breaking off of our relationship.

As promised, I showed up a week later for dinner. Thereafter, Ruth, my girlfriend and future wife, and I came over for dinner weekly. Anyway, two to three months and a number of visits later, we dropped by my parents' house for another free meal and conversation. My dad proceeded to tell us how happy they had been since I had left. He then told me how glad he was to have suggested that I leave and how he wished he had thought of it earlier. He was absolutely serious. He was taking credit for "his" brilliant idea. Ruth and I looked at each other in disbelief and just smiled. "Forever" sometimes does not last all that long.

Dad continued to be very critical of me, and I was so sensitive that we continued to have difficulties. Yet we were much happier not living under the same roof. Although we no longer yelled at each other, we rarely had a normal, relaxed conversation. Through all this I still loved my dad; I just could not get along with him.

Ruth and I were married in 1964. Mom and Dad were living in Tulsa at the time and drove back to Ohio for the wedding. Ruth graduated in 1965 and began teaching English and Russian in the Upper Arlington school system. During spring break in 1965, hoping to bring the family together, we drove from Columbus to Tulsa for a visit. About one and a half hours after we arrived at my parents' apartment, Dad began to be very critical of me. His criticism was like a flood of hot coals pouring over me. It was unbearable. I had to leave. Although I remained civil, I became so upset that I turned to Ruth and said, "We have to leave. We have to leave now." Ruth was embarrassed and my parents were shocked, but I had to get out of there. We drove home.

After I graduated from college and was a well-paid engineer, my relationship with Dad improved significantly. He was much less critical, and I suppose I was not as touchy. I don't know what was going on in his head, but it may have sounded like, "I guess this son of mine, who seemed so incapable, is actually going to turn out OK."

A few years later I was finally able to forgive my dad and he was able to relax around me. Maybe he also forgave me. From then on, whenever I visited my parents, it was no longer tense. I remember sitting and talking with Dad and enjoying our conversations. Mom was always somewhere in the background, smiling and absolutely enjoying the two former combatants getting along. Through all those numerous rages and beatings, she had always had to be silent. Finally there was peace.

Dad died at the age of fifty-eight when I was thirty-two. His death came way too early. He had so many unfinished plans, like owning a machine shop and publishing math books. His time as a POW, malnutrition, hunger, and stress after the war had taken its toll. As a relatively young adult, Dad had lost most of his teeth. We now know that poor dental health often results in heart damage. Until we came to America, dental care was nonexistent. If you had a toothache, someone with a pair of pliers pulled the offending tooth. And as a POW, even that was not always an option.

I am so thankful that I forgave my dad and that we had several years of peace. This allowed us to enjoy each other's company before his death. Without that forgiveness, I would have had regret and pain in my heart for the rest of my life.

In recent years I have realized even more what an impact growing up without a male role model can have on a boy. I've mentored young men in a youth correctional facility. The incarcerated youth did plenty of nasty things before they were finally convicted. Each of them came from a dangerous environment that is a bit like a war zone. That environment impacted them all in a negative way. The one thing all the young men had in common involved their fathers: Dad left Mom, Dad is in jail, Dad is gone, Dad is not in my life, or I don't know who my dad is. When I compare myself to these young men, I know I am blessed. My father was not perfect, but he was there. He was loyal and hardworking. And in his own way, he loved me.

I remember talking with an incarcerated seventeen-year-old who had a terrible relationship with his father. I shared with him my own relationship with my father. I explained that I was blessed to have been able to forgive Dad and reach a point where I have absolutely no ill feelings toward him, giving me peace. The young man and I discussed how forgiveness can be a long, gradual, but important process. He shook his head and was not sure he could ever forgive his dad. I hope someday he will be able to let go of his animosity and forgive. Forgiveness is a blessing that lasts a lifetime.

For more than ten years after Dad died, I had "visit dreams." In these dreams Dad would appear, and I would say, "I thought you died. But you are still around. It is good you are here." We would talk very little—we'd just spend time with one another and Dad's presence was comforting. It felt good to be together again. After a while, he would leave. When I woke up from those dreams, I always felt calm and happy to have seen Dad again. I don't know if these "visit dreams" were just in my head or if Dad visited me in spirit. In either case, his visits were of great comfort because in these dreams we felt only love for one another.

–NOTES–

1. In the days before preservatives, bread would become stale in one day, making it considerably cheaper.
2. http://www.ibtimes.com/how-many-people-did-joseph-stalin-kill-1111789.

Chapter 17

Paying Back

WANTING TO SERVE MY COUNTRY

Air Force, Here I Come

As I was growing up in America, I was a serious young man. I was also seriously patriotic. I felt I owed a debt to the United States for being allowed to come here and live. In my own mind, the best way to repay this debt was to serve in the military. I joined the Air Force ROTC (Reserve Officer Training Corps) at OSU and planned to become a fighter pilot. After taking the required tests, I was told that I qualified to be a navigator, but not a pilot. This meant I would sit behind the F-4 pilot in the two-seater F-4 fighter. Only a bit disappointed, I was still eager to serve in the air force.

Rejected

After two years in basic Air Force ROTC, I took the required physical at the age of nineteen. To be accepted into advanced Air Force ROTC, I needed to pass the physical and sign up for a six-year service commitment. Well, I flunked the physical. A urine test showed I had albumin in my urine. Later tests by a private doctor showed I had postural albuminurea. When I was flat on my back, my kidneys passed albumin, and when I was vertical, they did not. Albumin in the urine is a possible indicator of kidney disease, but postural albuminurea is a benign condition that is outgrown. Six months before my physical, the air force had decided to automatically reject people with albumin in their urine and not bother with further testing.

I could not serve in the air force. I was devastated and cried like a baby. Ruth will attest to the bitter tears. It was hard, but I decided that if the military did not want me, I did not want it. I left it behind me—no military service for me.

Invited to Serve

The first year of college, I lived with my parents, but I paid for my own tuition and books. Even though I also lived rent-free while they lived in Tulsa in 1963 and until I got married, often I did not earn enough to be a full-time student. At the end of my fifth year at OSU, I had been married for two years and had two years of school remaining. That year, 1966, I received the "invitation." President Johnson was increasing the US fighting force in Vietnam to four hundred thousand. Planning for a buildup to a fighting force of five hundred thousand in 1967 was also underway. To meet the manpower requirements, many young men were drafted into the military service. When I received my draft notice, all I cared about was finishing school and graduating. The draft notice did not concern me. I knew I could not serve for medical reasons.

The Fossils on the Draft Board

I was working toward my bachelor of mechanical engineering (BME), with two full-time years remaining. Full-time university students were exempt from the draft; however, my five years for the five-year BME was over, making me eligible to be drafted.

I expected to fail the army induction physical but chose to go through the process of seeking a two-year draft deferment from the local draft board, allowing me to finish school before being called up. In 1966 many young men purposefully delayed graduation to avoid the draft. My situation was different. I was determined to state my case, thinking that the draft board would grant an exemption because I was working my way through school.

I walked into the room where the draft board sat behind a long table. The five men on the board looked to me like they were all in their eighties. I stood about five paces in front of the table and politely introduced myself. But as I started to make my case, one of the fossils (yes, that is disrespectful) cut me off and said, "You can save your breath. Nothing you can say will change anything. Your five years are up and you are going to be drafted. We know how you people try to extend your graduation in order to avoid the draft. You can't fool us." The way he said it, I was sure that no matter how well I explained my case, it would make no difference.

I was allowed to speak for thirty minutes and I decided to state my case in spite of knowing it would make no difference. I explained that I paid my own way through school, had volunteered for the air force, flunked the air force physical, etc. I respectfully presented my prepared remarks as planned. As I was speaking, I thought (not so respectfully), *I'm going to make you old fossils sit on your bony asses for the entire thirty minutes.* As the old man had promised, my appeal was denied. They did offer the comment, "We don't recognize the air force physical."

For the army physical I had to pee in a bottle. You can guess the test results: no albumin in the urine. I had outgrown the condition.

The Master Psychologist

I was willing to serve my country but decided I preferred to serve as an officer and wanted to graduate before I served. The air force did not want me, but hey, the army did! After all, the army thought I was healthy. If I signed up for advanced Army ROTC, I could continue my education, graduate, and then serve as an officer. With high hopes, I walked into the ROTC building on campus and asked to whom I needed to speak about joining advanced Army ROTC.

I was directed to Lieutenant Colonel Tanner, the officer in charge of Army ROTC. Tanner was sitting at his desk. I approached him and introduced myself. I explained that I had received a draft notice, wanted to serve my country, but wanted to do so as an officer. I did not get very far before Tanner interrupted me and said, "We don't want your kind in the army officer corps." The implication was that I was trying only to avoid the draft.

I was stunned and said, "Excuse me?" He then said something like, "We want only good Americans in the army officer corps."

Well, Lieutenant Colonel Tanner had done it. He had pulled my chain. For the next minute or so I spoke at him heatedly while he said nothing. I said things like, "How can you say that? You know nothing about me or my background." I even pointed my finger at him to emphasize my point; he just sat there looking at me. I explained about coming to the United States from war-torn Europe and knowing damn well better about how wonderful America was than most other people will ever know.

Suddenly I came to my senses and realized how disrespectfully I had spoken. I stopped, was silent, and thought, *Gerhard, you dummy. Now you've really stepped in it. You just got angry at the one guy who can approve your entry into advanced Army ROTC.*

Still sitting, without saying a word, Tanner turned to his left, opened the top drawer of his desk, took out a piece of paper, and handed it to me. He said with a smile, "Here is your application." Over the next two years, Lieutenant Colonel Tanner and I talked occasionally. He was a wise man.

In the Army

I finished my studies at OSU and graduated in June 1968. As a second lieutenant, I served my first year at Aberdeen Proving Ground near Bel Air, Maryland. It was not a typical army tour. I worked an eight-to-five schedule as an engineer testing wheeled vehicles for the army. The engineer sitting at the desk beside me was a private; we addressed each other as Marvin and Gerhard. I enjoyed the work.

Hello, Vietnam

In January 1969 I flew from the Columbus International Airport on a commercial plane to Tacoma, Washington, and on to Vietnam. Ruth, Geoff (our son), Mom, and Dad were there to say goodbye. They all cried. Even Geoff, who was eight weeks old, cried because his mom was crying. This was the only time I had ever seen my dad cry. Mom and Dad knew what war was like. As I was walking up the stairs into the airplane, I was in good spirits and glad to finally be able to get my service in Vietnam behind me.

I served as a first lieutenant and was fortunate to avoid combat. I was keenly and unhappily aware of opposition to the war back home during my time in Vietnam. Because we were fighting Communists, I thought the war was justified.

I was in Vietnam for nine months; the normal tour was twelve months. Most wives were sure their husbands would survive and return home, but Ruth was convinced I was not coming home. That was a hard burden for both of us to bear. I promised her that I would be as careful as possible and would return stateside as soon as I could.

Since I had made that promise, I began to inquire about early releases. I found that I could depart three months early if I was accepted by and enrolled in a graduate school. I thought, *What a way to run a war.*

With Ruth doing the legwork at OSU and me working with the army in Vietnam, I was granted an "early out." I had kept my promise and came home as soon as possible. I was twenty-seven at the time and was looking forward to being a father, husband, and civilian engineer.

PAINFUL HOMECOMING

Coming Home

In late September 1970, I was on a civilian stretched DC-8 filled with 265 military personnel. Upon landing at McChord Air Force Base, we were directed to a large auditorium filled with soldiers and a few lower-ranking officers like me. A captain talked to us from the stage. I suppose this was the army's one-hour-long attempt to reintegrate us into civilian life. He mentioned that in spite of what we had heard about opposition to the war at home, the American people really appreciated our service. I knew better. I had such a negative emotional reaction to what the officer said that I nearly vomited. I had to consciously calm my stomach for a significant portion of his talk.

All returnees were required to undergo out-processing physical examinations before being released to return home. The captain's talk was over a few minutes before 5:00 p.m. on a Friday. At 5:00 p.m. the medical section closed down for the weekend. About 99 percent of the GIs were stuck at McChord till Monday. Since I was one of the few officers due to be released, I was first in line to see a doctor. The army doctor sat at his desk and asked me if I was sick. He asked if I had any unusual illnesses. Was I healthy? I smiled and answered his questions and told him that I felt fine. That was it! He signed my release papers and I headed off to the civilian airport at exactly 5:00 p.m. Friday afternoon. After waiting a few hours, I boarded a red-eye to Columbus, Ohio.

No one met me at the Columbus airport on Saturday, per my request. I took a taxi to the apartment in Columbus where Ruth and our son were living. I was home at 1:00 p.m. I hugged Ruth and my son, who did not know me. He cried.

Although I had not seen combat, my Vietnam service had been very stressful. When I arrived home, I was really not in a good or healthy frame of mind. I called my parents but did not visit them. Less than forty-eight hours earlier, I had been manning twin M60 machine guns on a three-quarter-ton truck heading toward Phu Cat Air Base. It was like being Captain Kirk beamed from Vietnam to home. The human brain, at least not mine, is unable to process such a sudden change. A couple of decades later, long after Dad had died, I discussed my homecoming with Mom. I found out that she and Dad thought I did not visit them the day I arrived because Ruth wanted me to herself. Mom finally understood my actions were a result of being distressed by how my fellow Americans felt about the soldiers serving in the war.

On Monday morning at 8:00 a.m., less than two full days after being welcomed home by Ruth, I was in the engineering department office at OSU, talking to a secretary. I introduced myself and inquired about my class schedule. I mentioned that I had just returned from Vietnam and was starting graduate school two weeks late. Also in the office, on my side of the counter and to my left, was a fellow with rather long, dark hair, to whom I paid little attention. After my conversation with the secretary, the gentleman walked up to me and from an uncomfortably close distance looked me in the face and asked, "Well, how many babies did you kill?"

I was devastated. Thinking back, I was in a fragile state of mind. I said nothing. After he left, the secretary informed me that he was my computer course instructor. I immediately dropped his course and never encountered him again. Little did he know that although I was eager to come home, it had been hard for me to leave several of my very good Vietnamese friends. Ever since the baby-killing question was asked, I've had an aversion to "peace-loving" people who betray their true natures by prejudging and demonizing others. There are true peace-loving people and pacifists; I have respect for them, but most "peace lovers" are self-righteous hypocrites who just have not found the cause for which they are willing to cause pain or even kill.

About a year after my return from Vietnam, I saw a newspaper picture of Jane Fonda sitting on a North Vietnamese antiaircraft gun surrounded by smiling enemy NVA soldiers. Something inside me broke in that moment. Maybe the pain I felt about the postwar treatment of my fellow servicemen and me was heightened by my love for the country that had given me sanctuary. The wound remains to this day.

While I was in Vietnam, I observed the army disintegrating. No one could have paid me enough to stay in the army. In later years I was heartened by the revitalization of the military under the leadership of officers who had been lieutenants during the Vietnam War. General Colin Powell was one of those lieutenants.[1] They experienced the leadership mistakes that occurred during the war and applied the lessons they learned. In the subsequent two decades, those capable officers rebuilt the military into a well-disciplined and capable fighting force.

Occasionally I've thought about how being rejected by the air force probably saved me from being shot down over North Vietnam. As a navigator I'd have been sitting behind the pilot of an F-4. The average number of missions in a twelve-month tour was one hundred. The chance of being shot down for each mission was 1 percent. Not good odds.

Neither being killed nor being a POW appealed to me. Who knows—had I been captured, I might have gotten to know the famous former POW Senator John McCain, or better yet, I might have met Jane Fonda when she visited with American POWs after she posed with North Vietnamese antiaircraft gunners. Now I'm glad I was in the army.

–NOTES–

1 http://colinpowell.net/colin-powell-biography.html; https://en.wikipedia.org/wiki/Colin_Powell.

Chapter 18

The Passing of a Generation

HE DIED TOO YOUNG

In 1975 Dad was again transferred to Tulsa. Mom and Dad liked Tulsa but were reluctant to move from Columbus and their dream home. With the up-and-down nature of the aircraft industry, moving to Tulsa was a requirement for him to keep his job. He had to work where the jobs were. They drove from Tulsa to my home in West Virginia to be present for our daughter Christine's baptism in June 1975. Looking back, I am sure that trip was exhausting for them because they were both in fragile health.

In late October, following their return to Tulsa, Mom underwent emergency gallbladder surgery. At the time, gallbladder surgery was invasive, requiring six to eight weeks of recuperation. Dad's health had been deteriorating for some time; he had serious heart disease. Mom had been home for two weeks after surgery and was still experiencing pain when he was admitted to the hospital's cardiac unit for tests.

Not long after he was admitted to the hospital, Dad died of a massive heart attack. It was November 1975, shortly after his fifty-eighth birthday. The war and associated hardships had taken their final toll. Such an early and sudden death is always a shock. With Mom still weakened and recovering from surgery, this loss was even more devastating for her.

My brother got a call from Mom shortly after Dad died. He called me right away, about 6:00 p.m. He was living in Illinois and I was in West

Virginia. Mom needed us. We felt helpless. My brother and I could not arrive until the next day. Then I remembered the name of a family, the Deeses, who had been my parents' good friends when they had lived in Tulsa a few years earlier. I called Jane Dees and told her about Dad's death. I asked her to find Mom and stay with her. That night Jane sat and held Mom while she was shaking and in shock. Thank you, Jane. You are a good friend to our family. My brother and I arrived the following morning to help and support Mom during one of the most difficult times of her life.

The Spirit

Dad's funeral service was in Tulsa. Later there was a service in Columbus. I remember the Tulsa service very well and have no recollection of the service in Columbus.

At the church in Tulsa, there were pews on the right and left with an aisle down the middle and aisles next to the right and left walls. My mom, brother, and I were sitting on the right side in the second pew from the front. The first pew was unoccupied. Much of that day was a blur, but I remember parts of the funeral service very clearly.

We cried. Hearts were breaking. There was also some sniffling and crying from other mourners, friends, and Dad's Tulsa work colleagues.

Then my brother, who was sitting next to the center aisle, broke down and cried uncontrollably. My mother also began to sob. My heart was breaking, not only because of losing Dad, but because of the pain Mom and Günter were feeling. Perhaps in response to this grief, there was a corresponding intensification of crying in the rest of the congregation. I was overcome by emotion because of all their pain and sorrow. I prayed for God to please comfort Mom, my brother, and the others. Then a strange thing happened. I felt a warm, comforting breeze coming from right to left, slowly blowing over us. It seemed like it came through the wall. It was like being wrapped in a warm blanket, very gentle, almost an embrace. Within seconds the crying stopped. The sniffling stopped. I was comforted. Many years later I asked my mom about the service in Tulsa. She had not felt anything and remembered only the pain. But I know how I felt, and that all the crying stopped. My prayer had been answered.

Dad had many hopes for the future. He had plans to own his own machine shop. He wanted to write his own trigonometry textbook. He once showed me some of his ideas of how to better explain trigonometry concepts. It would have been a superior textbook. As I think about it, how many students study trigonometry and then decide they can write a better textbook?

Dad's life was filled with great hardship. Each time he was knocked down and demeaned, he got up and bravely started doing his best again. He never lost his courage or resolve. He was always strong. He never wavered. Like everyone else, he was not perfect, but he was a loyal family man driven to help his family and driven to succeed. He died too soon.

Well done, Dad.

LIFE WITHOUT GUSTAV

The First Year

Mom and Dad had been through so much together. Suddenly living alone was even more difficult because Dad was an old country husband who took care of many family responsibilities, including all the finances. She was alone and unprepared to manage life's demands. Her learning curve was steep. Life was difficult for her. She was living in a fog.

Mom moved back to Columbus soon after Dad's funeral, hoping to live in their beautiful home on Norwell Drive. The renters, who had just signed a one-year lease, had no desire to move and stayed until the lease was up. A former coworker from Lazarus shared her home for several months. Then she stayed with us in Parkersburg, West Virginia, for a few months. For the remainder of the year, Mom lived with another good friend in Columbus and began working at Lazarus in the alterations department.

After the rental contract expired, Mom moved back into her house.

She discovered considerable damage and her heart ached for their lovely home. It took her several years to bring the house back to its original condition, but she accomplished it. The realtor, who was to assure that the renters took care of the home, collected his fee for his inspection services but never fulfilled his contract. The renters and the realtor were negligent at the expense of Mom's peace of mind and the joy of coming home.

When Dad died, there were eight more years until the mortgage would be paid off. Mom received a small pension from Dad's former employer, had a small savings account, and earned a salary at Lazarus, but not enough for her to pay both the mortgage and living expenses. Dad had no life insurance. He had gambled by not buying life insurance. She faced losing the house she loved.

Help from Abroad

Herr Lehrer Lorenz, a young teacher in Ohrenbach whom Dad had mentored, learned of Dad's death and contacted Mom. He told her that she was probably eligible for a widow's pension from the German government. The German government counted both teaching in Germany and teaching in the Transylvanian Saxon schools in Romania when calculating pension benefits. Fortunately, Mom and Dad had kept all important documents and she was approved to receive the benefits. Herr Lorenz took care of all the paperwork and Mom began receiving a monthly widow's pension check, which was more than the small pension check she received from Dad's former employer, North American Aviation (by then Rockwell International). The stack of paperwork required to accomplish this was about three inches high. Mr. Lorenz went the extra mile for Mom.

Independent Businesswoman

Some of Mom's regular customers at Lazarus suggested that she start her own alterations business. That is exactly what she did. Working from home, Mom started her own seamstress business. Mom earned enough to pay off the mortgage. What a proud day! I think Mom could have made much more money with her work. Over the years I convinced her only three times to increase her rates a little. I believe her customers would have paid more for her high-quality work and for the personal nature of the service she offered. If the customers had time, Mom would offer them tea and home-baked German cookies. Now that is not your standard service! Another bonus: the customers paid in cash, not in cigarettes like the Russian officers had! Forever honest, Mom paid taxes on all her income even though all customer payments to her were in cash.

The Attack Grandmother

The Transylvanian Saxon diaspora continued to locate each other after the war years through word of mouth. That was how Mom, when she was in her late fifties, learned of Hilda Fritsch, her best friend from her school days (see the appendix, 11).

Life without her husband presented Mom with many challenges. One of the challenges was traveling alone for the first time since 1944. She traveled twice to see her siblings in Europe, and she flew to Chicago to visit Hilda, who lived with her elderly mother.

When Mom was sixty-five, she visited Hilda. One day Mom, Hilda, and Hilda's mother were walking near Hilda's high-rise apartment. Two young thugs grabbed Mom's and Hilda's mother's purses. Mom's purse strap failed and her attacker sprinted off with the loot. But Hilda's mother's purse strap was very strong and the tiny, frail lady had a death grip on the strap. The mugger, with purse in hand, violently shook her back and forth like a rag doll.

Mom described the purse snatching to me, saying that when the young man began throwing Hilda's mother side to side and dragging her on the sidewalk, Mom snapped. In her fury she attacked the thug with her collapsible umbrella. Holding the umbrella with two hands, she repeatedly beat him on the head. After several blows, he ran away sans purse.

Mom's German-made collapsible umbrella was quite sturdy. The short center shaft was made out of chrome-plated steel. After the encounter, the shaft had a forty-five-degree bend.

When our children heard of their grandmother's exploits, they were quite proud of her and commented that they had an attack grandmother. But the sweet taste of victory did not last. She quickly realized that the purse snatcher had all of her personal information including her address. For a couple of months she worried that he would come and find her.

The Last Move

When she was about seventy-two and could no longer take care of her beloved house, she sold it free and clear, giving her a financial cushion for renting a very comfortable apartment in a nearby retirement community. She continued her seamstress work until she was seventy-five. She stopped working because she was losing her eyesight and the feeling in her fingers from the effects of diabetes.

Retirement communities are not inexpensive, but Mom was able to pay for her apartment with her own money. My brother and I could have helped her financially, but she did not need our help and was proud to manage on her own.

Mom was lonely but accomplished much in her twenty-seven years as widow. She kept the house she loved, paid off the mortgage, maintained the house in immaculate condition inside and out, had comfortable furniture, bought two new cars while continuing to manage her money, and live frugally. The last few years, she worried about running out of money. I explained to her that she would not run out of money even if she spent more money on herself. No matter how I explained it, she did not spend more. Having accomplished paying off the house and saving money with reasonably safe investments, she accomplished her last goal after her death: leaving some money for her sons.

MOM'S PASSING

***Es ist vorbei!* (It's Over!)**

As Mom weakened, she survived several serious illnesses and made numerous visits to the hospital. Following an especially severe downturn, the doctor approved hospice care. Ruth and I provided care in her independent living apartment. We worked twelve-hour shifts for four weeks. As Mom occasionally moved about, always accompanied by either Ruth or me, there were many times we had to catch her as she lost her balance. Without constant care she would not have survived. As sometimes happens, during those four weeks she got much better. At the end of the four weeks, my brother and his wife took over for us and were surprised by how well she functioned. Upon seeing Mom's condition, Günter commented, "Gosh, she is nowhere near as bad as you had been reporting." Anyone who has been a caregiver and has communicated with a family member who is living elsewhere can easily understand this type of situation. My brother and his wife stayed for one week in Mom's apartment and Mom continued to improve. Mom lived another year in her independent living apartment and then moved to the assisted-living wing of the retirement community.

Nobody lives forever and Mom was failing. She wanted to die and did not understand why the Lord did not take her. In spite of wanting to die, she fought for her life a number of times. The hardest time for me was when I sat beside her in the hospital and she could not catch her breath. It was terrible for both of us.

Eventually Mom was put in hospice one last time. The retirement center allowed the hospice caregiver to visit Mom in her assisted-living room. One special caregiver was a beautiful Christian lady from Tanzania. She was a kind and loving person. She had a green card and hoped to become a citizen. I hope she was successful. She would be a good addition to our country.

When we knew Mom was close to the end, Günter drove to Ohio from his home in Illinois. The three of us, the Tanzanian lady, my brother, and I took turns so Mom was never alone.

As the end neared, Mom was in a state of delirium for two or three days. She had her eyes closed and seemed to be dreaming. In these "dreams" she talked, but I could not understand her. Her eyes were active as if she were dreaming and reliving scenes from her life. On her last day she just lay there quietly with my brother by her side.

Late that afternoon my brother called me and said Mom was very close to the end. I was there about fifty minutes later, but she had already died. My brother had said his private goodbyes to Mom before I arrived. We informed the retirement community's director of Mom's death. They arranged for an ambulance to transport her to a funeral home. Mom was eighty-four.

While waiting for the funeral home ambulance, my brother and I sat beside Mom's bed for about three hours. It was good to just sit there and talk to my brother. We talked about the good old, bad old times. One story my brother told me was about the sack of potatoes Dad had carried from Romania to Rothenburg. I knew the story, but it had a new twist. My brother remembered from our time in West Germany that Dad would often tell Mom how he had sacrificed for her and schlepped potatoes all the way from Romania to West Germany. Mom had sacrificed plenty herself. One day she had heard the story one time too often and told him, "I'm tired of hearing about those seven damned potatoes." That was the first time I knew how many potatoes he had with him when we were reunited in Rothenburg. Günter and I talked a lot. We laughed. We did not cry.

Mom was finally picked up by an ambulance and taken away. I said goodbye to my brother and walked outside to my car to drive home. It was around 10:00 p.m. As I approached my car in the dark, I suddenly and involuntarily cried out loudly, "*Es ist vorbei!*" (It's over!). Then I wept, standing alone in the parking lot.

Later I thought about the words I had cried out in such a sudden, unplanned fashion. What was over? I guess what was over was my mother's struggle and the struggle of her generation. So much fear, so much loss, so much effort, so much pain, so much courage, so much hard work. It was over. Mom was at rest and released from the cares, troubles, and struggles of the world.

Well done, Mom.

Chapter 19

Traces, Learnings, Miracle

TRACES

Gustav, Helene, Günter, Gerhard—we were all marked by WWII.

Impact on Dad

Being a POW, with its associated stress, malnutrition, and abuse, damaged my dad's health. During the postwar period in West Germany, nutrition continued to be poor and job stress was high as he worked to provide for his family. Those events compromised his health and led to his early death. His childhood, the war, being a POW, PTSD, his head injury, and postwar stress negatively impacted how he interacted with his family. However, since his experiences did not break him, they strengthened his resolve to succeed.

Impact on Mom

Mom was less impacted physically but suffered from what we now call PTSD for the rest of her life. As my interest in our background increased, for more than two decades I occasionally interviewed her. There are audio recordings of the last two of those many interviews. During the visits I'd ask questions about our family's experiences during and after WWII. After one interview toward the end of the twenty-plus years of infrequent interviews, Mom was very sick and bedridden for one week.

That caused me to think back, and I realized past interviews might also have been followed by her getting sick. Were these bouts brought on by dredging up terrible memories? Months later I interviewed her again. The next week she spent in bed. Was that a coincidence? About six months later, I asked her questions about the difficult times for about an hour as I was taking notes. Again Mom spent the following week in bed. It was not a coincidence. That was my last interview.

Was that the end of learning about our past? Not really. From that time on, I was never the initiator of discussions about the past. For the rest of her life, Mom would occasionally offer a story from our past. While I asked questions for clarification, I never probed. When she was the initiator of telling a story, she was never sick afterward. I made mental notes while she was talking and would write down what she had said as soon as I got home, or even as soon as I got to my car. The dying-room story, which she told me when she was about seventy-eight, is one example. I continued to learn about our past, and my appreciation for what she had done for us grew.

Her impromptu recollections might even have been cathartic or reaffirmations of what she had done for us. I'm sure my interest and my responses as she told me stories reinforced in her mind my appreciation of what she had done for my brother and me.

Impact on Günter

In his own words:

> Within a few weeks of reaching these hallowed shores I made a conscious effort to divorce my mind from most things associated with Europe. When family reminisced about the good old or bad old days, my response was to quietly leave the room.
>
> Panic attacks were an almost daily experience and continued until I was fifteen. When I was twenty-eight, my

employer sent me to Germany, and wham, the sounds, smells, and foreign voices transported me into an almost surreal state of mind. A hundred such business trips later, the feeling of unease persists.

Although we were born into a structured society, in which authorities were respected, commencing at the age of six, while attending a Communist grade school, I learned to recognize self-serving frauds and liars. The discipline (a.k.a. torture) endured during my first and second grades in a Communist grade school sharpened that sense and freed me to resist all forms of groupthink indoctrination. My crime against the state was the refusal to tell my teacher about conversations I had with my mother, grandparents, and neighbors.

The nightly ritual of waking every hour on the hour for a "security check" stopped when I reached fifty—though even today at age seventy-nine, the slightest out-of-the-ordinary sound will jolt me wide awake.

But these seeming hardships had a mostly positive effect. Life in America was low-hanging fruit—all was doable for the price of a little elbow grease. As a paperboy, the ugliness of the past prepared me for the encounters with Billy Banks, the two "working girls" in Apartment D, and a pedophile on the floor below. When the couple from 134 Northwest Boulevard moved across town without paying, they were tracked. The bill was settled.

Life in business was a grand adventure and allowed me to see the gears that made America the premier engine of opportunity, a freedom machine which guaranteed not only that one's labor could be sold to the highest bidder but that one could "fire" an incompetent boss. America seemed like

> Disneyland. Whether working the canyons of downtown Pittsburgh selling my company's engineered wares, working month after month in a Harlan County, Kentucky, coal mine, or growing the bottom line as a chief operating officer—the ride was heady, sweaty, and oh so sweet.
>
> But most of all, it's the Americans you meet along the way. It is their influence that begs one to strive for more. The Mormon mining engineer in Salt Lake City, the Baptist entrepreneur in Sumiton, Alabama, and the nonbeliever in Tulsa—we all had one thing in common: we loved our freedom, our work, and our America.

Impact on Me

Although I do not consciously remember the war, I know it deeply impacted me over the years. The postwar experiences in Europe also shaped me. Those experiences have instilled in me a great appreciation for my life, my family, the lifestyle I lead, and America. It is easier to be thankful for what one has when one has experienced life without.

Knowing what life was like under both Communist and National Socialist (Nazi) regimes modified my behavior. I knew people were persecuted and arrested for their religious beliefs and for having non-government-approved ideas and non-government-approved political views. For much of the Cold War, the outcome was uncertain. I always considered the possibility that Communist Russians might win the Cold War and I might someday find myself in a Communist United States.

I've grown up with a feeling that things will not necessarily always be good. I have enough to eat, but it may not always be so. I am safe, but that may change. I have a place to live, but that can change. Things are calm, but in an instant life can be taken over by chaos. Our government is here to protect us, but even that can change. Taken too far, this mindset can lead to paranoia, but a healthy wariness can make a difference in critical times.

Knowing that what we have today may be gone tomorrow can make us more thankful and encourage us to work to preserve it. A demonstration of this thankfulness occurred at every family dinner beginning when our son Geoff was about one year old, right after I came back home from Vietnam. It continued until he was about four or five. First, I need to tell you that my dad's nickname for Geoff was Hosch Kirai (Belly King in Hungarian, written phonetically in German), an old-country term of endearment for a young child who loved to eat.

We always enjoyed a family dinner after I came home from work. During each dinner, without fail, for three or four years, I would look at my young son eating his fill and tear up. I was overcome by thankfulness that my son had enough to eat. How my parents must have suffered when they could not provide adequate food for their children! Ruth noticed the tears and understood. Geoff did not notice the tears. He was too busy enjoying his meal.

After our son was born, I better understood a peculiar habit Dad had at holiday meals in the United States. Whenever there was a special holiday meal such as Thanksgiving or Christmas, Dad had to take pictures of the set table laden with many wonderful prepared foods. We sat there smiling, not touching the food as it cooled, until he had taken the picture. The sight of a full table brought him great joy and tears to his eyes. But setting all the hot food on the table only to have it cool while Dad set up his tripod and timer and took pictures drove Mom nuts. I did not fully understand Dad's joy at the sight of a bountiful table until I had children of my own.

As I matured, I became aware of how my experiences impacted my behavior. For decades I did not sign a church roster or join a political party. I avoided any public statements about my political convictions. My only foray into political expression in my younger years occurred in the early 1960s, when I was about twenty and attending OSU. I was the sole demonstrator against a Communist speaker at OSU. At that time, there was a strong leftist and Communist sentiment among some college students, and Students for a Democratic Society (SDS) was active on many campuses.[1]

I was somewhat of an oddity expressing an anti-Communist viewpoint. I held my large poster-board homemade sign and walked around the Oval. The Oval is the traditional campus center. It is a large, mowed grassy area with occasional large trees, crisscrossed with sidewalks and surrounded by the earliest university buildings.

On that sunny and warm day I was the only "anti" demonstrator. Being the only anti, I drew the attention of a *Columbus Dispatch* reporter. When he asked to interview me and take pictures, I reflexively refused. I could have had a large platform to communicate my views. The instinctive refusal was a direct result of knowledge gained mostly by osmosis of the risks of exposing one's political views. I believed with my whole heart in freedom of speech but was fearful of expressing my views.

Someone from my high school was part of the large group of students demonstrating for the Communist speaker. In the course of my walking around and holding up my sign, our paths crossed. I said, "Hi, Carol," in a friendly manner. She did not speak but turned away. The look she gave me before she turned her back spoke volumes. Her look could be compared to the look someone might give when being too close to maggot- and fly-covered roadkill. So much for political dialogue. I'm sure she felt both morally and intellectually superior.

In recent years I finally outed myself and have written letters to the editor to respectfully share my views. Years ago, I would not have done that. I waited until the age of the internet, where everything can be googled and there is no anonymity. Now that's courageous!

America is the land of opportunity. In high school I decided to pursue two careers: air force pilot and engineer. The air force pilot option was taken away, but I achieved the other. I attained one of my dreams by graduating with an engineering degree from OSU. My wife and I raised a family and, although during the first few years money was tight, we never had real need. I enjoyed my career as an engineer and was able to work on some challenging projects. I worked with very capable people and traveled to Europe and Japan numerous times on business. My work helped to make several industrial products more competitive and profitable. Manufacturing plants stay open when it is profitable to produce a product. Having worked in manufacturing my entire career, I knew the operators, mechanics, and supervisors personally. In some cases I also knew their families. Having a small hand in helping a business to stay profitable, allowing my coworkers steady employment, gave me an enormous sense of satisfaction. Those workers were able to attain their dreams of retiring with well-earned pensions.

I retired from industry at age fifty-nine and started a new career as a high-school teacher of German. What a great country, where you can reinvent yourself and do something completely different! I absolutely love teaching and loved my students. My career path was the opposite of Dad's, whose first career was teaching and second career was engineering. Although I enjoyed my first career, with my second career I was what I call "occupationally reborn." Many days, as I was walking toward the school and about to enter the building, I would quietly say, "Thank you, Lord, for allowing me to teach another day." I wrote and published five German short-story books for students and a teacher's manual.[2] I am now retired from teaching on the high-school level and am teaching adults in the evenings at a coffee shop called Das KaffeeHaus. I've discovered that coffee, pastries, and German go well together.

And finally I wrote this book—in English. America—the land of opportunity, dreams, and reinvention.

LEARNING FROM THE PAST

Play the Hand You Are Dealt

From my parents' story I draw a lesson. Dad was unfairly dealt a bad hand to play in Romania. He played it the best he could, and failed. He was again given a bad hand in West Germany. He played it as well as he could, but failed. In America he started out with a weak hand, having nothing at the age of thirty-five and no recognized university degree and working at an entry-level job. He played it as well as he could. He succeeded. He succeeded because this is America. America rewards hard work. To quote Condoleezza Rice, an American whom I admire, "America is the most minority friendly country on the face of the earth" and "the essence of America—that which unites us—is not ethnicity, or nationality or religion—it is an idea—and what an idea it is: That you can come from humble circumstances and do great things."[3]

I take our family's experiences and Condoleezza Rice's experiences as lessons for life. Many are dealt a bad hand. What to do? There is only one answer: play the hand well. It's not easy. It is up to each individual. It looks like a lot of hard work because that is what it is. It takes a will, hard work, and perseverance. Dwelling on the unfairness of the situation one finds oneself in and not concentrating on one's objective can lead to inaction and failure. Nothing paralyzes an individual more than seeing oneself as a victim. America is not perfect, but it is biased toward rewarding hard work and celebrating success.

I Have Learned That America Is a Great Country

I will be forever thankful for being allowed to immigrate and share in the freedom and opportunity given to me as a citizen. Americans are a kind, tolerant, and generous people. America is a land of opportunity with the rule of law. It is a land of individual rights and religious freedom. The inherent nature of America and Americans has given me the opportunity to succeed.

The Future of a Nation

I have learned that the future of a nation is not assured. For eight centuries the people of Transylvania maintained local autonomy. They had freedom of speech, property rights, and rule of law. They never had an aristocracy. In Transylvania there was the flowering of freedom. When the Saxons arrived in Transylvania, they settled a largely unpopulated wild area as a free people. I see some parallels between tiny Transylvania and the United States.

Because Transylvania was small, its fate was sealed. It was overrun by the armies of larger nations, and the oasis of prosperity and freedom ceased to exist. I look at the future of my new homeland, America, through the prism of having lost my homeland in 1944. Both history and the experience of my family teach that the life of nations is finite.

America is a continent-wide country rich in natural resources and endowed with industrious people. If we lose our freedom, that loss will not come by our nation being conquered; it will come from within. I've lived long enough to have observed political trends. For some time now, with each president, the executive branch of government becomes more powerful. At the same time, Congress has willingly ceded power. The citizens are OK with this trend as long as "their" president is in office but complain bitterly if the president belongs to the other party. We are experiencing a time when the executive branch usurps more power and Congress acquiesces. My fear is that we are heading toward an imperial presidency with a weak Congress.

As the executive has grown in power and Congress has become less powerful, the influence of the judiciary has grown. In the absence of congressional action to change the Constitution, as our forefathers envisioned, the judiciary has increased its power and influence through interpreting the Constitution to fit some prevailing political biases. The increasing power and influence of the coequal Supreme Court has intensified our political strife and is dangerous to our republic. This trend is welcomed by those who cannot see a way to change the Constitution via legislation, as designed by the Founding Fathers, so they seek to make law via court rulings. If these trends are not reversed and the three branches of government are not coequal, tyranny will be the result. Living under a tyrannical regime is nothing I want my children and grandson to experience.

Another trend I have observed is an ever-expanding federal government far beyond what was envisioned by the founders. While we live in a very different and complex world, which dictates new roles for the federal government, we are unnecessarily concentrating power at the highest level. The ever-growing government and the promises made by politicians, especially at the federal level, have resulted in ever-growing and unsustainable federal debt. At the time of this writing, the federal debt per taxpayer is $178,338 and growing.[4] If the trend of ever-expanding government is not reversed, it will not end well. We are potentially heading for an economic crash that will dwarf the Great Depression.

Two quotes from Thomas Jefferson are worth pondering. The first is this: "My reading of history convinces me that most bad government results from too much government."[5] Here is the second: "It is incumbent on every generation to pay its own debts as it goes. A principle which if acted on would save one-half the wars of the world."[6]

What Makes America Great?

In its short history, America has become the most prosperous, free, and powerful nation in the history of the world. What are the reasons America has flourished?

The foundations of our greatness are as follows:

- Faith in our Creator
- A system of government run by the people and for the people, designed by wise founders who threw off the yoke of an oppressive aristocracy
- Self-reliant and independent-minded citizens who have been free to pursue their dreams without unnecessary government interference
- Specific and limited powers granted to the three branches of the federal government
- A society built upon a stable family structure

We abandon these foundations at our peril. I fear that we are drifting away from all five. A house without a firm foundation will fall.

It is easy to dismiss a belief in God as a founding principle. The second sentence of the Declaration of Independence speaks to the belief in God by our founders: "We hold these truths to be self-evident, that all men are created equal, that they are endowed by their Creator with certain unalienable Rights, that among these are Life, Liberty and the pursuit of Happiness."

The painting of George Washington on one knee beside his horse, praying at Valley Forge, tells much about this man of faith. Our Founding Fathers were highly educated men of faith. Each year, Congress is opened with a prayer. This practice was initiated by our Founding Fathers.[7]

There is one great stain on our history and our greatness—slavery. Slavery has existed from the beginnings of mankind. All nations, peoples, and cultures throughout history enslaved others. It is not an invention of the Western world. England and then America outlawed slavery for the first time in history. In both nations, Christian abolitionists successfully fought against and ended slavery. It was the abolitionists in America who ran the Underground Railroad, opposed slavery, and were the driving force for its abolition. The Western Christian-based culture not only abolished slavery but patrolled the seas, interdicting slave ships and making the practice uneconomical. As a people, we Americans needed to—and did—evolve morally and ethically. As demonstrated by the Voting Rights Act of 1965, we have the governmental structure to right wrongs and make progress without violent revolution.[8]

Our nation has been blessed. We as citizens have been blessed. The way to retain this blessing is to work at maintaining and supporting the core values that made us great. May it be so.

Good People

Good people and bad people have entered and exited my life and the life of my family. I have learned that no people, no race, no ethnicity has a corner on good or evil. Character has no relationship to race, background, education, religion, pedigree, or wealth. Without the help of kind people during the war and when we were refugees, we would not have survived and been reunited. Without us helping others, some of them might not have survived. I survived due to the love, caring, and kindness of many.

MIRACLE AND PLAN

It is a miracle that I wrote this book. It is a miracle because there were many times when I could have died or been killed. I once commented to my mother that it is a miracle that we all survived WWII and the postwar years, were reunited as a family, and came to America for a new beginning and a new life. She responded, "Our Lord had a plan for us." About six years ago I came across a twenty-eight-year-old recording of my mom saying those exact words. I've been thinking about what she said.

I do believe God had a plan for us.

If Mom's statement is true, I'm part of the "us" for whom God has a plan. What I've been pondering is, *What is His plan for me? What should I do now?*

I am thankful to have been spared and been able to live my life. I feel this was part of God's plan. However, there were millions of people, uncounted people, who perished during and after the war. There were many who were broken by the war and were never at peace again. Was my family better than all those people, and families, who were extinguished or broken? I think not. Why were we spared? Who knows God's mind?

I do not often think about all the suffering and pain that people endured, because when I do, I am covered with a great, dark blanket of sorrow, pain, and sadness. The knowledge of their suffering overwhelms me. The feeling can be so strong that it can cause me to totally break down. For a supposedly tough old man of German descent, breaking down and uncontrollably crying can be quite embarrassing. My way to avoid becoming overwhelmed is to not visit Holocaust museums or concentration camps and to avoid movies that show the suffering of many people. When I am away from those influences, I assure you I can be fun to be around, and you don't have to worry about me suddenly becoming a blubbering old fool.

I thank God for my life. I hope to somehow discern His plan for me and hope to live my life so that I may fulfill at least part of His plan.

Maybe His plan for me is as simple as living the commandment to "love thy neighbor as thyself," imperfect as I am, to the best of my ability. And maybe His plan for me is to honor my parents by writing this book and sharing our remarkable story with others.

Thank you, Mom and Dad. Thank you, God.

–NOTES–

1. The SDS did not claim to be Communist, but they were avowed opponents of anti-communism. A later faction of the SDS was the Weather Underground, a domestic terror organization that bombed and killed. Two famous Weather Underground members are Bill Ayers and Bernadette Dohrn.
2. http://germanreaders.com/.
3. https://www.brainyquote.com/quotes/authors/c/condoleezza_rice_2.html.
4. http://www.usdebtclock.org.
5. http://www.creators.com/opinion/daily-editorials/relevant-wisdom-of-mr-jefferson.html.
6. http://www.brainyquote.com/quotes/authors/t/thomas_jefferson.html#vXqi1cGGvuOQj0Lp.99.
7. http://chaplain.house.gov/archive/continental.html.
8. http://www.justice.gov/crt/about/vot/intro/intro_b.php.

Appendix

1 Gustav Günter Maroscher.

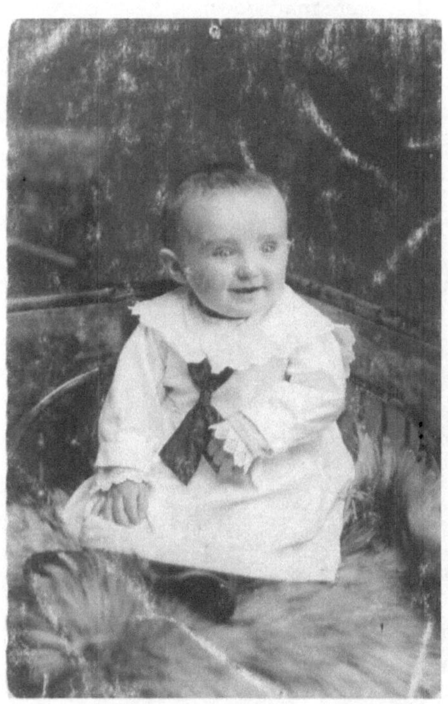

Gustav Günter Maroscher (Dad) was born on November 11, 1917. This is the only baby picture of him.

2 Gustav Friedrich Maroscher

My father's father, Gustav Friedrich Maroscher, as a student. He was born in 1890 and died in 1920 when Dad was two years and seven months old.

3 **Dad's parents: Gustav Friedrich Maroscher and Käthe Knopp.**

Shown in 1915, the year they were married

4 **Dad with his Knopp family relatives in the summer of 1924, when he was six years old.** The picture was taken four years after Dad's father died. Bruno Knopp, Dad's uncle, lived with Käthe Maroscher (Dad's mother, whose maiden name was Knopp) in Bistritz for several years while attending a gymnasium (college-prep high school) in Bistritz. Dad is the boy in the middle of the front row.

Top row, left to right: Karl Rudolf Knopp Jr., Adalbert Belo Aikelin, Karl Rudolf Knopp Sr. (my great-grandfather). *Middle row, left to right:* Maria Knopp, Anna Aikelin, Käthe Maroscher. *Front row, left to right:* Grete Knopp, Bruno Knopp, Gustav Maroscher (Dad), Annemarie Aikelin (daughter of Anna and Belo), Ernst Knopp.

5 Translation of the original document that verifies Dad's education. The original document was in Romanian and was translated into German for the German education administrators. The document was part of Dad's case that he was a qualified teacher. The English translation of the German follows.

Duplicate copy

Central Office
for Foreign Education
Head: Dr. Walter Wienert
Tab.Nr. 943/51/Wi
(Please include in response)

Göttingen 22 May 1951
Wilhelmsplatz 1
Phone: 3992/93, 2773

Assessment

Mr. Gustav Maroscher, born 10 November 1917 in Transylvania, presents a number of certificates, which include the following information about his professional background:

a) Attended elementary school in Transylvania for 4 years
b) Attended the first four years of a Romanian lyceum (similar to the German grammar school)
c) Attended the Protestant Theological-Pedagogical Church Seminary in Sibiu/ Transylvania for 5 years (diploma dated June 1937).

The above mentioned seminary, which was run by the state, served as an institution for educating the future teachers of German elementary schools in Transylvania. There are no objections to consider Mr. M.'s education as equal to the previous seminar-like education of German elementary school teachers.

He received his permanent employment as a Transylvanian elementary school teacher (both under the Romanian and Hungarian rule) after having served as a "provisional teacher" for 2 years. In Hungary, the competent school inspector paid teachers a visit after they had completed this probation period. The school inspector issued an assessment based on this visitation, which then led to the employment decree. The detailed assessment of Mr. M. is also present. Subsequently, Mr. M. was appointed as a "definite teacher" and hired as such (see the enclosed Employment Decree issued by the German Protestant Presbytery of Mettersdorf).

In Hungary, there is no second exam for becoming a teacher—nor has there ever been one; instead teachers are visited by the school inspector. In Hungary, Mr. M. was a fully licensed and qualified Elementary School teacher; his appointment as "definite teacher" and his employment were in accordance with the Civil Service Law provisions as they apply in Germany. Since the quality of his education is on par with the seminar-like education that was once offered in Germany, there are no objections to considering him an equal to German Elementary School teachers who underwent the seminar-like examination and fulfill the requirements for a full employment.

[Signature]
(Dr. Wienert)

6 Tuition stipend document by the Bistritz City Council (Stadtmagistrat Bistritz). The contents of the original document are summarized below.

The bilingual document (Romanian on the left and German on the right) is dated November 16, 1931, and states that the income from the property Käthe owns and her small widow's pension is barely enough to support two persons. The document also describes the property owned by her and enthusiastically supports the granting of a scholarship to enable Gustav, who was fourteen at the time, to attend the university. The total size of the property owned by Käthe Maroscher was 14.3 acres and consisted of the following sections: 6.4 acres cultivated, 6.8 acres meadow, and 1.1 acres orchard. All farm labor was manual, which required the hiring of farmhands.

7 Résumé. Dad wrote a résumé that covers his education, employment as a teacher, qualifications, military service, POW time, and severe health issues. Other teachers from Romania had been recognized and paid for their previous teaching, but the regional Bavarian education administration did not recognize Dad's previous experience. Dad wrote the résumé on December 12, 1950.

Gustav Maroscher, Teacher a.Dv.
(13a) Ohrenbach near Rothenburg o.T.

Résumé

I, Gustav Maroscher, son of the elementary school teacher Gustav Friedrich Maroscher and his wife Käthe, née Knopp, was born on 11/10/1917 in Deutsch Budak, Northern Transylvania. After my father passed away in 1920, my mother and I moved to my paternal grandparents in the district capital Bistritz, where we had a larger estate, house and property. My mother received a pension.

In Bistritz, I attended four years of elementary school and grammar school. In 1936 I completed the five years of the Evangelical Theological-Pedagogical A.B. Church Seminary in Hermannstadt. Because I suffered from a severe case of typhus during the examination session in 1936, I could not take the teacher qualifying examination until 1937, which I passed as the second best of five candidates.

I held the following positions at these elementary schools of the Protestant Church in Romania and (after 1940) at elementary schools of the Evangelical general church district A.B. in the Transylvanian regions of Hungary:

1936/37 Substitute teacher at the 4-year elementary school in Botsch.
1937/38 Active military service.
1938/42 Teacher and headmaster of the 2-year elementary school in Senndorf.
1942 until the collapse of the Axis powers: Teacher and headmaster at the 4-year elementary school in Mettersdorf.

In Senndorf I was first hired as a provisional teacher (the Romanian term for this: învăţător cu titlu provisoriu; this term matches the German LAA-Hilfslehrer). On March 21st and 22nd 1941, I underwent a 2-day school visitation by a public school inspector and as a result of this visitation I was retroactively—starting on Sept. 1st 1939—appointed a definite teacher for life on April 16th 1941. This legal title is the equivalent of the German title Civil Servant for life. Unlike here, there was no second qualifying exam in Hungary, but in its place, they had a thorough school visitation with in-depth methodic discussion and evaluation.

I got married in 1939. In the fall of 1944, my wife Helene, née Maurer, was evacuated from our homeland to Germany together with our two sons, Günter (born in 1940) and Gerhard (born in 1943). Because of our escape, we lost all of our immovable and movable possessions.

I served in the compulsory military service of Romania and Hungary; most recently as a Lieutenant in the reserve. During the collapse, I was captured by Americans who then released us to the Russians after two days. I was released from Russian captivity in 1945 (September). While I was a prisoner of war as well as the following year, which I was obligated to spend in Romania, I had to endure severe physical and emotional distress. In September of 1946, I fled from Romania to Vienna, from where I was repatriated to Germany that same month in my attempt to find my family. I found my family in Rothenburg o. T.

I immediately reported to continue in my employment and was soon after, on October 22nd 1946, hired as a teacher at the elementary school in Ohrenbach. So this is my 5th year working as an elementary school teacher in Bavaria!

After having worked in this position for 3.5 years, I was asked this spring to take the second exam. Because I had been a definite teacher and therefore a civil servant in my homeland, and because this employment follows the general principles of the Civil Servant Law, I requested from the ministry and the government on multiple occasions that this second examination be waived. However, this was not granted, and neither were my two attempts to have the examination procedures shortened.

Because there was not sufficient time to prepare for the qualifying examination in 1950 and because my health unfortunately does not allow me to add another heavy burden without it inflicting severe physical or emotional harm on my person, I was not able to take the examination this summer. Based on the last notification from the Middle Franconian government dated 12/1/1950 (which was issued because of the ministry's decision from 7/26/1950), I will now have to register for the qualifying examination in 1951.

I am going to thoroughly prepare for the examination. But with the same diligence and energy, I will continue to insist on my right to tenure without having to pass another examination. To that end, I will utilize all available legal channels and continue to provide the authorities with the necessary information regarding my situation.

I was recently informed that the ministry had already created a precedent back in 1948 regarding the employment of teachers who had received tenure in Hungary; in our administrative district there was the case of Mrs. Schlarb (née Treuchtlingen) whose case is identical to mine. I see this different treatment, which leaves the verdict up to chance, as a severe social injustice as my case wasn't taken up until 1950. So if the past decisions are not taken into account for my case, my tenure would not be reinstated until spring 1952 at the earliest, meaning after I had worked as an elementary school teacher in Bavaria for 6.5 years and 13 years after I received definite employment for life!

This situation is a bitter and undeserving deprivation of rights for my family!

Ohrenbach, 12/9/1950

Gustav Maroscher

8 Diploma. Gustav Günter Maroscher's diploma from June 1937. Dad became severely ill with typhus during the teacher qualification exam in 1936 and had to wait to take the exam in June 1937. That is why he did not receive his diploma from the seminary until June 1937 (see the appendix, 7).

Aprobat de Înaltul Minister al Educațiunii Naționale (Direcția Învățământului Particular și Confesional) sub No. 101853/937.

No. 165.

ROMÂNIA
MINISTERUL EDUCAȚIUNII NAȚIONALE
Direcțiunea Generală a Învățământului Particular și Confesional

DIPLOMA
DE CAPACITATE PENTRU ÎNVĂȚĂTOR

Școala normală de învățători ev. C. A. - Sibiu -

Având în vedere rezultatul examenului pentru obținerea diplomei de capacitate pentru învățători din Sibiu, ținut în sesiunea de Iunie 1937 la școala normală ev. C. A. de băeți, care funcționează cu limba de predare germană și cu drept de publicitate conf. autorizației No. 92 din 1928 Min. Instr. No. 72.293|1928.

Potrivit legei asupra învățământului primar și normal-primar și legei asupra învățământului particular.

Noi, Ministru Secretar de Stat la Departamentul Instrucțiunii,

Liberăm prezenta diplomă Domnului Gustav Günter Maroscher născut la: ziua 10, luna Noemvrie, anul 1917, în comuna Budacul de jos, județul Năsăud, și care a absolvit cu bună purtare cursurile școalei arătate mai sus.

Domnia sa, reușind la examenul de capacitate, a obținut media 7·81, fiind clasificat al 2 între cei 5 absolvenți ai școalei.

În baza acestei diplome numitul candidat are dreptul de a funcționa în învățământul particular la școale primare cu limba de predare germană conform legilor și regulamentelor școlare.

Pe verso s'a notat rezultatul din cei 8 ani de studiu.

(L. S. M.) p. MINISTRU,

Directorul Învățământului Particular și Confesional,

Candidatul, Gustav Maroscher

Ziua 16 Luna Iunie 1937.

9 Final college exam. Among the documents my parents kept is Dad's final exam (with grades for all subjects), which he took before graduation. In part, the document states, "Der Schüler Maroscher ist in den Tagen 19–26 Juni, 1936 in allen Gegenständen geprüft worden" (From June 19 to 26, 1936, the student Maroscher was tested in all subjects). To be certified to teach, prospective teachers needed to pass a teacher qualification exam. During that exam in the summer of 1936, Dad became extremely ill with typhus. He was therefore not able to take the exam again until the following summer. Because he had not been able to take the teacher qualification exam, he was employed as a substitute teacher in the 1936/37 school year (see the appendix, 10). The final exam document is in both German and Romanian. The actual two-page document is rather large and therefore not included in this appendix.

10 Dad's teaching history starting in the 1936/37 school year. Dad started teaching in the 1936/37 school year in Botsch as a substitute teacher. This affidavit is from Hans Sierel, a Lutheran minister who took part in an observation and evaluation of Dad teaching school

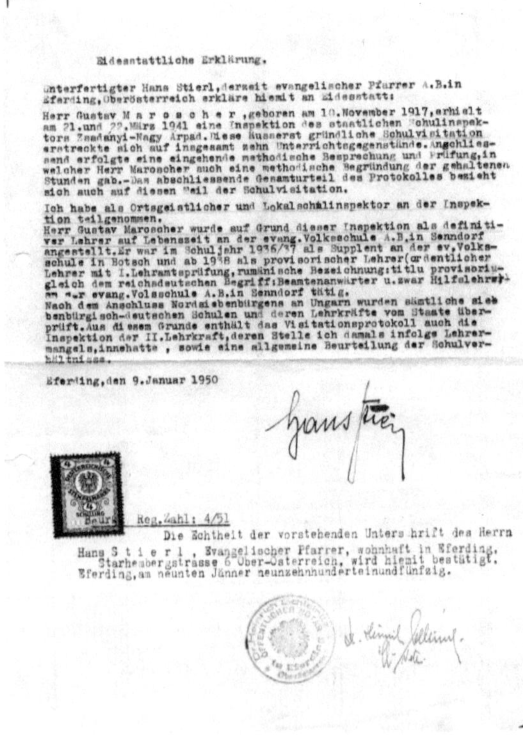

Eidesstattliche Erklärung.

Unterfertigter Hans Stierl, derzeit evangelischer Pfarrer A.B. in Eferding, Oberösterreich erkläre hiemit an Eidesstatt:

Herr Gustav M a r o s c h e r, geboren am 10. November 1917, erhielt am 21. und 22. März 1941 eine Inspektion des staatlichen Schulinspektors Zsadányi-Nagy Árpad. Diese äusserst gründliche Schulvisitation erstreckte sich auf insgesamt zehn Unterrichtsgegenstände. Anschliessend erfolgte eine eingehende methodische Besprechung und Prüfung, in welcher Herr Maroscher auch eine methodische Begründung der gehaltenen Stunden gab.-Das abschliessende Gesamturteil des Protokolles bezieht sich auch auf diesen Teil der Schulvisitation.

Ich habe als Ortsgeistlicher und Lokalschulinspektor an der Inspektion teilgenommen.
Herr Gustav Maroscher wurde auf Grund dieser Inspektion als definitiver Lehrer auf Lebenszeit an der evang. Volksschule A.B. in Senndorf angestellt. Er war im Schuljahr 1936/37 als Supplent an der ev. Volksschule in Botsch und ab 1938 als provisorischer Lehrer (ordentlicher Lehrer mit I. Lehramtsprüfung, rumänische Bezeichnung: titlu provisoriu-gleich dem reichsdeutschen Begriff: Beamtenanwärter u. zwar Hilfslehrer) an der evang. Volsschule A.B. in Senndorf tätig.
Nach dem Anschluss Nordsiebenbürgens an Ungarn wurden sämtliche siebenbürgisch-deutschen Schulen und deren Lehrkräfte vom Staate überprüft. Aus diesem Grunde enthält das Visitationsprotokoll auch die Inspektion der II. Lehrkraft, deren Stelle ich damals infolge Lehrermangels, innehatte, sowie eine allgemeine Beurteilung der Schulverhältnisse.

Eferding, den 9. Januar 1950

Reg. Zahl: 4/51

Die Echtheit der vorstehenden Unterschrift des Herrn Hans S t i e r l, Evangelischer Pfarrer, wohnhaft in Eferding, Starhembergstrasse 6 Ober-Österreich, wird hiemit bestätigt.
Eferding, am neunten Jänner neunzehnhunderteinundfünfzig.

in Transylvania (in Hungary at the time). He mentions Dad's prior teaching jobs also. This document was part of my dad's effort in Germany from 1946 to 1952 to be recognized and paid for his experience and education in Romania. The translation follows.

Statutory Declaration

The undersigned Hans Stierl, currently Protestant pastor A.B. in Eferding, Upper Austria, hereby affirms that:

On 21 and 22 March 1941, Mr. Gustav Maroscher, DOB 10 November 1917, underwent an inspection by the public school inspector Zaahanyi-Hagy Arpad. This extremely thorough school visitation covered a total of ten subjects. This was followed by an in-depth methodic consultation and examination, during which Mr. Maroscher also provided methodic reasoning for the lessons he had taught. The final assessment in the protocol also refers to this section of the school visitation.

As local clergy and local school inspector, I participated in the inspection.

Based on this inspection, Mr. Gustav Maroscher was hired at the protestant Elementary School A.B. in Senndorf as the definite teacher for life. During the school year of 1936/37, he served as a substitute teacher at the Protestant Elementary School in Botsch, and starting in 1938 he taught as a provisional teacher (full teacher who passed the first examination needed for becoming a teacher, Romanian title: bitlu provisoriu—which is the equivalent of the German title: Beamtenanwärter, specifically assistant teacher) at the Protestant Elementary School A.B. in Senndorf.

After Hungary's annexation of Northern Transylvania, all Transylvanian schools and their teaching staff were subjected to an examination by the state. This is why the visitation protocol also includes the inspection of the second "teacher," whose position I held at the time due to a teacher shortage, as well as a general assessment of the conditions at the school.

Eferding, on 9 January 1950

Signed Hans Stierl

(Austrian adhesive stamp)

Certification Register Nr.: 4/51

This hereby confirms the authenticity of the above signature by Mr. Hans Stierl, Protestant pastor, residing in Eferding, Starhembergstr. 5, Upper Austria.

Eferding, on the ninth of January nineteen-fifty-one.

Dr. Heinrich Schleinitz Signed Dr. Heinrich Schleinitz

Notary Public in Eferding Notary P.

(Illegible) Upper Austria.

The correct nature of the above text is certified by:

Ohrenbach, on 3 April 1951 [Seal: Ohrenbach] [Signature]

Note: The term *Beamtenanwärter* refers to individuals who are contenders for a position as a civil servant or similar position.

11 Photos of Mom. Hilda Fritsch was Mom's best friend since the first grade. Hilda and Mom were reunited after the war when Mom found Hilda in Chicago, where she lived with her mother.

Mom at eighteen before she was married. The picture was taken the year she completed her nurses' training.

Mom, at sixteen, and Hilda Fritsch as students

Mom as a homemaker

12 Dad's military history summarized. The following two-page notarized affidavit, dated November 11, 1951, outlines Dad's military history. In the document Dad explains his service in three separate armies. The document was sent to the US immigration office in Munich, West Germany, as Dad was in the process of applying for and being permitted to immigrate to the United States. The translation follows.

Eidesstattliche Erklärung

Ich, Gustav Günter Maroscher geb.den 10.11.17 in Budacul de jos-Deutschbudak, erkläre hiermit an Eides Statt:

Im Oktober des Jahres 1937 wurde ich zum "Bat.8 VM" /8.Gebirgsjäger-Bataillon/ nach Bistritz-Rumänien einberufen. Während meiner ganzen Dienstzeit im rumänischen Heere gehörte ich dieser Einheit an. Nach der Grundausbildung in der "compania de specialitati-ploton de recuneastere /Spezialitätenkompanie-Aufklärungszug/ wurde ich der Schipatrouille des Bataillons zugeteilt. Diese Einheit wurde im Winter 1937/38 in Dorna-Vatra, in den Karpathen, ausgebildet. Im Frühjahr erhielten wir eine speziale Gebirgsausbildung auf dem Suhard/Karpathen/.Am 1.1.1938 wurde ich "fruntas"/Gefreiter/. Im Sommer 1938 wurde ich mit meinem Aufklärungszug zur "Div.4 TM"/Gebirgsartillerie/ abkommandiert. Nach der Rückkehr machte ich noch die Ausbildung sämtlicher Züge der sogenannten Spezialitätenkompanie durch, u.zwar: Nachrichten, Granatwerfer und Pioniere. Nach den Herbstmanövern in den muntii apuseni/Siebenbürgisches Erzgebirge/ wurde ich im November 1938, nach Abdienung des Pflichtdienstjahres als sog."Einjährig-Freiwilliger",als Sergent TR/Einjähriger-Unteroffizier entlassen.

Im Rahmen der rumänischen Mobilmachung am 16.März 1939 einberufen, wurde ich, nach cca 2monatigem Einsatz bei der Grenzbewachung an der ungarischen Grenze, wieder entlassen. Am 6.September 1939 wurde ich wieder einberufen und auf die Offiziersschule nach Sf.Gheorghe geschickt. Ende Februar 1940 kam ich als "Plutonier elev"/Kadettfeldwebel/ nach Beendigung des Kurses zu meiner Einheit zurück und wurde sowohl bei dem aktiven Teil des Bataillons, beim Grenzschutz, als auch beim "PS"/Ersatzbat. als Ausbildner verwendet. Nach meiner Ernennung zum sublocotenent de rez. /Leutnant der Reserve/ wurde ich einer Marschkompanie zugeteilt(8.7.40).

Infolge des Wiener Schiedsspruches 1940 wurde meine Heimat Nordsiebenbürgen an Ungarn angeschlossen und ich wurde Anfang September 1940 aus dem Verbande des rumänischen Heeres entlassen.

Im Jahre 1941 wurde ich zum Wehrdienst in das ungarische Heer zum "M.kir. 26.honv.gyalogezred" /Kgl. ung. 26. Honved-Infanterieregiment/, stationiert mit seinen 3 Bataillonen in Bistritz, Des u. Klausenburg, nach Bistritz einberufen.- Die im rumänischen Heere erworbenen Dienstgrade wurden von den Ungarn nicht anerkannt, und ich mußte 1941 einen 5monatigen Offizierskurs in Des und Varpalota (Kriegsschule bei Veszprem) besuchen. Am 23.11.1941 wurde ich als "hdp.örmester"/Kadettfeldwebel/entlassen. Im Jahre 1942 habe ich cca 2 Monate Waffenübung zur Ausbildung am Granatwerfer Abgeleistet. Im Jahre 1943 wurde ich zum "tart.zaszlos" /Oberfähnrich der Reserve/ befördert und wurde wieder auf cca 2 Monate zur Waffenübung einberufen. Ungefähr im Juni 1944 wurde ich zum "26/II potzlj./26.Honved-Infanterieregiment, II.Ersatzbataillon/ nach Des einberufen. Im August 1944 wurde meine Einheit als Feldersatzeinheit feldmarschmäßig ausgerüstet und im August 1944, nach der Kapitulation Rumäniens an der Siebenbürgenfront eingesetzt. Meine Einheit, die ich damals befehligte, trug folgende Bezeichnung "26/II.tabori potzlj.nf.szd.av. szak. Die später üblichen Feldpostnummern, die auch wechselten, sind mir nicht mehr im Gedächtnis.

Ungefähr im Juli 1944 hatte ich von dem staatlichen Kreisnotariat der Gemeinde Mettersdorf-"körjegyzöseg Nagydemeter" auf Grund eines zwischenstaatlichen Abkommens(Ungarn-Deutschland) als Volksdeutscher eine Einberufung zur Musterung für den Eintritt in die Waffen-SS erhalten. Auf Grund einer Aussprache mit meinem Komandanten verblieb ich bei meiner Einheit im ungarischen Heere und stellte mich nicht zu dieser Musterung.

Nach einem Vormarsch im September 1944 in Rumänien folgten lange Rückzugskämpfe quer durch Siebenbürgen. Erwähnendswert erscheint mir noch, daß der letzte Volksdeutsche Angehörige,meiner Einheit, außer mir, Herr Ernst Otto Penteker, der in meinem Zuge diente, im September 1944 schwer verwundet wurde. Herr Penteker befand sich 1950 in der Lungenheilstätte

Kutzenberg bei Ebensfeld in Bayern.

Auf Grund meiner Sprachkenntnisse wurde ich Anfang November 1944 von der Front zu einem Ausbildungskurs an deutschen Waffen, mit denen unsere Einheit ausgestattet wurde, nach Westungarn zum Feldersatzregiment der SS-Kavalleriedivision Florian Geyer geschickt. Die Abkommandierten wurden verwaltungsmäßig (Verpflegung, Sold usw.) von dieser Einheit geführt, weil wir infolge der ständigen Rückzugskämpfe der eigenen Einheiten keinen Kontakt mit ihnen halten konnten. Durch den Einbruch der Russen bei Budapest wurde die Ausbildung abgebrochen und ich wurde zum Einsatz nach Budapest in Marsch gesetzt. Hier erkrankte ich an Gelbsucht und wurde Ende November in das Feldlazarett nach Tatabanya zurückgeführt und nach dessen Räumung und einem schweren Rückfall meiner Krankheit nach Baden bei Wien weitergeschafft.

In den letzten Wochen vor dem Zusammenbruch wurde ich aus dem Lazarett entlassen und auf einen Truppenübungsplatz in Böhmen (CSR) weitergeleitet, von wo ich zu meiner Einheit finden sollte. Diese war nicht aufzufinden und es wurde mir erklärt, ich müsse auf Grund eines zwischenstaatlichen Abkommens zwischen Ungarn und Deutschland als Volksdeutscher in der Waffen-SS dienen. Ich forderte meine Einstufung in den Offiziersrang, dadurch wurde mein Einsatz bis zum Zusammenbruch hinausgeschoben, weil auf Grund eines Befehles des Führungshauptamtes kein Volksdeutscher Offizier ohne vorherige Einstufung in den alten Rang eingesetzt und verwendet werden durfte. Infolge der Kriegsereignisse und des Zusammenbruches traf die Einstufung, die nur das Führungshauptamt vornehmen durfte, nie ein.

Nach dem Zusammenbruch wurden alle in Rumänien Beheimateten von den sowjetischen Truppen gesammelt und nach langwierigen Aufenthalten und einem ein Monat währenden Transport aus Budweiß (CSR) nach Focsani (Rumänien) überführt, von wo ich Anfangs September 1945 in meine Heimatstadt Bistritz entlassen wurde.

Im Juli des Jahres 1946 mußte ich mich bei der alljährlichen Meldung der Reserveoffiziere beim Cercul teritorial Nasaud meldem; ich wurde hier wiederum als sublocot.rez./rumänischer Leutnant der Reserve/ geführt, nachdem mein Fall als heimgekehrter Kriegsgefangener von einer Kommission überprüft worden war und ich den rumänischen Entlassungsschein ausgehändigt erhalten hatte.

Am militärischen Akten aus der Zeit vor dem 8.Mai 1945 besitze ich nur einige Schriftstücke, die sich zufällig bei meinen privaten Dokumenten zu Hause befanden, und die meine Frau bei ihrer Flucht 1944 mit denen mitnahm. Es sind dies folgende: 2 "Leszerelesi jegy" /Entlassungsscheine des ungarischen Heeres/ vom 23.XI.1941 und 29.Sept.1942, sowie eine Zuschrift meiner Einheit, "M.kir.26.Honved gyalogezred III.zlj.parancsnoksag" vom 20. November 1943.-Außerdem besitze ich den russischen Entlassungsschein vom 28.Aug.1945 und die rumänische "dovada de viza" /eine Bescheinigung über die alljährlixhe Meldung der rumänischen Reserveoffiziere/ vom 3.Juli 1946. und zwei "Foaie de drum" über militärische Dienstreisen aus dem Monat April 1946. Die militärischen Dokumente aus der Zeit vor dem 8.Mai 1945 mußte ich bei der rumänischen Kommission zur Überprüfung heimgekehrter Kriegsgefangener abgeben, die sie behielt und dem Dosar meiner militärischen Akten im rumänischen Heere beilegte.

Gustav Maroscher

/Gustav Maroscher/

Die Richtigkeit obiger Unterschrift bescheinigt:

Ohrenbach, den 11. November 1951

....

Why Can't Somebody Just Die Around Here?

Statutory Declaration

I, Gustav Günter Maroscher, born on 11/10/17 in Budacul de jos (Deutsch Budak), hereby confirm the following under penalty of perjury:

In October of 1937, I was drafted and served in the /Bat.8 VM/Gebirgsjäger-Bataillon/ (Eighth Mountain Troop Battalion) headquartered in Bistritz, Romania. I belonged to this unit for the entire time I was with the Romanian military. After basic training in the /compania de specialitati-ploton de recunoastere/Spezialitätenkompanie-Aufklärungszug/ (special reconnaisance company) I was assigned to the ski patrol of the battalion. This unit was trained during the winter of 1937/38 in Dorna-Vatra in the Carpathian Mountains. In spring we underwent special mountain training in the /Suhard/Karpathen/ (Carpathian Mountains). On 1/1/1938 I became a /fruntas/Gefreiter/ (lance lorporal). In the summer of 1938, I was directed to join the /Div4 TM/Gebirgsartillerie/ (mountain artillery) together with my reconnaissance platoon. After my return, I underwent training in various platoons of the special company. I was trained in intelligence, grenade launcher, and sapper. After the autumn military maneuvers in the /munyii apudeni/Siebenbürgisches Erzgebirge/ (Transylvanian Erz Mountains) and after I had completed my mandatory year of service as a so-called "one-year volunteer," I was released as a sergeant TR/Einjähriger-Unteroffizier/ (one-year sergeant) in November of 1938.

As part of the Romanian mobilization I was called up on March 16, 1939. After about two months duty guarding the Hungarian border I was discharged again. On September 6th 1939, I was called up again and sent to the Officer Candidates School in Sf. Gheorghe. After I had completed the course, at the end of February 1940, I returned to my unit as a /Plutonier elev /Kadettfeldwebel/ (beginning sergeant). I was then an instructor in both the active part of the battalion guarding the border as well as the / PS/Ersatzbataillon/ (reserve battalion). After being appointed to lieutenant of the reserve I was assigned to an infantry battalion (July 8, 1940).

As a result of the Second Vienna Award in 1940, my native North Transylvania was annexed to Hungary and I was discharged from the Romanian military in the beginning of September 1940.

In 1941, I was drafted into the Hungarian military and assigned to /Kgl. ung. 26 Honved-Infanterieregiment/ Kgl. ung. 26 Honved-Infanterieregiment/ (infantry regiment), which had its 3 battalions stationed in Bistritz, Des and Klausenburg. The rank I had been awarded in the Romanian military was not recognized by Hungary so in 1941 I had to complete a 5-month Officer's course at the Des and Varpalota (military college in Veszprem). On 11/23/1941, I was released as a /hdp. Örmester/Kadettfeldwebel/ (beginning sergeant). In 1942, I completed about 2 months of weapons training with the grenade launcher. In 1943, I was promoted to a /tart. Zaszlos/Oberfähnrich der Reserve/ (acting lieutenant in the reserve prior to commissioning) and was called up for another 2 months of weapons training. In about June 1944, I was ordered to go to Des to serve in the /26/II potzlj./26. Honved-Infanterieregiment/II Ersatzbataillon/ (II replacement infantry battalion). In August 1944, my unit was equipped for movement to the front as a field replacement unit. And in August 1944, after Romania had capitulated, we were deployed to the Transylvanian front. My unit, which I commanded at the time, had the following name: "26/II.tabori potzlj.nf.szd.av.szak." After that time I do not recall the commonly used military field addresses, which also changed.

In approximately July 1944, I—as an ethnic German—received a letter ordering me to report for a medical examination because I was being drafted into the Waffen-SS. The letter was from the district's notary public of the municipality Mettersdorf (*körjegyzöser Nagydemeter*). The draft notice was sent pursuant to the international treaty (Hungary–Germany). After talking to my commander, I stayed with my unit in the Hungarian military and did not report for the physical exam.

We gained ground in Romania in September of 1944, but this was followed by long retrograde operations straight through Transylvania. It seems noteworthy to me that the last Volksdeutscher (ethnic German) of my unit, except for myself, Mr. Ernst Otto Penteker, who served in my platoon, was severely injured in September 1944. In 1950, Mr. Penteker was staying at the sanatorium for lung patients in

[Page 2]

Kutzenberg near Ebensfeld in Bavaria.

Because of my language skills, I was sent from the front to a training course about German weapons, with which our unit had been equipped; so at the beginning of November 1944, I went to the Field Replacement Division of the SS Cavalry Division Florian Geyer in western Hungary. Individuals assigned to the division were administratively taken care of by this unit (rations, pay etc.) because we were not able to have contact with our own units due to the ongoing retrograde operations. When the Russians breached the front lines at Budapest, my training was abandoned and I was sent to Budapest. This is when I contracted hepatitis and was taken back to the field hospital in Tatabanya in late November. After the evacuation of the field hospital, I was moved to Baden bei Wien (Baden at Vienna) because I had had a severe relapse.

In the last weeks before the collapse of all military resistance, I was released from the hospital and redirected to a troop training area in Bohemia (Czechoslovakia) so I would be able to find my unit. My unit could not be located and I was informed that, as a Volksdeutscher (ethnic German), I would be required to serve in the Waffen-SS because of an intergovernmental treaty between Hungary and Germany. I requested my officer rank, which postponed my deployment until the collapse of all military resistance at the end of the war. This occurred because the Army Leadership Main Office (in Berlin) had issued an order that no ethnic German officer was to be deployed and used until his appointment to officer had been approved by the Army Leadership Main Office. As a result of the war and collapse at the end, I never received the order promoting me to officer from the Leadership Main Office, which was the sole entity authorized to make this decision.

After the collapse, all residents of Romania were gathered by the Soviet troops and—after lengthy delays and a month-long journey—taken from Budweis (Czechoslovakia) to Focsani (Romania), from where I was released to my hometown Bistritz in early September.

In July of 1946, I had to report to the Cercul Teritorial Năsăud for the annual check of all reserve officers; they then put me down again as a sublocot.rez./Romanian Leutnant der Reserve/ (lieutenant of the reserve) after my case as a returned prisoner of war had been examined by a committee and I had received the Romanian discharge papers.

I have only a few military documents from before May 8th 1945, which I just happened to keep with my private papers which my wife took with her when she fled in 1944. They are the following: 2 "Leserelesi jegy" /discharge papers from the Hungarian military/ dated Nov. 23, 1941 and Sept. 29, 1942, as well as a letter from my unit, "M.Kir.26.Honved gyalogezred III.zlj.parancsnoksag" dated November 20, 1943. I also have the Russian discharge papers dated Aug. 28 1945 and the Romanian "dovada de viza" / a confirmation regarding my annual reporting of Romanian reserve officers/ dated July 3, 1946 and two "Foaie de drum" regarding military duty trips from the month of April 1946. I had to hand all military documents prior to 8 May 1945 over to the Romanian commission for the screening of returned prisoners of war, which then kept the papers and added them to my Romanian military files.

[Signature]
/Gustav Maroscher/

The authenticity of the above signature was confirmed:
Ohrenbach, 11 November 1951

[Seal] [Signature]

Note: The *Foaie de drum* (military travel ticket that can be used for multiple trips) from April 1946 referred to in the translation is still among the documents kept by Gustav and Helene.

13 Dad with students in Transylvania (part of Romania). Both boys and girls are wearing *Tracht,* the traditional Transylvanian Saxon costume. Four of the girls are each wearing a black cylinder hat (*Zylinderhut*), which indicates that she is not married. The girls without a Zylinderhut are younger and have not yet been confirmed in the Lutheran Church. The cylinder hats are hard to see. I suppose they did not anticipate the lighting requirements for the picture to print well in this book. Married women wore a scarf with their Tracht clothing. Dad is shown in the center.

Dad with a class of younger students in Transylvania. They are wearing the Transylvanian Tracht for young children. Dad is in center of picture.

14 Hospital train evacuation approval. Mom kept the document giving us permission to travel to Germany on the hospital train as a three-by-five-inch carbon copy (made by typewriter with carbon paper). A translation of the document is below.

Local military hospital
Geb.-san.- Company 1/8 O.U. September 1944

Approval.

Mrs. Helene Maroscher and two children

with Mrs. Käthe Maroscher

to travel with the train for the wounded from the local military hospital of the Geb. – San. Company 1/8 (Evacuation per order of the army doctor 8). It is requested to support these ethnic Germans in each and every case to enable their further travel into Germany.

Headquarters doctor
and company chief
of Staff

Note: *O.U.* is a code word used in written communication to hide the location of military units. It is short for *Ortsunterkunft,* which means "cantonment" (temporary billets for troops).

15 Herzogenburg refugee camp departure certificate. The document was used as a certificate of registration and permission for departure from the camp, which was located in the district of St. Pölten, Austria. The title of the document, *Fl-Abreisebescheinigung,* means "Departure Certificate." The actual document is a three-page booklet. Mom's intention was to travel to her sister in Weimar, Germany, as soon as possible. The location of where we came from is given as "Bistritz/Ungarn" (Bistritz, Hungary). After the war, Northern Transylvania, where Bistritz was located, returned to Romania. The last date stamp on the document is February 6, 1944. On or shortly after that date, Mom traveled with my brother and me to her sister's house in Weimar, Germany. Note the stampings with the eagle and swastika. The refugee camp was run by the Nazi regime.

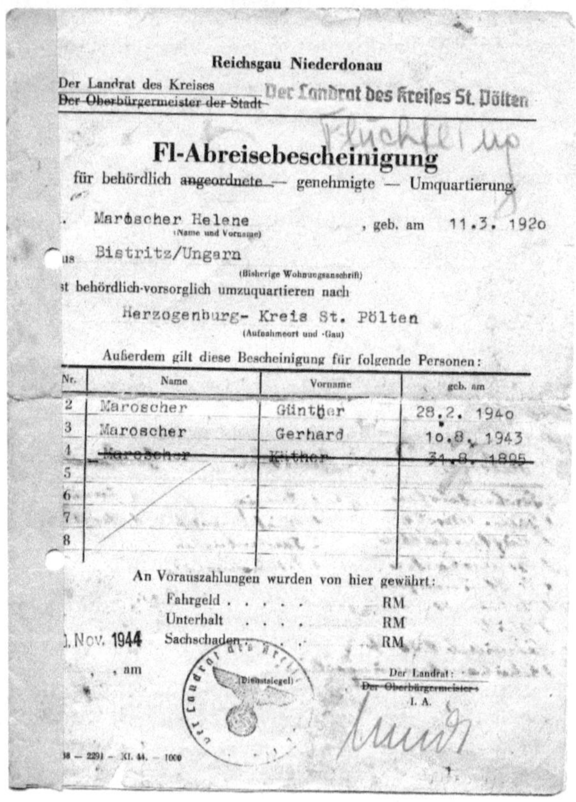

Reichsgau Niederdonau

Der Landrat des Kreises
~~Der Oberbürgermeister der Stadt~~ Der Landrat des Kreises St. Pölten

Flüchtling

Fl-Abreisebescheinigung

für behördlich ~~angeordnete~~ — genehmigte — Umquartierung

Marøscher Helene (Name und Vorname), geb. am 11.3. 1920

aus Bistritz/Ungarn (Bisherige Wohnungsanschrift)

ist behördlich-vorsorglich umzuquartieren nach

Herzogenburg- Kreis St. Pölten (Aufnahmeort und -Gau)

Außerdem gilt diese Bescheinigung für folgende Personen:

Nr.	Name	Vorname	geb. am
2	Maroscher	Günther	28.2. 1940
3	Maroscher	Gerhard	10.8. 1943
4	~~Maroscher~~	~~Käther~~	~~31.8. 1895~~
5			
6			
7			
8			

An Vorauszahlungen wurden von hier gewährt:

Fahrgeld . . . . . RM
Unterhalt . . . . RM
Sachschaden . . . RM

].Nov. 1944
, am

(Dienstsiegel)

Der Landrat:
~~Der Oberbürgermeister~~
I. A.

38 — 2291 — XI. 44. — 1000

First page of Departure Certificate. The earliest date on the document is November 10, 1944 (*lower left*). The "10" in front of "Nov. 1944" can be seen clearly with backlighting when viewing the actual document. *Flüchtling,* the handwritten word in red (*top right*), means "refugee."

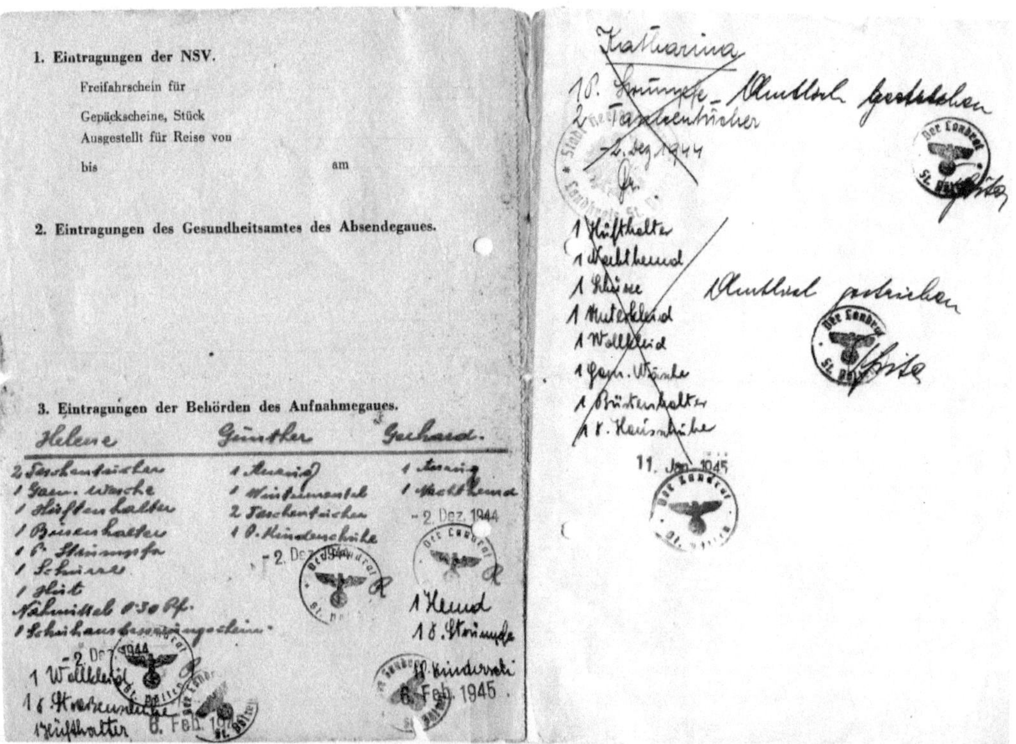

1. Eintragungen der NSV.
Freifahrschein für
Gepäckscheine, Stück
Ausgestellt für Reise von
bis am

2. Eintragungen des Gesundheitsamtes des Absendegaues.

3. Eintragungen der Behörden des Aufnahmegaues.
Helene Günther Gerhard

- 2. Dez. 1944

6. Feb. 1945

Katharina

11. Jan. 1945

Third and fourth page of Departure Certificate. Item three (*left page*) reads, "Eintragungen der Behörden des Aufnahmegaues" (Entries by the district administration). Listed are clothing items in our possession. The name and belongings of Katharina Maroscher (*right page*) are crossed out. She left the refugee camp for Cologne, Germany, before Mom, my brother, and I were able to leave for Mom's sister's house in Weimar, Germany.

16 Russian military government residency permit. The permit is for the Hungarian citizen Helene Maroscher and her two children, Günter and Gerhard, to reside in Weimer, which was then in Communist East Germany. At the time, our address was Rosa-Luxemburg Siedlung 1/6 in Weimar. The Russian military government used the American residency permit until it issued its own permit on October 3, 1945, and notarized it on October 5, 1945. The top half of the document is in German, and the bottom half is in Russian.

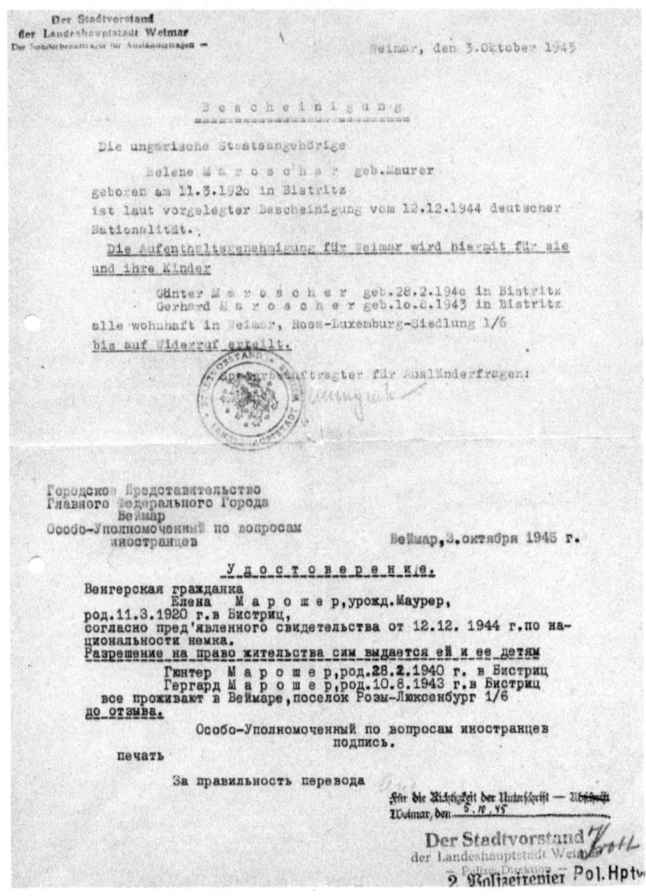

Der Stadtvorstand
der Landeshauptstadt Weimar
Der Sonderbeauftragte für Ausländerfragen –

Weimar, den 3.Oktober 1945

Bescheinigung

Die ungarische Staatsangehörige

Helene Maroscher geb.Maurer
geboren am 11.3.1920 in Bistritz
ist laut vorgelegter Bescheinigung vom 12.12.1944 deutscher Nationalität.

Die Aufenthaltsgenehmigung für Weimar wird hiermit für sie und ihre Kinder

Günter Maroscher geb.28.2.1940 in Bistritz
Gerhard Maroscher geb.10.8.1943 in Bistritz

alle wohnhaft in Weimar, Rosa-Luxemburg-Siedlung 1/6
bis auf Widerruf erteilt.

Sonderbeauftragter für Ausländerfragen:

Городское Представительство
Главного Федерального Города
Веймар
Особо-Уполномоченный по вопросам
иностранцев

Веймар,3.октября 1945 г.

Удостоверение.

Венгерская гражданка
Елена Марошер,урожд.Маурер,
род.11.3.1920 г.в Бистриц,
согласно пред'явленного свидетельства от 12.12. 1944 г.по национальности немка.
Разрешение на право жительства сим выдается ей и ее детям
Гюнтер Марошер,род.28.2.1940 г. в Бистриц
Гергард Марошер,род.10.8.1943 г.в Бистриц
все проживают в Веймаре,поселок Розы-Люксенбург 1/6
до отзыва.

Особо-Уполномоченный по вопросам иностранцев
подпись.

печать

За правильность перевода

Für die Richtigkeit der Unterschrift — Abschrift
Weimar, den 5.10.45

Der Stadtvorstand
der Landeshauptstadt Weimar
— Polizei-Direktion —
2. Polizeirevier Pol.Hptw

17 Dad's letter to Mom, dated August 8, 1944. The English translation follows.

My dearest!

I am writing in a huge rush. That is how it always is in the military, including now. Our departure *(to the front)* is temporarily postponed for 10 days. They are "forcing" us by all necessary means to stay here and not rush to the front. And that is supposed to "offend" us. Who knows what this was good for? What date did Mr. Prediger last write and from where? Hopefully he made it; otherwise it would be horrible for Mrs. Prediger.

Otherwise it's business as usual, we have lots of work to do. Hopefully I can leave again on Saturday. In any case I will telephone you so that you can come to Bistritz and we can go to the movies. Or if I leave in the evening, we can rent a car *(it might mean "wagon")* for Sunday at noon. In that case I will reserve a bus ticket and return on Monday.

Please write right away. My new address is on the envelope.

Kissing you, your

Daddy

It is awful when one writes in such a hurry. When one is always interrupted, one can hardly write anything that is loving. But I want to drop off the letter now so that you will receive it in a timely manner.

You sweet thing!!!!

I talked with my commander. I will definitely be able to come. I expect to arrive in Bistritz before 4:00 p.m. So that we don't pass each other in buses, please ask Mr. Nofär to communicate with Foto Sport that you will be there if you can only get a seat on the one at 3:30. I will then go in and determine if you are there. If not, I will take the bus to you *(to Mettersdorf; it is likely that Dad was arranging for a family picture. This is probably the family picture of the four of us together in Bistritz. That was the last picture of us together until pictures taken in Ohrenbach, West Germany, around 1950.)*

Kissing you, your

Gusti

Looking forward to being reunited soon. Hopefully you will get the letter in a timely manner.

18 Dad's letter to Mom, dated August 26, 1944. The English translation follows.

My dearest!

We are ready to decamp. If it is true, it will be quite a while till we are deployed to the front.

I'm lonely and thinking of you! I'm thinking about the time when we got to know each other. We have had so many happy hours together since then. But how much hardship have we undergone, especially you. And now you are alone again.

I am so happy that I have you! You and our dear children give meaning and purpose to my life. You and the kids mean everything to me. Considering this, my going to the front makes sense, to stand firm out there, so that you all can be home, living in peace with bread to eat.

How short is such a farewell. One has so much to say and yet finds no words to say it.

[Page 2]

But words are not needed in such moments, because the heart speaks. One is united in thoughts and feelings. Each one reads the other's soul, and our souls are one.

In my heart I am still thinking about our farewell, yet at the same time it also feels like a reunion, as if you were really with me. I can see you in my mind's eye as if you were here with me and then I feel how you are thinking about me and how you love me.

My sweetie! Someday the time will come when we can be happy again and untroubled. When we will always be together!! And live our lives only for each other and our children. My dear!!

[Page 3]

Don't wait by the telephone, because for the foreseeable future I will not be able to call. *(Note: there was one phone in Mettersdorf—at the post office.)* I must have left my pocketknife at home; just today I bought a Knödelwürger. (*Knödelwürger literally means a "dumpling slayer" and refers to a type of knife that was traditionally used for eating dumplings.)*

Now life in the field is beginning and it's pretty much like it was in 1939 and 1940. It will be hard at first. Then one gets used to it. This too shall pass.

My dearest! Please write often! And take good care of yourself! I am so worried about you! Don't work too hard, because in this situation one must take care of oneself.

It is evening again. Think of me! Dearest!!!

Kissing you

Your Gusti

Your daddy!!! My sweetie! When I come home on leave !

[Page 4]

Since I do not know our new address, please write me at the old address: 26 II. Aábon potzlj

Zlj.

Jf. Szd.

Dés

(The letter continues, written in a different-color ink, dated August 28, 1944.)

We went on maneuvers yesterday. That meant sweat and dust, but had a good bath and a great meal from the field kitchen. Today we are out again, then a bath and duty station. It is starting. The seriousness of the situation does weigh on one's soul. This uncertainty and anxiousness, one should rather not continue to think about it.

I believe that our Lord will lead us through this also.

We've been married now for more than five years. I think we love each other even more than before. My dearest! If only the time would come when we are together again. Until then we will just have to bear the weight of our fate.

Please take care of yourself.

Kissing you, your Gusti

My sweetie!!!!

19 Dad's letter to Mom, dated August 11, 1944. Mom did not keep the envelopes for many of the letters she saved. This letter had an envelope, so we know the address to which it was sent. The letter was sent to Lene Maroscher in Nagydemeter (Mettersdorf). The address was written in Hungarian since Northern Transylvania had become part of Hungary in 1940. The translation follows.

My dearest!

I received both of your dear letters and the solemn invitation to muster. I submitted the latter of the two to my commander and am waiting on a decision by "higher authority."

(This was an order to report to Bistritz to be drafted into the Waffen-SS. Based on an agreement between Germany and Hungary, all ethnic German men living in Hungary were required to serve in the Waffen-SS. Since a prior agreement between Germany and Hungary had ceded the northern part of Transylvania to Hungary, this order included my dad. This order to muster had the force of law behind it.)

First question, did you receive some Pengö from Klausenburg? I need some money now, since here in the boondocks we have to pay for our own room and board. (So one is better off "economically" when one is on the front. But I think we can both gladly accept this reduction in net income.)

Sweetie! Yesterday our Gerhard was one year old. How worried I was about you one year ago. *(Not long before my birth, Dad had had a serious motorcycle accident that resulted in a depressed skull fracture. I'd say Mom had lots to worry about when I was born.)* You poor thing, you had to endure so much.

[Page 2]

Hopefully we will be spared now; it would be terrible for you! Because things are really getting serious. I'm writing you this letter because I am not sure I will be able to come home. It feels as if I am conversing with you, speaking with you.

I'm considering bringing you and our children here, because it is not at all certain when we will depart. I would just have to find an appropriate place to live. Lunch we would eat from the officer's mess. It is not too expensive. Hopefully it will work out. You could come by bus.

[Page 3]

I will write you with details if it works out. But *(illegible—maybe the name of a babysitter)* would need to come too so that you can have some free time. I am on duty from 6:30 a.m. to 11:00 a.m. and from 2:00 p.m. to 6:00 p.m. However, there are some duty-free afternoons too. So why don't you think about it!

Kissing you

Your Gusti

My little one!

Saturday!!!

If it works out, then??

(The letter continues with a few lines written on August 12, 1944.)

This time we had bad luck. I was so looking forward to being with you on Sunday, now our plans are dashed! Such a shame. It would have been so nice!!! But if my commander keeps his word, I can come to you sometime during the next week. The next thing on the agenda is to go on a duty-related trip.

20 Affidavit by Ernst Penteker swearing that Dad's draft notice for the Waffen-SS was torn up. In a sworn statement from 1951, Herr Penteker verifies and provides details of Dad's avoiding the Waffen-SS draft. The affidavit was important for our family to immigrate to the United States. US immigration authorities investigated potential immigrants to weed out war criminals and other undesirables. We immigrated to the United States in 1952. The translation follows.

Copy

Statutory Declaration.

I, Ernst Otto Penteker, born on 11/25/12, currently residing at the sanatorium Wöllersdorf, hereby confirm upon request that I knew Mr. Gustav G. Maroscher, born on 11/10/17, resident of Ohrenbach, back in our homeland. We were classmates at the seminary and later worked for the same school district.

From the summer of 1944 until I was wounded, Mr. Maroscher was my platoon commander as a Fähnrich and I was his noncommissioned officer in the heavy weapons company of the second battalion of the 26th Hungarian Honvéd-Infanterieregiment. As a result of the treaty between the German and Hungarian governments of the time, Mr. Maroscher, an ethnic German, was obligated to undergo the physical examination for the Waffen-SS. I remember quite well that he did not follow similar instructions even though he had the opportunity to do so. He also talked to me about this and said something along the lines of not feeling like becoming an SS recruit after having undergone the Romanian and Hungarian basic training. He had also expressed these thoughts when talking to the commander, whose adjutant had then torn the request in half.

On 19 Sept. 1944, I was injured near Torda and Mr. Maroscher remained with the 26th Honvéd regiment as the only Volksdeutscher (ethnic German). In mid-October he sent me a Hungarian military postcard to the military hospital in Komorn telling me about the ongoing retrograde operations and that my appointment to Feldwebel had appeared in the order from the regiment.

Wöllershof, on 12 November 1951 Signed by Ernst Otto Penteker

(13a) Dinkelsbühl, Muckenbrünnlein 21
Currently residing at the sanatorium
Wöllershof
Postal service Neustadt/Waldnaab

The authenticity of the signature is hereby confirmed.
Township Lanz (Seal)
Lanz, on 11/14/1951
The Municipal Council
Signed on behalf of *(illegible)*
The correct nature of the above copy is certified by:
Munich, 11/20/51

[Seal] [Signature: Dr. Bruckner]

21 Affidavit by ethnic Romanians swearing that Dad was threatened by Nazis. The affidavit below was signed June 3, 1946, a time when Dad was trying to restart his life in Communist Romania after the war. The affirmation was given by six ethnic Romanians (not Saxon Romanians). These six Romanian friends and acquaintances of Dad's were good people and were willing to testify to the truth at a time when the Romanian Communist government was actively discriminating against and arresting Saxons. Lieutenant Jacon, an ethnic Romanian police chief, signed the document. The affidavit

Abschrift

Legiunea Jand. Nasaud
Postul Jand. Dumitra

A d e v e r i n t a

Se adevereste de noi ca Dl Maroser Gustav, de origina etnica germana, fost invatator in Comuna Dumitra Judetul Nasaud, nascut in Budacul de jos Jud. Nasaud, a fost urmarit si chiar amenintat cu moartea de catre membrii S.S.-ului german si ai partidului Hitlerist din Comuna Dumitra, din pricina ca nu facea parte din armata germana S.S. Deasemenea tot pe aceasta tema si familia Dsale a avut de suferit din partea acestor membrii amintiti mai sus.-

Acestea s'au petrecut in timpul ocupatiei maghiare in Ardealul de Nord.

Cele de mai sus, sunt adeverite si de Dnii Reduic Joan, actualul director al scoalei primare din Dumitra, Ilovan Alexandru, Ciont Toma, Plaian Mihai, Unchi Mihai si Chifa Catarina, toti din comuna Dumitra, care au dat declaratii la post in sensul celor aratate mai sus.

Pentru care i-am eliberat presenta.
Seful postului — 3 Junie 1946

Plut. Jacon

Die Richtigkeit obiger Abschrift bescheinigt:
München, den 20.11.51
Dr. Bruckner

was important in Dad's case to US immigration officials that he tried to avoid serving in the Waffen-SS. The notarized Romanian document was translated into German by Diethard Knopp. The English translation of the German transcript follows.

Transcript

Police Legion District Nassod
Police-Station Mettersdorf (Dumitra)

Affirmation

It is affirmed that Mr. Gustav Maroscher, of German ancestry and former teacher in the municipality of Mettersdorf, who was born in Deutsch-Budak, District of Nassod, was pursued by members of the German Waffen-SS and the Nazi-Party representatives from Mettersdorf. He was even threatened with death, because he did not belong to the German Waffen-SS. Even his family suffered from the above named parties.

This occurred during the Hungarian occupation of North Transylvania.

The above portrayed situation is testified to by Mr. Ioan Rednic, who was at the time the principal of the Mettersdorf elementary school, as well as by Alexandru Ilovan, Toma Ciont, Mihai Plaian, Mihai Unchi, and Catarina Chifa, all of whom reside in Mettersdorf. We submitted the above at our police station.

Therefore we have submitted the above affirmation.

Chief of the police station June 3, 1946
Sergeant Jacon

The accuracy of the above transcription is attested to and signed by Dr. Wilhelm Bruckner on November 20, 1951.

Seal: Aid committee of the Transylvanian Saxon and Schwaben from Banat aid-organization of the Evangelical Church in Germany, Headquarters Munich.

22 Dad's letter to Mom, dated January 26, 1946. Thanks to the tiny slip of paper smuggled to Romania in a cigarette, Dad had just learned that his family had survived. Dad immediately wrote the letter below to Mom at her address in Weimar, Germany. It was the first letter she had received from Dad since September 1, 1944.

Dad was living in his mother's house in Romania, having been released from Russian captivity. Written below the date in the upper right is Mom's writing indicating the date she received the letter, February 28, 1946. The English translation follows.

1/26/46

received Feb.28

Günter's birthday

My dearest!

Finally I can write a few lines. You are surely worrying about me as I worry about you and the kids.

I arrived here in good health after being released from a Russian POW camp. *("Here" refers to his mom's property in Bistritz, where his paternal grandmother, Therese Maroscher, was living. Dad was not in good health. He had been released because he was near death from dysentery and the aftereffects of hepatitis. Grussi was one of the nicknames of his grandmother.)* Grussi's funeral was on November 23, 1945. Edda was also at the funeral. She rented a room for herself, her children, and her father. They are healthy. I received your dear letter to Grussi, at least it was a sign that you are alive. But now it is six months since you mailed it.

My dearest! I have such a longing for you and I am so worried about you!

Regarding the trip afterward, look into what they are doing in Oberdonau. Do what they are doing. *(This may refer to a possible return trip by Mom and us kids to Romania. All borders were closed at the time and nobody traveled anywhere without proper government travel documents.)* Tilde and the kids are also in the country! They are doing well. Julius also visited me. You should sell the things you still have and buy food. Sell the goat too! We will manage things again in the future. The main thing is that you and the kids stay healthy.

Bruno and Minchen received my mother's letter and also wrote me. Rudi, Erna and Bubi are alive; he is however still a POW, but he did write.

Kissing you all

Your daddy

Heartfelt greetings to all!

Greetings from Mrs. Marx.

23 Dad's letter to Mom, dated May 11, 1946. He wrote this one-page letter right after he received his first letter from Mom since 1944. The envelope indicates that the letter was mailed on May 14, 1946 from Bistritz and was addressed to Lene Maroscher, 15, Weimar, Rosa Luxemburg, Gartenstadt 1/6, Germania, Russische Zone

(Russian Zone). The translation follows.

My dearest!

I received your dear letter of March 19, 1946. Finally after 1½ years a letter, yet only a letter, since we cannot be together! God grant that we will be together again. Everything is easier to bear together. Otherwise everything is as you have written, waiting and more waiting. You poor thing. I cannot support and help you during this hard time. I am now moving to be the administrator of a small property in the boondocks. It does not pay well, but at least it is a job. But please write to my old address because Mrs. Marx will be forwarding my mail. I wrote to Franzi to see if it is possible for you to move there, but that does not seem feasible. *(Franzi, Mom's oldest brother, was living in Austria, which was under American control.)*

Some of our dear relatives in Austria are sending letters with such naïve questions about property and estates. It is as if they are living on the moon. *(Dad was living in Communist Romania. The Communist philosophy involved no personal ownership of property and required the redistribution of wealth as a way to make everyone equal. This philosophy later resulted in the government confiscating Dad's small property, making him homeless, and giving his property to someone with a greater need—in the eyes of the government.)*

Regarding such questions you should turn to Franzi. He seems to be in touch with reality. Edda, Tilde, etc. are doing well. Hopefully they can be on their own, and then it will be significantly easier. *(Dad was helping support these relatives. Tilde might have been the wife of Josef, one of Mom's brothers).*

I am always thinking of you. My longing for you and my worry about you are accompanying you! Day and night, in my dreams, and when I am awake, I am with you!

Kissing you, Günter, and Gerhard,
Your daddy

Give everyone my warm greetings! They should not have hurt feelings that I don't always mention them individually—Mom, Dad etc.

24 Dad's letter to Mom, dated May 22, 1946. The letter was postmarked in Bistritz on May 24, 1946, and sent to Lene Maroscher, 15 Weimar, R.L. Siedlung Str. 1/6, Germania Russische Zone (Russian Zone). The translation follows.

My dear!

In the course of a week I received nine precious letters and postcards from you. You cannot imagine my joy, but also my worry about you. I've already written you several times; hopefully at least one letter will arrive. *(The political situation must have settled down after the war, allowing the mail, at least between fellow Communist countries, to flow more freely.)* I can endure everything, but worrying about you gives me many sad and bitter hours. Not to be able to help you . . . But God willing this separation will also end. Just so you and our boys stay healthy, everything else we will be able to manage. Therefore, please, please take care of yourself! Even if you have to sell all the clothes and other things, everything except for your health I can work for and obtain again. *(Actually, we had almost nothing in Weimar—not much to sell in order to buy food.)* Please dear, fulfill this one wish of mine! I am so anxious about you. Without you, life just has no meaning for me! And we really need to stay alive so we can raise our dear little innocent children. And if the time ever comes, I force myself not to think about it, yet my one and only hope and my most beautiful dream is that we are together again!!! Then you will be with me, to be protected by me and taken care of by me and you will then be able to forget all tribulation and worry. After so many ordeals and tests, God must grant us this happiness. My dear little one! You are writing that you are aging. With me, too, fighting on the front and being a POW did not pass by without leaving its marks. But I believe with certainty if we are together again—yes, if and when! Sometimes I could bang my head against the walls when I think about the happiness, were we together! And what remains are lonely hours, closing the eyes, and dreaming, dreaming of happiness, my happiness: of you! Even now, as I write this letter I am dreaming of you. I want it! Because it is the only fulfillment of my yearning. I want to fill these lines

[Page 2]

with words of love so that you can sense how much I love you and how much

I long for you. But you know it. You know that you are my one and only, my everything! I just do not want to awaken from this dream. I want to forget my surroundings. I am at the point, if I had the money, I'd be drunk all the time and forget everything and just feel you, sense you. Why? My soul is screaming, why must this happiness bypass us? Is our cup still too full? Have we not drunk from it enough already and always to the last bitter drop! As there is a God on this earth, this suffering must end and we be together again. To be together again! How beautiful that sounds! Have you already thought about it? The hour of our reunion! Illusions? Nonsense! Certainly not, I believe in it! And then? I'm not going to dream anymore; otherwise the awakening will be too harsh, too bitter.

Kissing you fervently, and Günter and Gerhard
Your daddy

P.S. The Behreudischs wrote you about Gonsosch. I don't need to inform you!! Maybe something will come up to enable you and the boys to come here. Please stay in contact with Franzi regarding this. Should it be possible, travel to him. The food situation is good here, I'd be able to fatten you up in a short time, but there are still some difficulties here. *(Today we might say "regain strength" rather than "fatten up." In 1946 our diet in East Germany was a near-starvation diet.)* I quit my job as administrator of the small property on the first day. I'm looking for other work. I've cultivated Grussi's grounds and bought a milk delivery system, a goat, for 215,000 Lei. *(The lei was the Romanian dollar. Inflation was very high. Just before a revaluation of the lei on August 15, 1947, one US dollar equaled three million lei.)* I'm healthy and look good, although I look better in my birthday suit. My suit does not fit well anymore because of my captivity. Gusti (my mother's brother) is also in the country. Also Bruno etc. are healthy; Edda, Tilde, etc. too. Tilde is doing seamstress work. The sewing machine is waiting here for you. My black coat is still in excellent condition, so for the coming winter I have one thing less to worry about. Kifaneni was here, with no results! She greets you and the kids, also Mrs. Marx. My living as a bachelor is somewhat monotonous and unusual, but it will do.

Give my love to all

I'm also writing a letter today. Gusti is kissing her—tell my mother.

25 **Postcard dated May 31, 1946.** The translation follows a scan of both sides of the postcard.

ROMANIA

CARTE POSTALA

D. Numele și adresa trimițătorului Maroscher G.
Str. A. Mureșan 12
Comuna Bistrița
România

Doamnei
Helene Maroscher
R.L. Siedl. – K. Kautzky Str. 6
Weimar
Russische Zone
Germania

Pe această parte se scrie numai adresa

31.5.1946

Mein Liebstes!

Heute erhielt ich wieder 3 Briefe u. 3 Postkarten von Dir. Dass Du noch kein Schreiben von mir erhalten hast, ausser dem vom Januar?! Hoffe dass inzwischen doch welche eingetroffen sind. – Mein Liebstes Du! Ich habe solche Sehnsucht nach Dir!, nach euch! Trotzdem wäre eine Reise noch verfrüht, obwohl die Ernährungslage hier beinahe friedensmässig gut steht. – Ich gehe fleissig zum Mais hacken, bin bald fertig. – Sprach diese Tage telefonisch mit Ernst (Bukarest) eventuell besuche ich ihn demnächst. – Sonst ist hier alles beim Alten. – Es ist mir so gram, immer allein! Na und meine Kocherei kannst Du dir ja vorstellen. (Trotzdem würde sie Dir armes „Würmchen" gut anschlagen). Verlass Dich drauf, wenn Du wieder bei mir bist soll ich Dich auffüttern dass Du wie eine „Dulcinea" wirst! – Und zuletzt: doch wann?!

Es küsst Dich und unsere Jungen
euer Vaterchen

Today I received three letters and three postcards from you again. It is amazing that you have not received a letter from me, other than the one in January!! Hopefully in between some have arrived. My dearest you! I have such longing for you, and for the kids! But still, you traveling to here would be premature, although the food situation here is almost the same as in peacetime. *(Note: There was peace since the war ended in May 1945, but the situation in the new communist states was not in any way normal. Travel was greatly restricted, and people who were deemed not friends of the new regime were subject to arrest, being sent off to slave labor camps, being sent to concentration camps, and other harassment. The food situation was good in Romania where Dad was living, but not good in Communist East Germany where Mom, my brother and I were living.)* I am busily hoeing the corn, am almost done. Recently I talked by telephone with Ernst (Bucharest) and maybe I'll visit him soon. Otherwise everything is as usual. Everything seems so gray, always alone! Well, you can imagine my diet considering my culinary skills. (But it would still be good for you, you poor thing.) You can count on it, when you are with me again; I will fatten you up so you can be pleasantly rounded!....And lastly: When?!

Kissing you and our boys,
Your daddy

Last letter from you was May 3, 1946 *(This was written upside down on the top left of the card.)*

26 Dad's letter to Mom, dated June 23, 1946. Note the military censorship stamp in the top left. It is interesting that the letter passed through American or British censors on its way to Weimar in East Germany. The Communists also read all mail. They just did not bother to stamp it. The translation follows the two-page letter.

MILITARY CENSORSHIP 2736 CIVIL MAILS

23. Juni 1946

Mein Liebstes!

Endlich bin ich wieder zu Hause angekommen, für wie lange diesesmal weiss ich noch nicht. Ich habe verschiedene Reisen gemacht u. machen müssen, zuletzt war ich dann bei Bruno u. Erna, welche meine „Garderobe" aufgefrischt haben.

Es ist kein Leben so allein u. ferne von Dir, so im Ungewissen. Morgen sind es 7 Jahre seit wir verheiratet sind! Und — wir zehren an den schönen Stunden des Beisammenseins, wir zehren an der Erinnerung —— wie lange noch? Ich als Mann ertrag' es ja, obwohl es auch mir gibt grau ist dieses Leben, aber Du mein Ärmstes —— Vielleicht hat ja unser Herrgott ein Einsehen u. Erbarmen. Deinen lieben Brief vom 9.5.46 habe ich erhalten —, dass Du noch immer kein Schreiben von mir erhalten hast! Diesen Brief schicke ich über die Erna, vielleicht kommt er eher an. Um mich mache Dir keine Sorgen, ich habe wovon zu leben, habe auch für euch beiseitegestellt wenn ihr eintreffen solltet, und die anderen Schwierigkeiten mit denen werde ich schon fertig. Ich habe mich sogar für die Pfarramtsprüfung gemeldet, ich zweifle noch allerdings ob ich mich stellen kann (nicht wegen dem Lernen), aber vielleicht gelingt es doch; im September sollen die Prüfungen sein. — Trotz allem Elend würde ich doch einmal lächeln mit dem Gedanken an meine liebe kleine „frä Mätter"! —— Ich weiß nicht genau wie es mit Hedi steht aber hörte Bruno etwas erwähnen, jedenfalls kann der Gusti sich das leisten, da sie über eine gewisse Altersgrenze heraus ist. Mir wäre es jedenfalls lieber dich in Franzis Nähe zu wissen, obwohl ich so eine Sehnsucht nach Dir habe, aber auch ein wieder Beisammensein wäre dann leichter möglich. – Der Edda hatte ich 2 Kinderkleidchen u. Schuhe von der Schobel Hanni gebracht und jetzt ein paar Holzschuhe gemacht, daß sie was zum herumgehen hat. Na das sind so familiäre Sachen neben Größerem. Jedenfalls sind Reisen mit Gepäck schwierig, vor allem noch mit den Kindern.

Hoffentlich hast Du ja von mir inzwischen auch Post erhalten, damit Du nicht mehr im Ungewissen bist. Wieviel Liebes möchte ich Dir schreiben, aber auf dem Papier sind es kalte Worte. Vielleicht gibt Gott doch die Stunde des Wiedersehens, daß Du dann in meinen Armen all dieses Leid vergißt, daß ich mich dann um Dich, um euch sorgen kann.

Es küßt Dich u. den Günter u. Gerhard
euer Vaterchen

Grüße alle herzlich von mir
Gusti!

My dear!

Finally I arrived at home again. How long I will be able to stay this time, I don't know. I took several trips because I was required to. Recently I visited Bruno and Erna, who refurbished my wardrobe.

It is not a good life to be alone and so far from you, and with such uncertainty. Tomorrow it will be seven years since we were married! And we live off the beautiful hours of being together; we live off the memory . . . how much longer? As a man, I'm tolerating it, although now this life seems gloomy, but you, my poor thing . . . Maybe our Lord realizes and will have mercy. I received your dear letter of May 9, 1946 . . . that you still have not received a letter from me! I am sending this letter via Erna, maybe it will be more likely to arrive. Don't worry about me. I have what I need to live. I even have set aside food should you and the boys arrive, and I will manage the other difficulties I'm dealing with. I've even applied for the test to become a pastor. However, I doubt if I will be allowed (not because of my knowledge), but maybe it will work out anyway. The test is supposed to be in September. In spite of all the misery,

[Page 2]

in my thoughts I'd sometimes like to smile at my dear little one. I'm not sure how things are with Hedi, but I heard Bruno allude to something, anyway Gusti can afford it, since she is above a certain age. However, I would prefer to have you near Franzi, although I long for you so much. But being reunited would then be more feasible. *(This refers to Dad's expectation that fleeing across borders to Austria would be easier and more likely than Mom coming back to Romania.)* I gave Edda two sets of clothes for children, and shoes which I brought from Schobel Hanni. And I made a pair of wooden shoes for her so she has something to walk around in. Well, those are the normal things that occur along with the bigger concerns. Anyway, traveling with luggage is difficult, especially with the children.

Hopefully in the meantime you received some mail from me, so there is less uncertainty for you. Oh, how many loving words I want to write to you, but on paper they are cold words. May God grant the time of our reunion, and then in my arms you can forget all this misery. And then I can take care of you and our boys.

Kissing you and Günter and Gerhard

Your daddy

Give my warm greetings to all,

Gusti

27 **Dad's letter to Mom, dated July 10, 1946.** The translation follows.

My dearest!

Such a feeling of anxiousness and worry about you has grabbed me again. For over a month now I have had no mail from you. The last letter I received from you is from May 9, 1946. That you have not received a letter from me? And I wrote you so often. Even this letter I am sending via Erna, maybe it will be more likely to arrive that way? Everything is as always here . . . All my thoughts and longing revolve around you. What will our future be? When and where will we find each other again? It is so gloomy, always so alone! If I knew you were at Franzi's then a reunion would be easier. Of course we would have to start over, but if we were together again, my motivation would come back again—immediately. You have it much harder with the kids, so I do not want to complain.

Edda received a letter dated May 28, 1946, from your mother and from Medi via Reverend Meaning. It is difficult for her, too, no income and I can help only a little. Tilde is in Sankt Georgen and is sewing. Waretzi from Dürrbach is living with me now. He is working day to day. Otherwise I cannot complain, and I am looking better now. *(This is compared to deprivations of being a POW.)* Just my sense of hope should not leave me.

[Page 2]

If you were at Franzi's or Misch's, I could help support you. Should you possibly be able to travel there, immediately turn to Otto Horger. He already knows that you might contact him. I will give Pitsi, who is here, money and that way both of you will be helped.

Today I also wrote to Franzi and Misch. They also want to write to you so that you are not worried about me. But I still hope that a few lines from me have arrived in the meantime.

My dearest! I yearn for you so much!!

Kissing you and Günter and Gerhard

Your daddy

Give all my kind regards. I also wrote my mother. Hopefully she received the letters. In each of them was also a small note to you.

Gusti

28 Dad's letter to Mom, dated August 14, 1946. In this two-page letter he mentions that the government may confiscate his property. The translation follows.

My dearest!

When I came back again from a trip, I found another dear letter from you (according to the postmark from July 20, 1946, since it had no date). I was bringing boards back from Kolibitza with a wagon. That means two days including nights in one long drive, hard but at least an honest day's work. I'm not earning much but I can, in addition to setting aside some money for us, also help support Edda and others a bit more. Her hand is better. I am still hoping for a reunion here, but wait until I write. Should living in my house be disallowed, which is quite possible, I will travel to Franzi right away. But please continue to write to the old address until I tell you otherwise. Someone will send the mail to me. I'm sorry things can't work for you like with Hedi, but it is impossible for you and it is too risky. I would never have a moment of peace. Your parents and my mother should also stay put. I've written that to all of you already.

Is it possible to obtain food, other than with the ration card, i.e. by buying it? And how expensive are some of the items? I can possibly help you by giving Pitzi food here, and her husband who is in Linz *(Austria)* could send you money. Commerce here is much like before, enough but somewhat expensive. In spite of that, we could make ends meet with my current earnings here. Only clothes are unaffordable. If it were possible someday for you and the kids to come here, it would be good if you could bring yarn with you. For 20 spools of twine 1000 meters, one can buy a good horse.

[Page 2]

The outlook to teach again is not good. I'm actually considering to not teach in the future anymore. A coachman (like me) earns more than a teacher.

My dearest! One could bear everything easier; you just need to receive some mail from me! But maybe by now you are receiving more, meaning that the letters are arriving better. After all, there are two months between me writing a letter and receiving a response. I've now written my mother a few times, too, but if you have received no mail, she probably also has not received my letters. I've received only one letter from her. Luckily I'm staying out of serious difficulties—up to now. Well, this too will pass. Hopefully everything will be good in the end.

I came home late again tonight. I was busy looking for work. Now I am home again and alone, writing you and thinking about our lost happiness! Oh God, when will this being alone be over?! How gladly I want to work for you and the children to help you. My poor little dear! You should be with me again!

Kissing you and the kids
Your daddy
What do you think? Should I travel to Franzi?

Added at bottom of letter written in very small script:

August 19, 1946. Grussi's property has been confiscated. If that is carried through, I will travel to Franzi, because then I will be homeless. G.

There is more text written near the bottom right of the letter with a different-color ink (all pens had to be dipped in an inkwell) in my mother's handwriting. This was the address in West Germany of Dad's cousin where my parents were reunited when they both fled their respective Communist countries.

German
Grete Hermann Knopp
Lehrerin *(teacher)*
13a Rothenburg ob der Tauber
Bayern
Mittel Franken
US Zone

29 Vienna police registration. After escaping across borders, Dad arrived safely in the American sector of Vienna, Austria, on September 13, 1946. He registered with the Vienna police on September 14. The stamp reads, *Polizeidirektion, Wien* (Police headquarters, Vienna). He registered as a *Volksdeutscher* (ethnic German). Ethnic Germans from Eastern European countries, now under communism, were fleeing for their lives or to improve their lives, and many were forced to leave.

Registriert

am 14. Sep. 1946 Nr. ..../..........

als

VOLKS deutscher

MAROSCHER GUSTAV 10.11.17

Name — Vorname

zur Repatriierung.

POLIZEIDIREKTION

Stampiglie

c2

Unterschrift des Beamten

30 **Dad's letter from Vienna, Austria, to Mom in Weimar, East Germany, dated September 13, 1946.** Dad wrote this letter after successfully fleeing across two Communist-controlled borders. The first page of the letter was stamped on the lower left by Austrian censorship location 299. The translation follows.

My dearest!

On my way to you I am temporarily here in Vienna. If it works out I will travel to West Germany with a transport in about 10 days. We don't know yet where exactly the transport will go, but we were told that once we arrive at the reception camp we can depart with a residence permit. In any case I will then write to you right away. Should I not be able to travel to you right away *(from West Germany to East Germany)* I will go to Grete Knopp or Hansi. And should I be able to stay there, I will bring you and the kids to me.

[Page 2]

Therefore please write me at Hansi's and Grete Knopp's address. Grete Knopp, Rothenburg o.T. Topplerweg 4/2, Mittelfranken 13a. Unfortunately, I have no luggage except for two small suitcases. I could not lug more because I had to carry 20 days' worth of provisions with me for the trip. (For the second time I have absolutely nothing.) But all that is meaningless if we were finally together again, and I could provide for you and the kids. I simply cannot even imagine anymore that we will be together and happy again. I have such a longing for you!

Kissing you, your daddy
Warm greetings to all
Gusti

31 Dad's letter to Mom, dated September 17, 1946. The letter was stamped by Austrian censorship location 2313. The translation follows.

My dear!

I'm still in Vienna. So far the trip has gone well. Now I am waiting for a transport with which I can travel to West Germany. I am forced by circumstances to travel to Grete's (Knopp) first and will look for nearby accommodations for us there. Then I will go to you and bring you to Rothenburg. Should it be possible, I will go directly from the refugee reception camp to you! Were it only so already! Since I do not know the circumstances there, we will have to wait and wait. God, how much longer! Tilde, her children and I were to travel on the same day with a transport. I gave her 3000 Marks and some lard as well as cigarettes. Please write Seppi *(Mom's brother Josef)* and ask him if she arrived. She is supposed to send you half of the money. Maybe the mail will arrive undisturbed. Should it be too difficult for you to move, I will for sure come to you. Please write to Grete's address: Grete Hermann-Knopp, Rothenburg o.T., Topplerweg 4/2, Mittelfranken 13a. Should I also try to get an admittance permit for your parents? Or do you think we should travel to be near Hansi? Maybe I should travel to you first, so we can discuss the situation.

Kissing you
Your Gusti

In the lower right of page three are two additional notes written with a quill pen. Each of the additional notes was written with a different color of ink and with different handwriting.

One note is from Mom's mother and the other is from Mom's dad. The notes were written after they had received a telegraph stating that Mom, Dad, Dad's mother, my brother, and I were reunited in Rothenburg odT. Therefore, Dad's letter to Mom written on September 17 from Vienna, containing the two additional notes, was mailed from Weimar to Rothenburg after we had fled to join Dad.

Note from Mom's mother

Dear Leni, Gusti, Günter, and Gerhardt *(misspelled)* and Käthe,

We received your telegram. Thanks be to God that the time has come and you are reunited. Write to Bubi *(Mom's brother Josef, also known as Seppi)*. He has another address. He will be overjoyed. Please ask Gusti about the address. We got a room in Str. *(Street)* 8/2. Not much bigger than Mrs. Birkfeld's. But we do not have a stove. Were the children good during the trip? We wish for you that you will always be together.

Greetings, your Mama

Note from Mom's dad

Dear Gusti, Leni, and children.

Praise God that the reunion happily succeeded. Wishing the newlyweds lots of joy in your honeymoon. Did the luggage and everything arrive?

Love to you all,

Tata und Mama

The letters Mom kept

This is the last letter of the collections of letters Dad sent to Mom. The first letter was written on June 3, 1944, and the last on September 17, 1946. During this time, Mom and my brother and I lived in Mettersdorf (Romania), the refugee camp Herzogenburg (Austria), and several residences in Weimar (Germany). Mom then took these letters with her when she, Käthe (her mother-in-law), Günter, and I fled to Rothenburg odT in West Germany. The final journey for the letters was when we came to America as Romanian displaced persons—refugees. Mom obviously valued the letters. Her keeping the letters was a great gift. Thanks, Mom.

32 Grete Herrmann Knopp's escape to West Germany. Grete, who was also a Transylvanian Saxon, fled from Lechnitz, which is located in the county of Bistritz. She fled on September 15, 1944, with her one-year-old daughter, Ingrid, along with nearly the entire population of the city running for their lives from the Russian army.[1] In the German language such an endeavor is called a *Treck*, meaning a large caravan of people leaving their homeland forever with farm wagons pulled by draft animals. The wagons were filled with people, household items, and food, not unlike the wagon trains heading west in the early history of the United States. Most Transylvanian Saxons were farmers, and most of those who fled toward the end of the war did so in these arduous Trecks.

The distance from Lechnitz to Vienna, Austria, was 490 miles by the most direct route through Hungary, which included crossing two mountain ranges. During the first weeks of this journey, the advancing Russian army was close enough that those on the Treck could occasionally hear artillery shells exploding in the distance. Along the way there were many hardships, dangers, and almost no paved roads.

The Treck ended in Austria. The "treckers" dispersed in Austria and West Germany. Most eventually settled in the Rothenburg, Nuremberg, and Dinkelsbühl area of West Germany.[2] Grete chose to live in Rothenburg odT. By the time Mom, Käthe, my brother, and I arrived, Grete had been established there for a while. Grete's address was made known to a number of people through the mail, and she became an important haven in the West for other family members and friends.

Grete Herrmann Knopp was an elementary school teacher. Grete's husband was MIA and she never saw him again. She was to marry another man, who also served in the military, but he was killed in 1945. Ingrid had to grow up without a father and sometimes stayed with family in Rothenburg due to Grete's heart problems that required her to be hospitalized. Ingrid also stayed with us in Ohrenbach. I remember playing with Ingrid. We were the same age and were compatible playmates.

---

1 Lechnitzer Heimatbuch, zusammengestellt von Georg Felker, 1968, Herausgeber: Hilfskomitee der Siebenbürger Sachen. Druck: Schweinfurter Druckerei und Verlagsanstalt.

2 This area was the ancestral home of the Saxons prior to traveling to Transylvania in the twelfth century at the invitation of the Hungarian king Gysa II.

33 Rothenburg ob der Tauber police registration. Dad registered with the police in Rothenburg odT, Bavaria, on September 27, 1946. This was ten days after his last letter to Mom in Weimar, Germany. Item seven reads, "Citizenship." Filled in that space is "Stateless. Hungarian. Romanian." The street name he gave was "Topplerweg."

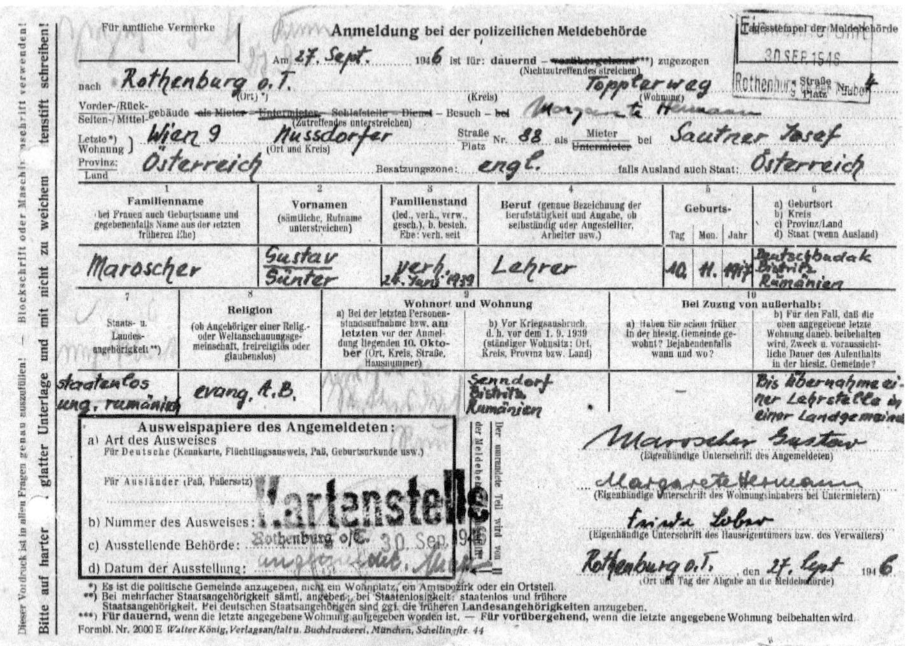

Bitte auf harter, glatter Unterlage und mit nicht zu weichem Tintenstift schreiben!

Dieser Vordruck ist in allen Fragen genau auszufüllen! — Blockschrift oder Maschinenschrift verwenden!

Für amtliche Vermerke

Anmeldung bei der polizeilichen Meldebehörde

Tagesstempel der Meldebehörde: 30 SEP 1946

Am 27. Sept. 1946 ist für: dauernd – ~~vorübergehend~~***) zugezogen (Nichtzutreffendes streichen)

nach Rothenburg o.T. (Ort) *) (Kreis) Topplerweg (Wohnung) Straße/Platz Nr. 4

Vorder-/Rück-/Seiten-/Mittel-gebäude ~~als Mieter – Untermieter – Schlafstelle – Dienst~~ – Besuch – ~~bei~~ Margarete Hermann (Zutreffendes unterstreichen)

Letzte *) Wohnung: Wien 9 (Ort und Kreis) Nussdorfer Straße/Platz Nr. 88 als Mieter ~~Untermieter~~ bei Sautner Josef

Provinz: Land: Österreich Besatzungszone: engl. falls Ausland auch Staat: Österreich

1 Familienname (bei Frauen auch Geburtsname und gegebenenfalls Name aus der letzten früheren Ehe)	2 Vornamen (sämtliche, Rufname unterstreichen)	3 Familienstand (led., verh., verw., gesch.), b. besteh. Ehe: verh. seit	4 Beruf (genaue Bezeichnung der Berufstätigkeit und Angabe, ob selbständig oder Angestellter, Arbeiter usw.)	5 Geburts- Tag	Mon.	Jahr	6 a) Geburtsort b) Kreis c) Provinz/Land d) Staat (wenn Ausland)
Maroscher	Gustav Günter	verh. 24. Juni 1939	Lehrer	10.	11.	1917	Deutschbadak Bistritz Rumänien

7 Staats- u. Landesangehörigkeit **)	8 Religion (ob Angehöriger einer Relig.- oder Weltanschauungsgemeinschaft, freireligiös oder glaubenslos)	9 Wohnort und Wohnung: a) Bei der letzten Personenstandsaufnahme bzw. am letzten vor der Anmeldung liegenden 10. Oktober (Ort, Kreis, Straße, Hausnummer)	b) Vor Kriegsausbruch, d. h. vor dem 1. 9. 1939 (ständiger Wohnsitz: Ort, Kreis, Provinz bzw. Land)	10 Bei Zuzug von außerhalb: a) Haben Sie schon früher in der hiesig. Gemeinde gewohnt? Bejahendenfalls wann und wo?	b) Für den Fall, daß die oben angegebene letzte Wohnung daneb. beibehalten wird, Zweck u. voraussichtliche Dauer des Aufenthalts in der hiesig. Gemeinde?
staatenlos ung. rumänisch	evang. A.B.		Senndorf Bistritz Rumänien	–	Bis Übernahme einer Lehrstelle in einer Landgemeinde

Ausweispapiere des Angemeldeten:
a) Art des Ausweises
Für Deutsche (Kennkarte, Flüchtlingsausweis, Paß, Geburtsurkunde usw.)
Für Ausländer (Paß, Paßersatz)
b) Nummer des Ausweises:
c) Ausstellende Behörde:
d) Datum der Ausstellung:

Stamp: Kartenstelle Rothenburg o/T. 30. Sep. 1946

Der umrandete Teil wird von der Meldebehörde ausgefüllt

Maroscher Gustav
(Eigenhändige Unterschrift des Angemeldeten)

Margarete Hermann
(Eigenhändige Unterschrift des Wohnungsinhabers bei Untermietern)

Frieda Lober
(Eigenhändige Unterschrift des Hauseigentümers bzw. des Verwalters)

Rothenburg o.T., den 27. Sept 1946
(Ort und Tag der Abgabe an die Meldebehörde)

*) Es ist die politische Gemeinde anzugeben, nicht ein Wohnplatz, ein Amtsbezirk oder ein Ortsteil.
**) Bei mehrfacher Staatsangehörigkeit sämtl. angeben; bei Staatenlosigkeit: staatenlos und frühere Staatsangehörigkeit. Bei deutschen Staatsangehörigen sind ggf. die früheren Landesangehörigkeiten anzugeben.
***) Für dauernd, wenn die letzte angegebene Wohnung aufgegeben worden ist. — Für vorübergehend, wenn die letzte angegebene Wohnung beibehalten wird.

Formbl. Nr. 2000 E *Walter König, Verlagsanstalt u. Buchdruckerei, München, Schellingstr. 44*

34 Employment ID and ration booklet for Gustav G. Maroscher. Upon arriving in Rothenburg odT, Dad immediately registered at the employment office. He registered on September 29, 1946, two days after registering with the police. On the following page is the multipage employment ID document booklet, which also served as a ration card to receive food from the authorities. A translation of part of the document follows below. Only the first page of the booklet is shown.

Vom Arbeitsamt ausfüllen
Pers.-Kreis
Ber.-Gr. u.-Art
Wzw.
Monat IX
Jahr 46
voll e.
beschr. e.
nicht e.

Arbeitsamt Ansbach
Nebenstelle Rothenburg o.T.

Ausweiskarte Nr. 284/Ro/4478
über die Registrierung beim Arbeitsamt

Name Maroscher Vorname Gustav
(Bei Frauen auch Geburtsname)
Geburtstag 10.11.17 Familienstand verh.
Wohnort Rothenburg o.T. Topplerweg Straße Nr. 4
Beruf[1]) Lehrer
Stellung im Beruf[2]) Lehrer u. Schulleiter
tätig bei[3]) Volksschule – Ohrenbach
(Name, Sitz, Art des Betriebes oder der Behörde oder der Schule)
Staatsangehörigkeit ungeklärt
schwerbeschädigt: Ja / nein (nur nach amtlicher Feststellung)
(Nichtzutreffendes durchstreichen)
Zahl u. Geburtsjahre der Kinder 2 (40 + 43)
Maroscher Gustav
(Unterschrift des Inhabers)
Registriert durch das Arbeitsamt
(Dienstsiegel und Datum) 30.9.46

[1]) z. B. Landwirt, Bauschlosser, Hausfrau, Student, Sozialrentner usw.
[2]) selbständig, Arbeiter, Angestellter, Beamter, mithelfender Familienangehöriger, Heimarbeiter usw.
[3]) bei Arbeitslosen ist hier „arbeitslos", bei Personen, die nach ärztlicher Bescheinigung arbeitsunfähig sind und ihr Arbeitsverhältnis gelöst haben, „arbeitsunfähig" einzutragen.

0755 7. 46. 200 000

Birthdate.........Nov. 11, 1917 Marital status......married
Residence.........Rothenburg oT, Topplerweg 4
Occupation......Teacher
Position..........Teacher and principal *(Note: Dad worked as a teacher and principal in Ohrenbach but was hired as an assistant teacher)*
working at.......Elementary school—Ohrenbach
Citizenship.......undetermined
Number and birth years of the children......2 (40 + 43)

19 49/50 **Bayerische Jagdkarte** Nr. 37/50
für Herrn Gustav Maroscher
geb. 10.11.17 zu Budak (Rum.)
Wohnort Ohrenbach 14
Wohnung — " — 14
Kreis Rothenburg o. T.
gültig vom 15. 8. 49 bis 31. 3. 1950
Rothenburg o. Tbr., den 15. Aug. 1949
Landratsamt:
(Ausstellende Behörde)
Maroscher Gustav
(Eigenhändige Unterschrift)
(Dienstsiegel)
Kovo-Druck 2891. S. (41048) Kommunalschriften-Vertrieb J. Jehle, München 34, Barer Straße 32

35 Hunting license. To hunt rabbits, one needed a hunting permit from the state of Bavaria. Shown is Dad's hunting permit for 1949/50.

36 Grade card, first half of third grade. My grade card for the first half of the third grade shows forty-one excused absences from my doctor-induced illness. Maybe fifteen of those days were a result of living at the refugee processing center in Munich starting in late January 1951. The teacher, Herr Lehrer Lorenz, described me as "Ein freundlicher und brauchbarer Schüler" (A friendly and satisfactory student). As the principal and head teacher, my dad signed the report card.

Volksschule Ohrenbach

3. Jahr der Schulpflicht   Schuljahr 1951/1952   3. Schülerjahrgang

Zeugnis

für Maroscher, Gerhard

Charakterliche Würdigung:
1. Halbjahr Ein freundlicher und brauchbarer Schüler.

2. Halbjahr

Benotung	1. Halbjahr	2. Halbjahr	Benotung	1. Halbjahr	2. Halbjahr
Religionslehre	2		Hauswirtschaft	-	
Deutsche Sprache	2		Rechnen und Raumlehre	2	
Schrift	2		Zeichnen - Werken	2	
Singen	1		Turnen und Sport	2	
Heimat-Erdkunde	2		Mädchen-Handarbeit		
Geschichte-Sozialkunde	-		Englische Sprache		
Naturkunde	-				
Versäumnisse schuldlos	41		Versäumnisse schuldhaft		

Unterschriften: 15.2.1952   19

Schulleitung: Maroscher

Klaßlehrer(in): H. Lorenz

Erziehungsberechtigte(r):

Notenstufen: 1 = sehr gut, 2 = gut, 3 = befriedigend, 4 = ausreichend, 5 = ungenügend

028k Druck: Carl Link Kronach   Vordruck 7

37 *Capital Chimes* **article from Tuesday April 24, 1952.** There are several errors in the article, but it is still a nice piece. The errors are as follows:

- Dad learned of our address in Weimar from the cigarette paper, not a letter.
- He did not decide to leave Germany because there was "no position to occupy him." He left because the Regional Education Administration did not pay him for his achievements, experience, and education.
- We did not travel to a POW camp in Munich before we came to the United States. We went to the United States displaced persons out-processing camp in Munich.

SPORTS LITE PREDICTS LOOP LEADERS PAGE 4

COLUMBUS 9, OHIO, TUESDAY, APRIL 24, 1952 — CAPITAL UNIVERSITY

German Family Adopted By Cap Family

Russian War Prisoner Seeks Peace In America For Wife And Family

Editor's Note: When Herr Arthur Grossman consented to act as translator for an interview, he and Sally Butts rang the bell at the Mound Street Annex A door. They were cordially greeted by a thin, red-haired gentleman and his short, pleasant wife, the Ethnic Germans, Mr. and Mrs. Gustav Maroscher, who are being sponsored by the University. Mr. Maroscher is now employed as a maintenance man by the music school.

There are tales of the valor that has stood up against uneven odds which send chills of admiration up and down one's spine. Among these falls the story of a man and his family who not only came out on top of adversity, but came out smiling.

For the whole picture of how Gustav Maroscher and his wife Helene found their way to peace in the United States, it is necessary to go back to the year 1940 when political unrest was sweeping the world and venting its anger on the German states.

Maroscher fought for five years with the Hungarian army, and the end of those five years found him a prisoner in Focsan, Russia. After six months of imprisonment, he was freed and returned to his native Rumania to see his family—only to find that a ruling that all people with German ancestors as far as 800 years back had forced them to return to the Fatherland. His wife, however, sent a letter to his grandmother in Rumania telling her that the Maroschers were residing in the Russian zone of Germany.

German Zones Postpone Reunion

Because of his former imprisonment at a Russian camp, it was impossible for Herr Maroscher to go to his wife, nor was it possible for him to write explaining that he couldn't come! By means of an ordinary letter speaking volumes more to the people reading between the lines, the family was reunited at the residence of Mr. Maroscher's aunt in the Western zone at Rothenburg o.T. (Rothenburg on the Taube River).

It looked as though life would go on in a normal fashion when Maroscher acquired a position in a city school in Bavaria. But here again, a change was necessitated when the predominately Roman Catholic community refused to give a deserved promotion to him purely on the basis of his Lutheran religion. With no position to occupy him in Bavaria, Maroscher moved his family to a Prisoner of War camp in Munich, and later, in Bremen from where they came to the United States and Capital University.

The two Maroscher boys, Guenter, 12 years, and Gerhard, 8, are now attending the Main-Montrose Elementary school, and, unlike most American kids, bombard their

(Continued Page 3)

ACP Critical Review Finds Chimes Improved

Chimes, Associated Collegiate Press member, this week received a certificate of award for its first semester entry in the ACP Critical Review Service.

The last time *Chimes* entered this contest was in 1950 when they received a Second Class (good) rating scoring 700 points.

Scoring 870 points, missing a First Class rating by just 30 points, the paper again received a Second Class award. The area showing the greatest improvement in comparison with the last report was in news writing and editing, although improvement was made in almost every rating area.

The letter accompanying the survey report stated that in line with its policy ACP has again raised its sights with respect to scoring standards and honor rat-

Alumni Help

LSA, League Quit

37 Continued. Capitol Chimes article.

Marschers Says 'It Takes Time'

(Continued from Page 1)

mother with the query of "Isn't it time to go to school yet?" With only the father able to speak any English, the children's conversation is still swiftly becoming punctuated with "Hello!" "Good-bye!" and "Thank you!"

Maroscher Educated As Teacher, Minister

College life is no mystery to Herr Maroscher who received an education in a combination theology-education university. Passing the exam at the completion of the study endowed him with both a teaching and a preaching vocation. The system in use was somewhat like the vicar system in the Lutheran Church, except that while not preaching his "duty-sermon" or substituting for the minister, Maroscher was occupied with teaching.

When the family arrived in Columbus at 5:45 AM on Easter morning, Mr. Maroscher laughingly related, they were met at the station by Miss Alphie Peters, who had them in a German church service by 11:00 AM. He expressed the family's appreciation at being introduced to Capital by such a family as the Peters; he said it was one of their most delightful experiences.

Capital comes as a relief to the travel-weary Maroschers; here they hope to find peace and quiet, and, what may be even more important, they won't have to move from place to place.

When asked whether or not he would like to return to the teaching profession, Mr. Maroscher smiled and said that he must first learn the language and *then* make further plans. And in the best Oxford English manner he declared, "I can understand more than I can speak." Shrugging his shoulders, he exclaimed, "It takes time!"

38 Inventory of our household goods in the cargo hold of the ship. On February 25, 1952, our entire household was packed in five small wooden crates. The total value was DM 1,200, or about $300 (about $2,700 today). The contents of the five crates (*Kisten*) are listed in the table below under *Inhalt* (Contents). At the time, goods were very expensive in West Germany; therefore, the value in today's dollars may actually be overstated.

Translation of *Inhalt* (Contents) list is below.

VERZEICHNIS

der mitgeführten Gegenstände

von

NAME	VORNAME	GEBURTSJAHR	GEBURTSORT	STAATSANGEHORIGK.
MAROSCHER	Gustav	10.11.17	Budak	Vd
— " —	Helene	11.3.20	Bistritz	— " —
— " —	Günter	28.2.40	— " —	— " —
— " —	Gerhard	10.8.43	— " —	— " —

PACKSTÜCKE	INHALT	WERT in DM
5 Kisten	Kleidung	400.-
	Wäsche	200.-
	Schuhe	50.-
	Hausrat	200.-
	Decken	50.-
	Violine	50.-
	Bücher	100
	Plattenspieler u. Linguaphone	100.-
	Werkzeug	20.-
	Radio	30.-
		1200.-

Siehe Rückseite!

clothes
washables
shoes
household goods
blankets
violin
books
record player
tools
radio

38 Continued. The signature and declaration of value page was signed by Gustav Maroscher on February 25, 1952.

PACKSTÜCK	INHALT	WERT in DM

GESAMTWERT DM: 1200,-
(Wertgegenstände und Luxusgegenstände sind gesondert aufzuführen)

ERKLÄRUNG

München, den 25. 2. 1952

Ich erkläre hiermit an Eidesstatt, dass in den angeführten Gepäckstücken nur die in obigem Verzeichnis aufgeführten Gegenstände enthalten sind. Es befinden sich darin weder verbotenes Eigentum noch grössere Maschinen, Lebensmittel, Devisen oder Rauschgifte.
Der Wert der genannten Waren übersteigt nicht die Höhe von 5000. DM für das Familienoberhaupt, zusätzlich DM 500.- pro jedes weitere Familienmitglied.

Gustav Maroscher
(Unterschrift)

4750 IRO-8-51 30000

39 Alien registration at the port of New York. The front and back of my card are shown whereas only the fronts of Mom's and Dad's cards are included here. The stamp date is April 12, 1952. That was a Saturday, one day before our Easter Sunday arrival in Columbus, Ohio. My brother's alien registration card was missing from my parents' records—but no need to worry, I assure you that he came with the rest of the family and was a legal immigrant.

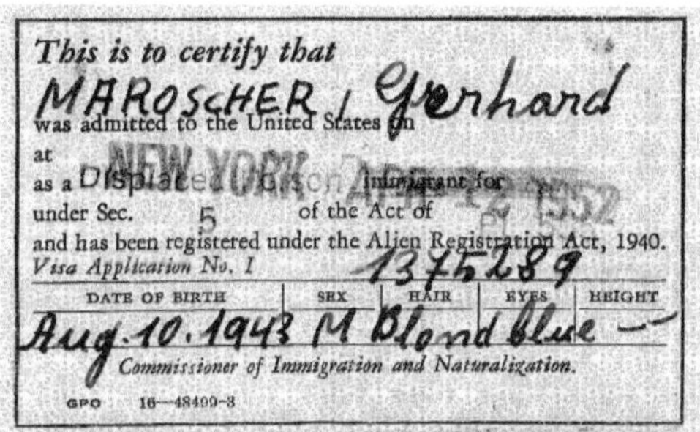

This is to certify that
MAROSCHER, Gerhard
was admitted to the United States on
at NEW YORK APR 12 1952
as a Displaced Person Immigrant for
under Sec. 5 of the Act of
and has been registered under the Alien Registration Act, 1940.
Visa Application No. I 1375289

DATE OF BIRTH	SEX	HAIR	EYES	HEIGHT
Aug. 10. 1943	M	Blond	blue	—

Commissioner of Immigration and Naturalization.
GPO 16—48499-3

TEMPORARY RECEIPT
PHOTOGRAPH OF HOLDER
VALID
FOR 3 MONTHS after date of admission shown on Reverse Side

UNITED STATES
DEPARTMENT OF JUSTICE
IMMIGRATION AND NATURALIZATION SERVICE
Alien Registration Receipt Card
Registration Number
FORM I-151 (1-14-49) 16—48499-3

This is to certify that
MAROSCHER, helene
was admitted to the United States on
at NEW YORK APR 12 1952
as a Displaced Person Immigrant for
under Sec. 5 of the Act of PL 555
and has been registered under the Alien Registration Act, 1940.
Visa Application No. I 1375287

DATE OF BIRTH	SEX	HAIR	EYES	HEIGHT
March 11. 1920	F	Brown	blue	5-2

Commissioner of Immigration and Naturalization.
GPO 16—48499-3

This is to certify that
MAROSCHER, Gustav
was admitted to the United States on
at NEW YORK APR 12 1952
as a Displaced Person Immigrant for
under Sec. 5 of the Act of PL 555
and has been registered under the Alien Registration Act, 1940.
Visa Application No. I 1375286

DATE OF BIRTH	SEX	HAIR	EYES	HEIGHT
Nov. 10. 1917	M	Red	blue	5-11

Commissioner of Immigration and Naturalization.
GPO 16—48499-3

40 ***Columbus Dispatch* Crusade for Freedom article, March 1, 1955.** This article discusses my brother's and my involvement in collecting money for the Crusade for Freedom on our paper routes, Dad's view of informing people behind the iron curtain, and his job at Accurate Manufacturing. A picture of our family is in the upper-left corner of the front page.

Article continues on the following page.

WEATHER
Fair, colder Tuesday night, low 33. Partly cloudy and mild Wednesday, high 55.
High 65 at 4:15 a. m. Tuesday
(Weather Map on Page 3B)

Columbus Eveni

OHIO'S GREATEST HOME

VOL. 84, NO. 244 ★★★★★x Telephone—CApital 1-1234 COLUMBUS 16, OHIO, TUESDAY

RECALL LIFE IN ROMANIA—Scrapbook relics of older days, in now-Communized Romania, are relived by the family of Gustav G. Maroscher, 906 W. 11th Av. The boys are Gerhart, 11, left, and Guenter, 15.—(Dispatch Photo.)

KNOW VALUE OF TRUTH

Freedom Crusade

FREEDOM CRUSADE FILM AVAILABLE AT THE DISPATCH

Church Can La

City Asked To Halt Bus Service Cut

Strong Stand Urged By Tipton; Officials Are Non-Committal

City officials Tuesday were non-committal about attempting to halt service reductions by the Columbus Transit Co. on March 14.

John Robert Tipton, president

40 Continued. Front page article under a picture of our family.

My brother, Günter (Guenter in the article), told the reporter he did not remember much about his homeland. That was a lie. He remembered everything. He just did not want to talk about it.

KNOW VALUE OF TRUTH

Freedom Crusade Family's Project

By SAM HARVEY

With the Gustave G. Maroschers of 906 W. 11th Av, the Crusade for Freedom is a family project.

All four are natives of Romania, although 11-year-old Gerhart was only a baby when they left.

Guenter, 15, doesn't remember much of his homeland. But his parents remember vividly their lives of peace and happiness while Maroscher was a school teacher there.

They also remember when the Russian Army moved in. That was in 1944. Less than two hours before the soldiers arrived, Mrs. Maroscher was fleeing the other direction with her two young sons.

Her husband, then a Romanian soldier, didn't escape until two years later. In those two years he learned about Soviet prison camps and about the Communist "system" for civilians.

Today, both Maroscher boys are helping the Crusade for Freedom by soliciting from customers on their Dispatch routes.

And their father talks fervently of the unique radio stations supported by the Crusade, the stations that beam "truth broadcasts" to citizens of five satellite nations behind the Iron Curtain.

"We must convince those people that we have not forgotten them," Maroscher stresses.

"We must keep freedom in their mind. We must give them courage, and that will keep their rulers always under tension.

"We must help keep the peace by stirring up trouble for the Reds behind their lines."

There are 70,000,000 people in the five countries of Hungary, Romania, Bulgaria, Poland and Czechoslovakia. And among them,

Continued on Page 4, Col. 3

40 Continued. Final portion of the Crusade for Freedom article appears below.

CRUSADE

Continued from Page 1

Maroscher points out, are millions of young people who have never known a non-Communist government.

"Just imagine a young citizen of 24. Since he was a boy he has heard and read nothing but Communist propaganda.

"Everything—the books, the newspapers, the radios, the schools, the posters—everything that's written down or spoken publicly is propaganda.

"Even the children's books were destroyed in a huge bookburning. Today the school children read about youth heroes who betray their own parents to the secret police.

"But if they keep hearing lies and lies and lies alone, maybe someday . . ."

Maroscher paused, and the pause told eloquently his fears for the homeland he loves and for the people there.

"I know how they feel," he said simply.

The Maroschers left Romania penniless. They were reunited in 1946 in West Germany.

Mrs. Maroscher then had but one memento of her former home, a family wristwatch. She sold it so her husband could buy the overcoat he needed to get a job as a teacher in the American occupation.

Under Lutheran sponsorship the family came to America in 1952. They landed in New York on Easter Sunday and were in Columbus the next day.

The former teacher decided to go into the drafting and designing business in America. But first, he worked as a janitor. Then came a job as lathe operator.

Careful work and correspondence study courses made him a "Class A" machinist. He now works at the Accurate Manufacturing Co. He's still studying for the day when he'll be a full-fledged draftsman.

His sons, because of their background, took great pride in collecting Crusade for Freedom funds as they delivered their Dispatches.

"I explained that we needed stronger stations to get through the Russian jamming," said Gerhart.

"I told my customers that their donations might prevent another war," said Guenter, who remembers hearing some similar broadcast when he was in West Germany.

Their father summed it up:

"Those people, they have no other way to know what's going on in their own countries."

41 History of Transylvanian Saxons. As a result of WWII my family and most Transylvanian Saxons were driven from their homeland forever. Toward the end of the war, some decided to flee while others stayed. Those who fled underwent danger and deprivation. Not all survived. Those who stayed and lived under the Communist Romanian government did not fare well either. Some were arrested and became slave laborers. All were discriminated against and eventually left their beloved Transylvanian homeland.

Transylvania, or *Siebenbürgen*[3] as the Transylvanian Saxons called it, is located in the Carpathian Mountains in the center of what is now Romania. Transylvanian Saxons have had a number of crests over the years, all featuring the seven fortresses that were the first seven settlements.

Cross-stitch of Transylvanian Saxon Crest. Stitched by Helene Maroscher.

3 The German name *Siebenbürgen* means "seven fortresses," after the original seven Transylvanian Saxons' cities in the region. The order in which they were settled in Transylvania was as follows: Mediasch in 1142; Mühlenbach in 1150; Hermannstadt, the capital, in 1160; Clausenburg in 1178; Schässburg in 1178; Reussmarkt in 1198; and Broos in 1200. The city of Bistritz (Bistrita in Romanian), where my family comes from, was first settled in 1206. That is the year that Genghis Kahn unified all the Mongol tribes and the Mongolian Empire was rapidly expanding. http://en.wikipedia.org/wiki/Transylvania.

Transylvanian Saxons are ethnic German people, originally called Franks, who traveled from the Duchy of Franconia to Transylvania in the twelfth century. The center of Franconia was located where Frankfurt, Germany, is today. Franconia was part of the Holy Roman Empire. In the year AD 1141, the Hungarian king Gysa II asked Kaiser Konrad III to send Germanic people who were willing to settle in the wilderness of the Carpathian Mountains to an area called Transylvania. About thirty-five thousand Franks with courage and the hope of a better life began to settle in the sparsely-populated area and became known as Transylvanian Saxons. They were accompanied by knights, who taught the farmers how to build fortifications and defend themselves. Transylvania is located in north central Romania.

The offer the Hungarian king made to the settlers was quite an enticement. The settlers received free land grants and were allowed to govern themselves, keep and develop their own culture and religion, and speak their own language. The Saxons, although autonomous, were still under the dominion of the king and were obligated to pay taxes and supply soldiers in case of war.[4] King Gysa II also expected a positive impact on the economy of his kingdom from the settlers because the Franks (Germans) were more technologically advanced than the Hungarians. In those days, advanced technology included blacksmithing, wagon building, and weaponry.

Why did the king offer such generous terms? Europe and much of the world was in danger from the Mongol tribes, who had developed an unstoppable "horse blitzkrieg." You may remember from high school history class the name of Genghis Kahn, under whose leadership the Mongol empire grew rapidly. The Mongol empire, which originated in the steppes of Central Asia, was the largest contiguous land empire in history. At its maximum size, it extended from the Sea of Japan to Central Europe, including Hungary. The Hungarian king wanted to populate the unsettled areas to provide more manpower to strengthen his military and establish this area as a buffer for the rest of his kingdom and Europe.[5]

Transylvanian Saxons survived in spite of serious losses early in their history from Mongol invasions. Estimated population losses from the Mongol invasion of 1241

---

4 http://www.siebenbuerger.de/portal/land-und-leute/siebenbuerger-sachsen/.

5 http://en.wikipedia.org/wiki/Genghis_Khan#Sole_ruler_of_the_Mongol_plains_.281206.29.

Crest of Transylvania depicting seven fortresses (1659 design)

vary from 15 to 20 percent. Some estimates are as high as 50 percent. The Mongol army numbered five hundred thousand soldiers on horseback.[6]

In 1224 the status and rights of the Transylvanian Saxons were codified by Hungarian king Andreas II. Subsequent kings continued to honor King Andreas II's proclamation. The Transylvanian Saxons flourished. The Saxon population increased from the original thirty-five thousand settlers to about 275,000 by WWII. What's surprising for that time is that the Saxons never had a noble class. They elected their own leaders. The top elected official interacted with the king and was the people's representative. They had their own judicial system, freely practiced their own religion, had property rights, and had a free-market economy. They established elementary education in the fourteenth century—about 150 years before England—and instituted compulsory education in 1722.

The Protestant Reformation, initiated by Martin Luther, was accomplished peacefully by the Transylvanian Saxons. In 1547 Johannes Honterus led the previously Roman Catholic Saxons to become Lutheran. While much of Europe fought the bloody Thirty Years' War (1618–1648) to a stalemate over political power and religion, the Transylvanian Saxons practiced freedom of religion since 1568 and no blood was spilled.

I think the Transylvanian Saxon history is in some ways similar to the history of the United States. We Americans threw off the yoke of aristocracy and had a new birth of freedom. We were a new nation never before seen on the earth, with freedom, rule of law, and individual rights. The Transylvanian Saxons were given a similar history by the wisdom of King Gysa II and subsequent Hungarian kings. The Saxons kept their autonomy for centuries through the turmoil of war and political machinations. Only in 1867 did the Saxons lose their political autonomy after a brief war in reaction to the Austro-Hungarian Empire imposing its authority after defeating the Ottoman Turks. Al-

6 https://en.wikipedia.org/wiki/Military_history_of_Romania#Early_Middle_ages.

though they lost their autonomy, the Saxons continued to thrive under the Austro-Hungarian Empire and controlled their own churches, schools, and local governments.

The Transylvanian Saxon language is an Old German dialect spoken in Franconia about 850 years ago. The German language changed during that time, but Transylvanian Saxon remained true to the original language. Even after 850 years of separation, Transylvanian Saxons—at least those who retained their native language—and native Luxembourgers can still understand each other.

Tartlau plan view. Image from https://en.wikipedia.org/wiki/Prejmer_fortified_church.

The Saxons built formidable fortifications to defend against horse-blitzkrieg warfare. The Saxons called such a fortification a *Kirchenburg* (church fortress). About 250 such church fortresses were built in Transylvania. The Christian faith was central to the Transylvanian society. Located in the center of every Kirchenburg was a church.[7]

The Tartlau fortification, built between AD 1212 and 1213 under the direction of the Teutonic Knights, was the largest and most effective fortification.[8] The fortifications continued to be upgraded through the centuries.

The walls of Tartlau were up to sixteen feet thick and thirty-nine feet tall, sur-

7 http://en.wikipedia.org/wiki/Prejmer.

8 https://en.wikipedia.org/wiki/Prejmer, https://www.flickr.com/photos/andra_mb/4062825229/.

rounding the church in the center. The method of fighting the hordes was to provide early warning of the coming Mongol invaders and move all people inside the fortification. As many livestock and other farm animals as possible were moved inside the fortification to deprive the enemy of food and protect the animals from being killed. The single entrance into the fortress was quite narrow so as to be easily defendable. In the history of Mongol invasions, the enemy successfully overran church fortresses a few times, but their successes were short lived because the Saxons were able to retake the fortifications quickly.

Centuries later, the Saxons fought many battles against the Ottoman Turks, who had conquered much of southern Europe, Hungary, Poland, and Romania. Casualties were heavy, but Transylvania was never occupied. The fortifications were very effective against the Ottoman army. The cost of the fighting was high on both sides. The Ottomans offered and the Saxons accepted the paying of a tribute. In 1683 the Ottomans were finally defeated at the gates of Vienna.[9]

Restored Tartlau today. Picture from http://en.wikipedia.org/wiki/Prejmer.

9 http://en.wikipedia.org/wiki/Battle_of_Vienna; http://en.wikipedia.org/wiki/Ottoman_Empire.

The Army of the Ottoman Empire Found the Tartlau Kirchenburg a Formidable Defensive Structure

When Ottoman forces or other invaders would break through the Buzău Pass, Prejmer (Tartlau) was the first place they encountered; the village was destroyed over 50 times between the 13th and 17th centuries, while the church (Tartlau) was only rarely captured. Due to this strategic position, the church was strongly fortified in the 15th-16th centuries. After Sigismund of Luxemburg ordered defensive systems to be built in the Burzenland, high, strong walls were built and surrounded with a water-filled moat. It seems that a subterranean tunnel linked the church to the exterior. The circular walls are up to 5 m thick and reach nearly 12 m in height. The circular walls surround the church, while a second and smaller wall sits atop the arched passage at the entrance gate. Other defensive features include five towers and a battlement. On the interior side of the wall, there are four levels containing rooms and storage space and backed by the battlement. The over 270 rooms could offer shelter to some 1600 villagers in case of attack. Entry into the complex is made through a 30 m long tunnel protected by a portcullis with wooden grilles strengthened by iron and powerful oak doors. To the right of the entrance stands a large barbican.

Frequently damaged or altered, with the last stage of extensions and modifications happening in the 18th century, Prejmer was restored to its original form following a restoration between 1960 and 1970. The site is now a museum, visitors can see some of the wall rooms, climbing the many stairs and walking the corridors that join them along the wall, eventually reaching the battlements on the outside. In 1999, Prejmer, together with five other places, was added to the already-listed Biertan to form the villages with fortified churches in Transylvania UNESCO World Heritage Site. Additionally, the church is listed as a historic monument by Romania's

Ministry of Culture and Religious Affairs, with the following being listed as separate entries: the inner wall and rooms, the outer wall, the barbican, the battlement and the arched gallery.[10]

Restored Tartlau courtyard.
Picture from https://en.wikipedia.org/wiki/Prejmer_fortified_church.

Captain John Smith in Transylvania

Before founding Jamestown, in 1607, Captain John Smith fought in Transylvania against the Turks in the year 1602. Smith was given the assignment to fight in Transylvania by Queen Elizabeth I of England because of the danger to Europe from the expansionist Muslim Ottoman Empire. Captain Smith was captured in the fighting and sold as a slave. He escaped and returned to England in the winter of 1605/06[11] and continued to serve the Queen.

The Fate of the Transylvanian Saxons

For most of their eight-hundred-year history, the Transylvanian Saxons enjoyed a privileged status regarding citizens' rights, unheard of in the rest of the world. They sur-

10 https://en.wikipedia.org/wiki/Prejmer_fortified_church.

11 http://apva.org/rediscovery/page.php?page_id=25; http://historicjamestowne.org/history/pocahontas/john-smith/.

vived the Mongols, Ottoman Turks, and various political intrigues. But they did not survive the Soviet invasion during World War II and communism. They lost their homeland, were persecuted, and chose to flee. Today's ethnic German population in Romania is 0.2 percent, reduced from 4.1 percent before the war (this includes Transylvanian Saxons).[12]

Starting in late 1944, as the Russian army was advancing into Transylvania, many Saxons, including my family, fled from Transylvania. They hoped to reach either Germany or Austria. Many eventually settled in the area from which their ancestors had departed in the twelfth century. Decades later, most of those who had stayed behind in Romania left because of discrimination and difficult living conditions under the Ceausescu Communist regime.

Map from
http://www.siebenbuerger.de/portal/land-und-leute/siebenbuerger-sachsen/wer.php

12 https://en.wikipedia.org/wiki/Demographics_of_Romania#Population_evolution.

The Long Journey

In the map at the bottom of page 334, the arrow labeled *12. Jh* (twelfth century) pointing to the right depicts the journey of the Transylvanian Saxons leaving Franconia for Transylvania. The two arrows pointing left show the routes by which they fled their Transylvanian homeland starting in late 1944.

Note: *nach 1944* in the thick part of the departing arrow means "after 1944."

The distance from the center of Franconia to Transylvania is about 975 miles, extending across four to six national borders depending on the route. The dark area in the map to the right is *Siebenbürgen* (Transylvania), in the center of Romania. The numbers *200,000* and *18,000* in the left-pointing arrows represent the number of Saxons who left their homeland.

42 Our parents and their families.

The Maroscher family name comes from the northern Transylvanian county of Marosch and the river that borders it, also called the Marosch. The Romanians call it the Mures. Since the last name "Maroscher" is derived from Transylvanian geography rather than an occupation or physical characteristic, I assume Dad's ancestors were likely among the early German settlers of Transylvania.

Dad's parents and grandmother

Dad's father, Gustav Friedrich Maroscher, was a teacher and minister. (2) He married Katharina Knopp at the age of 25 (3). Gustav Günter Maroscher (Dad) was born in 1917 in Deutsch-Budak, (1) about four miles south of Bistritz. His father did not live long enough to see his son grow up. He died at the age of 30 when Dad was 2 years 7 months old. Gustav Friedrich contracted pneumonia as a result of officiating at a funeral in cold and wet weather. The picture below, taken the same month his father died, shows Dad with his mother. Dad's mother, Katharina, nicknamed Käthe, did not remarry. In her teenage years, Käthe injured her knee. At that time there was no surgical fix for such an injury. From that time on that leg was stiff and did not bend at the knee. It did not seem to hinder her movement much, even into old age.

After her husband died, she moved to Bistritz with her young son Gustav and lived with his paternal grandmother, born Therese Zekeli. Therese had two nicknames, Tesi and Grussie. Grussie was occasionally quite difficult to get along with. At the outskirts of Bistritz they made their home on a small farm, which was the dowry from Käthe's parents. The small family was not well off financially and relied on income from farm activities and Käthe's small widow's pension.

Dad's childhood

Dad grew up on the farm, raised as an only child. His mother, grandmother, and he spoke Transylvanian Saxon in the home. Dad remained fluent in his first language his entire life.

43 Living in Bistritz. My brother, Günter, recalls the farm Dad grew up on, where Käthe and Grussi (Therese Maroscher, Dad's paternal grandmother) lived until we fled from the Russian army:

> I say "farm property" because it was located at the edge of town (Bistritz) and was replete with farm, yard, and barn. The main house was large and had an ample porch that ran the length of the house. I recall a substantial stone-and-wood wall between this and the neighbor's property. It was on this wall that Vati (Dad), as a tender lad, shot and killed the neighbor's cat. The single-shot .22-caliber handgun was manufactured by our father, who bored and rifled a large iron spike to manufacture the gun's barrel. He had found an old rusted firing mechanism in the barn's tool room and bingo—a dead cat.

Although Dad never discussed the subject, family lore indicates that he missed having a normal upbringing with adequate adult supervision and motherly love.

From what my brother remembers Dad telling him, Dad shot the neighbor's cat at the age of about eight. Because he was so young, we can maybe excuse Dad's lack of good judgment and at the same time marvel at his ingenuity. Dad worked on his mother's farm together with the farmhands. He received lots of practical experience with hard work, repairing farm equipment, cursing (learned from the farmhands),

Käthe Maroscher and her son Gustav (Dad) in 1920

and enjoying the freedom to exercise his imagination. Dad had great curiosity and amazing mechanical and electrical skills. When he was a young boy, Bruno Knopp, cousin Diethard Knopp's father, lived with the family while attending a Romanian college-prep high school in Bistritz. Bruno was five years older than Dad (see the appendix, 4).

I know of two of my father's experiences as a teenager: First, Dad came upon a Jewish peasant grandmother and her grandson. The grandson had cut an artery in his foot, and the grandmother's treatment for the wound was to put his foot in a bucket of water. The child was slowly bleeding out. Dad took charge. He took the boy's foot out of the water, applied pressure to the wound, bandaged the wound, and saved the grandson's life. He must have been applying a first aid lesson from school. The other story is about one of the things he and the other boys at school did to pass time. It cannot be repeated here, however.

Dad's Education

The Transylvanian Saxons provided their own school system, which was run by the Lutheran Church. In the Lutheran schools, instruction was in High German, not Transylvanian Saxon. Dad attended the German elementary school for grades one through four and then a college-prep high-school equivalent. The prep school was the same school Bruno Knopp, Dad's uncle and Diethard Knopp's father, had attended. Instruction was in Romanian (see the appendix, 7).

The income from the farm and the widow's pension his mom received was barely enough to provide for the family. Dad, who was an excellent student, was awarded a scholarship to enable him to continue his education following completion of his high-school-equivalent education (see the appendix, 6). At the seminary, he received an excellent education in science, languages, music, pedagogical skills, theology, and athletics. Part of the theological training included preparing and giving sermons (see the appendix, 5, 7). He also learned discipline, cleanliness, orderliness, leadership, and military bearing. German orderliness and discipline ruled in the seminary, except when the students were on their own time. Later in the military he honed his orderliness and discipline skills, none of which I inherited. Dad kept several files of graduation papers from his school and university.

Mom's Dad, Josef Maurer, and Family

Because Josef was of Austrian descent, he grew up speaking German and had little contact with Saxons. Josef endured a terrible childhood, constantly being severely beaten and abused. At the age of thirteen, he ran away from home. A barber in Bistritz and his wife, who had no children, took him on as an apprentice, thus allowing him to learn a trade and eventually own a barbershop. Josef Maurer, a Roman Catholic, married Maria Pauline (Paula) Groh, a Lutheran. At that time, interfaith marriages were unthinkable. One day, a Catholic priest visited Josef's house to discuss the situation of this unacceptable marriage. The priest told Josef that his children were bastards because of the mixed marriage, whereupon Josef physically threw the priest out the door and said something in German equivalent to "Don't ever darken my doorstep again." Josef never went to mass again. However, my mother said that whenever he passed a Catholic church, he would tip his hat in respect. The children were raised as Lutherans.

Josef had a successful barber business with several barbers working for him. He did well enough to live downtown, the desirable part of town, and was able to feed and clothe his ten children. I could find no record of two of the ten children, who must have died at an early age. One of Mom's brothers, Otto Maurer, died as a young adult as a result of WWII. He had been discharged from the military due to illness and died at home. The remaining seven siblings survived the war. In fact, Mom and five of her remaining siblings lived into their eighties.

I don't know anything about the history of my mother's mother other than the fact that she became deaf and heard constant, loud ringing in her ears for decades.

Mom's Childhood

Mom was born in 1920 and was named Helene Maurer. She was the second youngest of ten children. She grew up in a German-speaking home and did not speak much Transylvanian Saxon until she married Dad. Josef was a good father and beat Mom only once. Her brothers had done something unacceptable and shifted the blame onto Mom. This one undeserved beating affected her deeply. She never forgot the emotional pain of being beaten by her father.

Mom was a very fearful, shy, and sickly child, very much sheltered by her mother. Growing up as the ninth child in her family, Mom was not treated kindly by her older siblings, except for her sister Medi. Being the sheltered youngest girl, Mom was kept ignorant about many things in life like menstruation and other things a girl should know. The one bit of advice her mother gave her when she got married: "Don't have ten children."

Mom's brothers were not model citizens growing up; they were always getting into trouble, both in general and with girls. One time, one of them was splitting wood with an ax. Another brother put his hand on the chopping block. The one wielding the ax said, "Move your hand or I'll chop your fingers off."

"No you won't. I dare you," was the response. Several fingers suddenly became a little shorter. All the sons grew up to be responsible, productive adults, but when they were young, they caused great worries for their parents.

Mom's Values

Family was central to Mom's value system. She honored her parents and family. In her early years as a wife and mother, she frequently visited her parents, mother-in-law (Käthe), and Grussi by hitching up Wilma the horse and traveling the six miles to Bistritz with my brother and me. Her loyalty toward family explains why she fled Bistritz with her mother-in-law despite the fact that Käthe was unkind to her. It also explains the two extended visits to the United States by Käthe years later. For each of the visits, Dad, who was loyal to his mom, hoped Käthe could live with us. Both times it did not work out. Käthe made life too difficult for both of them. In America many families are not as close and do not share the family-above-all-else philosophy. As Mom grew older, it became difficult for her to accept the attitude of the younger generations who did not visit as often and pay homage as she had done.

Mom's Schooling

Her nurses' training served her well over the years with Günter and me and many others. I know she saved the life of a choking child in Tulsa. The child was turning blue; the mother panicked and became ineffective. Mom took charge and saved the girl.

For many of her school years she had a male teacher who was extremely cruel to her. He always called her stupid and would belittle her. Mom suffered for the rest of her life from those years of mental abuse. She often felt incapable although she was, in fact, very capable, smart, and courageous.

Saxon school girls participated in various sports including track and gymnastics, both of which Mom excelled in.

As she gained confidence in her role as an American, she became fluent in English. She never studied English and spoke with an accent, but she wrote well and was an avid reader of English novels. Through lack of use she lost her fluency in Romanian, Hungarian, Yiddish, and Saxon.

Acknowledgments

Many who know of my life story encouraged me to write this book. Without their input I may not have begun to write. Of special mention is Barbara Wilson, who experienced WWII herself while serving as a nurse in the English armed forces. For more than fifteen years she kindly, but pointedly, asked many times if I had begun to write.

I thank the students from my high-school German classes and my current adult students of German, who asked me to write a book about the history of my family. When I began writing, friends who knew of my work on the book would ask me, "How is the book coming along?" Their interest reminded me that there is value in recording my family's history.

My parents kept a treasure trove of documents and letters, and my wife stored them safely after Mom died. At the time, I was unaware of how many valuable documents they had brought from abroad. I could have written a book about my family based on the stories I had heard from Mom and Dad, combined with my own memories and those of my brother. The information contained in the documents and letters, along with my own research and the inclusion of some scans of the documents, resulted in a more complete book—a book with more personal, vivid, and accurate reminiscences.

My older brother, Gus (Günter in the old country), had an important role in the writing of the book. His amazing memory of his early childhood provided a glimpse into our simple rural life in Romania before we fled our homeland. His input also enriched the book by providing eyewitness accounts of his experiences during and after WWII. It was a pleasure to interact with him during the three years of writing and research. He never got tired of my numerous questions in emails and telephone calls. He gladly shared his memories. He also gave me the title, *Why Can't Somebody Just Die around Here*? and the story behind the title. Thanks, bro!

Excerpts from the hand-written memoir of the late Hanna Rothmann-Gellfart, a cousin, give a first-person account of being arrested in the night and becoming a slave laborer in Russia. She also describes her harrowing escape to the West. Her daughter, the late Ruth Lechner-Gellfart, was kind enough to share her mother's collection of memories when I was in Germany doing research for the book in 2014.

My cousin Diethard Knopp and his family continued to live in Romania after the war. Diethard provided a compelling glimpse into his life after communism descended upon Romania in 1945. His personal account of the loss of freedom, discrimination, hardship, arbitrary arrests, and surveillance by the secret police are a counterpoint to the dangers my family faced by fleeing communism.

Writing this book has been a consuming, fascinating, and sometimes emotional journey. Were it not for my parents' courage and perseverance, I would not have survived to tell this story. All mothers give their children life once. My mother gave me life several times.

As I was writing this book, I was often transported back in time to relive my experiences. Not infrequently, reliving those events brought tears to my eyes. I also gained a deeper understanding of and appreciation for what my parents had experienced. It was an emotional moment when I found the original Certificate of Release that authorized Dad to be released from a Russian POW camp. Reading the letters Dad had written to Mom during their separation made me realize the depth of their emotional suffering. It was a blessing to get to know my parents better and appreciate them even more long after their passing. Not many people experience such a blessing.

Few things in life are accomplished just by one person; *Why Can't Somebody Just Die around Here?* is no exception. Jennifer Brown and Robin Gile were brave enough to read the first rough draft and make suggestions. Their suggestions were invaluable. Dee Dawson proofread a second draft at a time when I had reached a plateau with little progress and got me writing again. Claudia Lawson, the editor of the first edition, helped make the book read better. Claudia also translated some of the official documents. Thanks also to Joshua Eno of Columbus Publishing Lab for his copy editing skills and feedback on the text.

Thanks also goes to Mark Dawson, photographer and friend, who helped me with some aspects of the publishing process, including graphic design work for the cover, researching publishing options, setting up and managing the website (www.themaroscherstory.com), and marketing consulting. You can see more of Mark's photography work at www.nomadicfrog.com and keep track of his current activities on his blog (www.journal.nomadicfrog.com).

My wife Ruth helped with organization and simplifying the telling of a great story. She discovered that being an author's wife required changes in our daily routine as happy and relaxed retirees. I have for too long neglected routine "man tasks" around the house. There is a long list waiting for me, which I will happily work on.

www.ingramcontent.com/pod-product-compliance
Lightning Source LLC
LaVergne TN
LVHW041145150826
845673LV00001B/68

* 9 7 8 0 9 8 1 6 0 7 9 9 3 *